Of His Glory

Our Heavenly God's Desire for His Eternal Saints

Jon Crowdus

Trilogy Christian Publishers
A Wholly Owned Subsidiary of Trinity Broadcasting Network
2442 Michelle Drive
Tustin, CA 92780

Cover design by: See Cover design—Purpose

For information, address Trilogy Christian Publishing
Rights Department, 2442 Michelle Drive, Tustin, Ca 92780.
Trilogy Christian Publishing/ TBN and colophon are trademarks of Trinity Broadcasting Network.

For information about special discounts for bulk purchases, please contact Trilogy Christian Publishing.

Manufactured in the United States of America

10 9 8 7 6 5 4 3 2 1

Library of Congress Cataloging-in-Publication Data is available.

ISBN 978-1-63769-144-1 (Print Book)
ISBN 978-1-63769-145-8 (ebook)

Note:
*e-book readers may 'Ctrl + Click' on the Links throughout this book for access to additional information/research on subjects presented.

*e-book is an electronic version of a printed book that can be read on a computer or handheld device designed specifically for this purpose.

READERS NOTES

CONTENTS

COVER DESIGN—PURPOSE

"NGC 2174" NASA & ESA Hubble Space
Telescope WFC3/IR PRC1418a

The front cover is a NASA photograph of a Star-Forming Region NGC 2174 in which stars/suns are being continuously formed in the universe, proving that our universe is endlessly expanding just as God planned at the very beginning of creation.

Look closely at this photo, and in the background, you'll see galaxies the size of stars and stars the size of galaxies. In the foreground is the Monkey Head Nebula, click on or insert the below link onto your browser to encounter (NGC 2174) from the Hubble space telescope. This beautiful patch of the starry sky is in the Constellation Orion, about 6,500 light-years away. The nebula gets its name from the shape it takes when viewed. This colorful region is filled with young stars embedded within bright wisps of the ingredients needed for star formation.[1]

https://www.spacetelescope.org/news/heic1406/

Note: One light-year is about 6 trillion miles or (9 trillion km).
Note: Imperial & US units: 6×10^{12} mi = 6,000,000,000,000 miles.

The three-dimensional computer-generated models of *star formation* predict that the spinning outflow of energy from the central *regions of* the star provides the most numerous stars in the *Universe* that may have lifespans of tens of billions of years. This stellar nursery contains many young stars that are embedded within the surrounding dust and gas.

I believe this star formation is proof that God in His Infinite Wisdom created the heavens and the earth (habitations) in preparation for what is about to become the *NeXt* big event ushering in the beginning of the tribulation, the 1,000 years Millennial Reign of Christ, and the perpetual Perfect Age of Ages awaiting the fulfillment of God's promise to Abraham, Isaac, and Jacob.

God made an everlasting promise to Abraham "Genesis 15:18-21" that his descendants would be as numerous as the dust of the earth, and God confirmed this to his son Isaac "Genesis 26:3", then repeated the same promise for the third time to Isaac's son Jacob "Genesis 28:13". The Promised Land was described by God in terms of the territory from the River of Egypt to the Euphrates river "Exodus 23:31". This promise has not yet been fulfilled, but its fruition is very close.

This book is focused on providing a better understanding of the literal and eternal "Kingdom of Heaven" throughout the perfect age of ages forevermore. The evangelist Billy Sunday (cir.1900) has said it best, "If we could get a real appreciation of what Heaven is, we would all be so homesick for Heaven the Devil wouldn't have a friend left on earth."

The heavens are part and parcel of God's creation, the Universe, some of which is seen and some unseen. It will, however, become a most glorious literal paradise in the future ages to come when all things are made new, and the universe is endlessly peopled with God's holy race of sinless immortal mankind, as purposely planned by God.

If only the people of earth could grasp the truth of this statement, they would be much more diligent in pursuing God's will in their own lives. They would be so much more devoted to teaching their children the importance of securing the significance of God's eternal rewards in the literal *"Kingdom of Heaven,"* attaining the greatest magnificence.

Of His Glory!

INTRODUCTION

Knowledge of God's Glory

> *"For the earth will be filled with the knowledge of the Glory of the Lord, as the waters cover the sea"*
>
> Habakkuk 2:14, NKJV).

I pray meditating on Habakkuk 2 will open your eyes to the Glory of God. Therefore, God created you. Therefore, you exist. Everything in your life is pointing to this, leading to the Glory of God, bringing Him glory, and dwelling in the Shekinah Glory, the visible manifestation of His presence. This meditation is a perfect opportunity to instill a vision of consistently praying and seeking the gift of "Revelation Knowledge" into any reader's spirit seeking a closer relationship with our Father God, Lord Jesus Christ, and His Holy Spirit.

I would love for all readers to experience this meditation at the beginning "Of His Glory," believing it will provide a more profound understanding of God's Eternal "Glory" presented in this meditation. I believe if you peruse the following written transcription and then later encounter the audio meditation, God's Holy Spirit will bless you with a revelation you may have never experienced. If there is a term in scripture most worthy of our meditation, it would be the word Glory, the Glory of God.

We certainly use it quite casually, but what is it? Well, defining the Glory of God is almost impossible, but encountering it is quite possible. Culture defines earthly glory as something of magnificence or beauty, and God's Glory is certainly that. But even more so, the Glory of God is the eternal magnificence and the infinite beauty of all that He is. But do you know His Glory? I hope you do because you were made to encounter it. Have you encountered the Glory of God recently? How do you know? Well, I pray this meditation from Habakkuk 2 will open your eyes to the Glory of God. Therefore, God created you. Therefore, you exist. Everything in your life is pointing to this, leading to the Glory of God, bringing Him Glory, and dwelling in the Shekinah Glory, the visible manifestation of the presence of God on the earth.

This time is a holy retreat set apart for you to rest in the presence of the Glory of God. A time for your mind to settle your breathing to relax and your eyes to close. So, for this next moment, just be still and showered by the presence of the Holy Father, Holy Son, and Holy Spirit.

Start by listening in your spirit and joining in this responsive reading and prayer from *Zechariah 14*, and respond *'Pause (30 sec)'*

> *Heavenly Father fill me with the knowledge of Your Glory, and may the Lord bless the hearing and reading of His Word. And the Lord shall be King over all the earth, and Heavenly Father fill me with the knowledge of Your Glory.*

On that day, the Lord shall be the only one worshipped. So *"Heavenly Father, fill me with the knowledge of your Glory. His name was, is, and will be the only one.* Spend a few moments now in reverent prayer, humbled before God, pointing to Him, inspired by Him, and in awe of His Beautiful Glory.

Continue now in silent prayer as you take note of the presence of God's Glory in and around you. How are you aware of Him right now? How are you being humbled by His Glory? Take note, too, of your posture before God. Consider kneeling or resting your face in your hands in a moment of reverence and humility. Scan your body and mind for any thoughts or feelings that may be blocking you from soaking in His Glory. What emotions are keeping you from accepting the assurance of dwelling in His presence?

As you continue to center on the Glory of God, does your mind drift back to thoughts of shame and unworthiness? Do you ever feel humiliation while resting in the Glory and Grandeur of God? Well, remember, those are thoughts from your mind and not the mind of God. So, allow unworthy thoughts to simply center you back on His Glory and how He created you to know it…

Continue as you whisper, *"Heavenly Father, fill me with the knowledge of your Glory."* Allow these words to become your centering prayer. Center too on your breathing, take several deep breaths, each breath full and deep from your belly. Become mindful of each breath. Each breath-in fills you with the presence of God. Each breath-out release's shame. Inhale the '*Pneuma*,' the breath of God. Your body is filled with the Glory of God, leaving no room for fear. Stay centered on your breathing and the sacred words, *"Heavenly Father, fill me with the knowledge of your Glory."*

Continue as you soak in God's Glory and listen to this, the first of three sacred readings from holy scripture. Listen for life application as you read from Habakkuk 2:14, and I'll begin in the New King James version. Just listen to God's response to the prophet Habakkuk as he cries out for God to reveal His divine Glory. *"My child, don't worry, for the earth will be filled with the knowledge of the Glory of the Lord, just as the waters cover the sea."* What in this passage were you most grateful to hear? Listen once more from God's Holy Word. *"For the earth will be filled with the knowledge of the Glory of the Lord, just as the water's cover the sea."*

What will you hold on to from the second reading? Allow this next minute to be a time to rest in the beauty of His divine presence…

Listen once more but, consider it now from a wider passage as you listen from the New Living translation:

> *What sorrow awaits you who build cities with money gained through murder and corruption! Has not the Lord of Heaven's Armies promised that the wealth of nations will turn to ashes? They work so hard, but all in vain! For as the waters fill the sea, the earth will be filled with an awareness of the Glory of the Lord.*

What in this passage brought you the deepest peace? Let that be your continuing contemplation for another minute longer…

In this third reading, let the words guide you to a deeper application as you listen once again, now from the New International Version:

> *For the earth will be filled with the knowledge of the Glory of the Lord just as the waters cover the sea. This is the word of the Lord; thanks be to God.*

What deep longings are you ready to share with Him? Let these reflections move you now into a time of worship, in prayer. Let the next minute be the beginning of a time of reverent worship and divine awe of God in His Glory…

Continue in imaginative contemplation as you listen to *Isaiah 6*. The prophet Isaiah here describes how he saw the Lord in a vision.

> *He was sitting on a lofty throne, and the train of His robe filled the Temple. Attending Him were mighty angels, each having six wings. With two wings they covered their faces, with two more they covered their feet, and with two more, they flew. They were calling out to each other, Holy, Holy, Holy is the Lord of Heaven's Armies.*

Now listen to the next things they say, *"the whole earth is filled with His Glory."* God's Holiness and His Glory are two different things.

Holy means *set apart*. God's Holiness is the truth that there is none like Him. But God's Glory is the eternal magnificence and infinite beauty of all that He is. So, take this next minute to contemplate the Holiness of His Glory. Beauty like none other. Let this be your meditation…

Rest your centering on the Holiness of God's Glory. Don't be burdened by your shame or thoughts of unworthiness. Those are not thoughts of God. You were created to know and encounter the Glory of God. And be mindful too of moments that God may use you to reveal His Holy Glory to another.

Now receive this prayer of benediction to remember to set aside shame and worry, for the earth will be filled with the knowledge of the Glory of the Lord, just as the waters cover the sea. So, may you know the beauty of Christ, the renown of the Holy Spirit, and encounter the Holy Glory of God, as you whisper without ending Heavenly Father fill me with the knowledge of your Glory, the beauty of the Father, and the Son and the Holy Spirit. *As it was in the beginning, it is now and forever shall be. Amen…*

Of His Glory!

The Encounter link below will provide access to the audio presentation of this wonderful meditation by clicking on the link if you are reading an e-Book or entering this link in your web browser.[2]

https://encounteringpeace.libsyn.com/knowledge-of-gods-glory

What is "Revelation Knowledge"

Have you ever been made aware of the Divine tension between the path you have chosen for yourself and the one God has chosen for you? One of the most needed things among the Body of Christ today is "Revelation Knowledge" of the Word of God. I believe you will find the following information will open your spirits to the Divine understanding of this heavenly gift of our Father God for your life.

> *[9]No eye has seen, no ear has heard, no mind has conceived what God has prepared for those who love Him. [10] But God has revealed it to us by His Spirit.*

Paul wrote this passage from the Revelation of the Holy Spirit, not from his own thoughts, but under the divine inspiration of the Holy Spirit, the actual thoughts and words of our God, not Paul's own imagination.

> *"We have not received the spirit of the world but the spirit who is from God that we may understand what God has freely given us"*
>
> *1 Corinthians 2:9,10, 12, (NIV).*

> *[14]But the natural unbelieving man does not accept the things (teachings and revelations) of the Spirit of God, for they are foolishness to Him.*
>
> *1 Corinthians 2:14, (AMP)*

There are two types of knowledge in our world, sense knowledge and revealed knowledge. Sense or natural knowledge is acquired through mans' five physical senses. We receive this knowledge from what we hear, see, taste, touch, and smell. This is the knowledge we receive from our education and our life experiences. In other words, we receive this knowledge from the *outside*.

Revelation Knowledge is revealed to us by God's Holy Spirit, who speaks to us by Revelation into our spirits on the *inside.* Revelation Knowledge from the Holy Spirit is transmitting knowledge from God direct into your spirit because you are a new creation in Christ Jesus.

> *However, when He, the Spirit of Truth, has come, He will guide you into all Truth; for He will not speak on His own authority, but whatever He hears He will speak, and He will tell you things to come. He will Glorify Me, for He will take what is mine and declare it to you.*
>
> *1 John 16:13-14 (NKJV)*

The Spirit will guide you into a further truth in granting believers today a fuller understanding of that Truth. The key to receiving "Revelation Knowledge" is obeying the Word of God, meditating in the Word of God, walking in the Love of God, and praying without ceasing as the Holy Spirit quickens God's will into your heart. Fasting along with prayer will lift your spirit, further benefitting your spiritual strength and receiving more "Revelation Knowledge" of the Word every day as you walk with God, meditating throughout your daily life and encountering the Glory of God.

It belongs to you, dear saint, allowing you to remain on the path God has assigned for you to take and helping you to avoid wavering down a rabbit trail, taking the lead instead of following God's directions.

> *That the God of our Lord Jesus Christ, the Father of Glory, may Give you a spirit of wisdom and of revelations in the Knowledge of Him.*
>
> *Ephesians 1:17 (ESV)*

"Don't change yourselves to be like the people of this world, but let God change you inside with a new way of thinking. Then you will be able to understand and accept what God wants for you. You will be able to know what is good and pleasing to Him and what is perfect.

Romans 12:2 (ERV) Easy-to-Read Version

We know that when He comes and is revealed, we will [as His children] be like Him, because we will see Him just as He is [in all His Glory].

1 John 3:2 (AMP)

Several links to "Encounter" meditations used in this book are available to you if you wish to become a subscriber. These meditations come to a subscriber's inbox daily and provide a prayerful audio meditation that lasts about fifteen minutes. Follow the path prepared by God for you and become focused now.

"The Path to The Kingdom" copy to your
web browser, and be blessed.

https://encounteringpeace.libsyn.com/the-path-to-the-kingdom

To subscribe to the free daily audio Meditations
of "Encounter," enter the following link onto your
web browser, click and follow instructions.[3]

www.encounteringpeace.org
or/ http://encounteringpeace.com/

Encounter was launched with a mission to offer a safe space to encounter the transcendent God in the midst of the noise of our daily routines. It is a podcast of over 500 sacred and mindful meditations to help you encounter the divine presence of God throughout your day, on-demand. Please install this app:

https://directory.libsyn.com/shows/view/id/encounterapp

PREFACE

In Genesis 1:28, God expected man and all His creation to be glorious reflections "Of His Glory." He expects us to be good servants and stewards of all he has given to us. Pay His love forward, advance the work of Christ, share the gift of grace with other people and expand His loving grace to reach the nations.

The back cover is exemplifying the Glory of the literal "Kingdom of Heaven" when the Vision is manifested in the spirit. Prior to Jesus dying for our sin, the "kingdom of heaven" was preached by Jesus and the disciples, but after Jesus rose from the dead and ascended into Heaven, the "Salvation Message" was preached exclusively.

My life has been one of a never-ending quest for truth. I always had questions about creation and the teachings of the church, but only got, "It's a Mystery. *When you're older, you will understand."* I never received any answers, but I did develop a very insubordinate attitude with many of my teachers due to never getting any answers to my questions. I was just ignored or embarrassed by the teacher calling me a troublemaker, a smart-aleck, or sending me out of class to stand in the corridor.

Matthew 7:7-12 gave me an answer, but not for several years after I accepted Jesus into my heart as Savior and Lord; after reading Matthew 7-7-12 (AMP), below I understood, I needed to search for the answers myself, to decern and hear the voice of God. *"You will seek me and find me when you seek me with all your heart."* I just recently purchased a new copy of the Amplified Bible* and loved the clear, well-defined language. I recommend getting a copy for your own personal study.

"Ask and keep on asking and it will be given to you; seek and keep on seeking and you will find; knock

and keep on knocking and the door will be opened to you

For everyone who keeps on asking receives, and he who keeps on seeking finds, and to him who keeps on knocking, it will be opened.

So then, in everything treat others the same way you want them to treat you, for this is (the essence of) the Law and the (writings of the) Prophets."

Mathew 7:7-12 AMP

Truth is found by allowing the Holy Spirit to guide us to the answers in our lives as we seek God's grace through prayer. When we walk with the Spirit, He will guide us to the Truth.

"You will seek me and find me, when you seek me with all your heart" (Jeremiah 29:13 NKJV, NIV, ESV, BSB, NASB ISV, NHEB)

God answers Habakkuk, 2:2-3 ERV (Easy to Read Version).

[2]The LORD answered me, "Write down what I show you. Write it clearly on a sign so that the message will be easy to read. [3]This message is about a special time in the future. This message is about the end, and it will come true. Just be patient and wait for it. That time will come; it will not be late.

[2] *The Lord answered me,* Write down this *vision; clearly inscribe it on tablets so one may easily read it.

Habakkuk 2:2 (CSB) Christian Standard Bible

*A vision inspires action. A powerful vision pulls in ideas, people, and other resources. It creates the energy and will to make change happen. It inspires individuals to commit to persist in sharing God's vision to help keep mankind focused on the "Kingdom of Heaven" and God's Long-Range Plan. We all need to be following the path of "Truth," professing the literal "Kingdom of Heaven" is at hand, and the Vision of God's Long-Range Plan is beginning to be fully revealed.

There remain several generations of humankind searching for the answers to the questions being raised in their spirits. It is now time to publish this Work and inform all of God's children that the literal "Kingdom of Heaven," which has been in God's Long-Range Plan since the creation of humanity, is more incredible than man has ever imagined. Praise God! The knowledge of the world is now opening mans' ability to better understand God's Master Plan, which establishes and enhances the true meaning "Of His Glory."

The subjects in this book may be controversial within certain fundamental segments of the ministry. However, I am confident that the Holy Spirit will direct and guide all final edits, assuring the finished product becomes the witness God wants this work to provide for all the Nations of the children of God.

Buckminster Fuller, an American architect, created the "Knowledge Doubling Curve"; he noticed that until 1900 human knowledge doubled approximately every century. By the end of World War II knowledge was doubling every twenty-five years. Today things are not as simple as different types of knowledge have different rates of growth. Experts now estimate that by the end of 2020, human knowledge will double every 12 hours. But the real question is, "How is it making us smarter? According to IBM, the build-out of the "internet of things" will alone lead to the doubling of knowledge every 12 hours. Look up the explanation of the "Internet of Things" on your browser. Become aware of this change!

I believe all of God's creation desires to know why they are here, what the future holds for them and how they go about getting the blessings God has prepared for them. Some form of belief, "religion," is important to them, but for the most part, Christianity is pretty much of a bore to many of them. They question the one-way to salvation through Christ.

God has a marvelous master plan for all His saints. We should all have a desire to know and understand what His plan is and how and where everyone fits into His plan. The literal Kingdom of Heaven" is close at hand, and God's magnificent paradise is waiting for a positive response to His calling within all of our spirits.

People from all global nations throughout the earth will all eventually listen to this informative message from Gods Revelation Knowledge. His intent is to bless all those who have earnestly listened, heard and believed in their hearts what His incredible purpose is for all of Eternity. He is providing this information today because the end-times are apparently approaching, and this vision has come from His "Revelation Knowledge".

They will receive insight regarding the millennial age to come and the 'Hope of Glory.' God has a great master plan, and my assignment is to share it with you and all the Nations of the world. I may be from a different generation, but I can honestly say I believe you should pass this forward! I have seen so many marvelous blessings in my life. I know that I know that God is everything He says He is, and His Word is truth. I have witnessed blessing after blessing in my life and in my family's lives providing confirmation of God's unconditional love for us all.

See the following testimony, one of many but the most wonderful of all my stories. *(a short departure to present an example of God's grace and mercy to His children)*

Several years ago, my wife and I were in a tragic automobile accident late one evening riding in the rear seat of a friend's car. We were rear-ended by an SUV that was calculated by the police to be traveling over 125 miles per hour upon impact. Immediately an angel appeared at the scene who told our friend, the driver of our car, *"have your friend's wife taken to 'a specific_hospital' or his wife will die."* Then the angel disappeared just as quickly after making this statement. After a much-heated discussion with the police and the EMSA driver, the ambulance took us both to the specifically designated hospital. Upon arriving at the hospital, my wife was pronounced clinically dead by the ER doctors who believed her brain stem had been severed.

Not according to my God! She remained in a coma for six weeks and, after almost two years of recuperation, was healed. Glory to God! There was only one location in this region testing a new medicine that was exactly what she needed to reduce the swelling in her brain stem and regaining her life. I learned an important lesson from the moment I became conscious in the crushed car, praying without ceasing and believing she would be healed. As horrible as this experience was, it became a blessing as we were both used by God to bring hope by ministering to people who had a like experience but had serious difficulty dealing with their own tragic events.

> *"Rejoice always, pray without ceasing, give thanks in all circumstance for this is the will of God in Christ Jesus for you"*
>
> *Thessalonians 5:16-18, (ESV).*

Back to the purpose: The three "heavens" implied in 2 Corinthians 12:2_(AMP) in the coming chapters are referencing the three different realms that we call "the sky," "outer space," and the "spiritual heaven." Paul was speaking of himself and what he saw and heard. There were no words in the human language that could describe his experience. However, he did believe he was in the third level of heaven, the location where God resides.

> *[2] I know a man in Christ who fourteen years ago was caught up to the Third heaven—whether in the body or out of the body I do not know, God knows.*

Not many authors have ventured into the age of the millennial reign of Christ or into the everlasting, eternal age of our triune God that He planned from the very beginning of creation. The Universe is often defined as "the totality of existence", or everything that exists, everything that has existed, and everything that will exist.

This book will be briefly discussing our known universe as a continually expanding universe leading to a belief there are other universes within God's creation. Is this leading to a notion God duplicated the human-race? No! We are God's only children, and His promise revealed in this book is real! Time in the realm of God is timeless and eternal.

The Hubble Space Telescope blasted off aboard the space shuttle Discovery on April 24, 1990 and was deployed a day later. After a nearly month-long checkout process, the observatory opened its eyes for the first time, capturing an image of several stars with its Wide Field/Planetary Camera on May 20, 1990, 31 years ago, proving the universe is continually expanding. Why do you think God would have set into motion an expanding universe, not just a small galaxy in which a tiny planet called earth resides? Why would He? His plan is actively being manifested and glorifying our Lord.

I will also be discussing the first resurrection of the Church that many, including myself, believe will occur at the time of the rapture, including all those who have placed their trust in Jesus Christ during the Church Age, and have died before Jesus returns, who will also be resurrected at the rapture.

There are several references to scientific subjects that may represent "TMI" (too much information). To better understand God's long-range plan, it is important to briefly discuss the unimaginable magnitude of God's creation. Forgive me if this causes any anxiety. I pray that you will read and understand the message I have been appointed to present with my discernment of the scriptures to understand the questions I have been asking about since I was nine years old. Now I know! That I know!

Note:

All italics in Scripture quotations are the author's emphasis.

"Red Letter" Scriptures are quotes from Jesus Christ as noted in the published Holy 'Bibles' noted in the following credits.

CREDITS

Published by: Trilogy Christian Publishing c/o Trinity Broadcasting Network, PO Box A, Santa Ana, CA 92711

Printed in the United States of America

Library of Congress Cataloging-in-Publication Data_______________________

Names: Jon C Crowdus, 2021—author. Copyright © 2021 by Jon C. Crowdus

Title: "OF HIS GLORY": About the "Millennial Reign of Christ" and the Literal "Kingdom of Heaven", throughout the perfect Age of Ages forevermore.

The Holy Bible, King James Version, KJV conformable to that of the Edition of 1611, known as the authorized or King James Version, Verse Reference Edition by A.J. Holman Company, Philadelphia. My very first Bible was presented to me on June 2, 1974, celebrating my new birth.

"GNT": Scripture taken from the Good News Translation—Second Edition, Copyright ©1992 by American Bible Society. Used by Permission. (The Good News Translation the Holy Bible Online)

Jack Van Impe Prophecy Bible (KJV): http//www.jvim.com, jvimi@jvim.com, ISBN: 1-884137-88-1, printed in the USA.

The Berean Study Bible (BSB) New Testament is a modern English translation of the New Testament. The Holy Bible, *Berean Study Bible*, BSB. *Copyright* ©2016, 2018 by Bible Hub.

The Christian Standard Bible (CSB). Copyright © 2017 by Holman Bible Publishers. Used by permission. Christian Standard Bible®, and CSB® are federally registered trademarks of Holman Bible Publishers, all rights reserved.

The Revised Standard Version (RSV) Up to 500 *verses* of the *RSV* or *NRSV* may be quoted in any form (written, visual, electronic or audio) without charge. Generally, *gratis* permission will not be granted to post or podcast.

The English Standard Version (ESV) is an English translation of the Bible published in 2001 by Crossway. It is a revision of the Revised Standard Version that employs an "essentially literal" translation philosophy. Unless otherwise indicated, all content is licensed under a Creative Commons Attribution License.

All Scripture quotations, unless otherwise indicated, are taken from The Holy Bible, English Standard Version. Copyright ©2001 by Crossway Bibles, a publishing ministry of Good News Publishers.

ERV (Easy to Read Version) The Easy-to-Read Version (ERV) is an accurate translation of the Bible created by the translation team at Bible League International. New readers sometimes struggle with reading older standardized translations of Bible text because of their unfamiliarity with the Bible. The ERV uses simpler vocabulary and shorter sentences while maintaining the integrity of the original texts. One of the basic ideas that guided the work was that good translation is good communication. In 2015, a major revision was completed in the English text. It uses broader vocabulary, and it is revised to reflect new cultural perspectives. The ERV is now in the process of revision for the other language texts while continuing to stay true to the original Biblical texts. In this process of revision, we are committed to keeping the text fresh and applicable to the global community of Bible readers.

Larkin, Clarence, 1850-1924: Dispensational Truth: or, God's Plan and Purpose in the Ages (enlarged and revised edition, 1920) (illustrated HTML at preservedwords.com)

Copyrighted 1918, Enlarged and Revised Edition © Copyrighted 1920.

Upon receiving instructions from our Father God to write "OF HIS GLORY," I began my quest for knowledge by researching various scriptures and searching for appropriate books about the Millennial Reign of Christ and the Age of Ages. God led me to Barnes & Nobel, and within a few minutes, I discovered the above book, and a vision of eternity was off and running.

> *17 that the God of our Lord Jesus Christ, the Father of glory, may give you the Spirit of wisdom and of revelation in the knowledge of him, 18 having the eyes of your hearts enlightened, that you may know what is the hope to which he has called you, what are the riches of his glorious inheritance in the saints, 19 and what is the immeasurable greatness of his power toward us who believe, according to the working of his great might.*
>
> *Ephesians 1:17-19 (ESV)*

God took Abraham outside and said, "Look up at the sky and count the stars-if indeed you can count them." Then he said to him, "So shall your offspring be."

Genesis 15:5 (NIV)

"When the Spirit of truth comes, He will guide you into all the truth, for He will not speak on His own authority, but whatever He hears He will speak, and He will declare to you the things that are to come."

John 16:13 (ESV)

Terry Dickinson is recognized as Canada's chronicler of record of our celestial canopy, in all its infinite and intricate wonders, unveiling a world of discovery and understanding. A guiding force behind *SkyNews*, Canada's national astronomy and stargazing magazine, founded by the Canadian Science and Technology Museum, from its premiere issue and continuing through its first 21 years of publication. He is the author of 15 books on astronomy, whose seminal work, *Nightwatch: A Practical Guide to Viewing the Universe*, still stands as one of the best-selling stargazing books in the world.

Named a Member of the Order of Canada, the President's Award from the Royal Astronomical Society of Canada, the Sandford Fleming Medal, the Klumpke-Roberts Award for outstanding contributions to public understanding of astronomy by the Astronomical Society of the Pacific; and a Lifetime Achievement Award by the County of Lennox and Addington; recipient of an honorary Doctor of Science Degree from Trent University; and commemorated with the nam-ing of Asteroid #5272 Dickinson by the International Astronomical Union. Terry's iconic photograph of the moon was immortalized in the issuance of a United States postage stamp in 2000.[4]

https://www.amazon.com/
Astronomy-2019-Terence-Dickinson/dp/0228100372

https://www.thriftbooks.com/a/terence-dickinson/211961/

https://books.google.com/books/about/Exploring_the_Night_Sky.html?id=SegOAQAAMAAJ

illustrations on pages: 61, 157, 296 & 297. Terry's love of astronomy and his selflessness to mentor and train anyone interested in studying the heavens. His links to books for adults, children & other products are a Treasure-trove of information as a hobby or professional career for one interested in learning more of our Universe of Universe's via the science of Astronomy to acquire the "Revelation Knowledge" and Vision of God's purpose for mankind to bring Eternal Glory to our Father God.

Illustration Credits

Page 61: Milky Way Galaxy, by written approval from Terence Dickinson

Page 62: Image Credit; NASA, ESA and M. Kornmesser (ESO). Milky Way Galaxy with 100 Billion Planets.

Page 72: Auguste Rodin's sculpture of the "Thinker."

Page 79: I Am the Door, credit by Permission of 'HavenLight', Jesus extended hand. Purchased unlimited use of illustration.

www.havenlight.com/yongsung-kim.

Page 102: Image Credit; NASA, Earth is seen from Apollo 17

Page 103: Profile of Earth's Atmosphere to the Height of New Jerusalem, NASA.

Page 104: Space Station 230 miles from Earth, NASA

Page 118: Holy Oblation, Map data ©2019 GeoBasis-DE/ BKG (©2009), Google, Inst. Geogr. Nacional, Mapa GISrael, ORION-ME. (noted on illustration)

Page 119: Jon Crowdus' drawing of "God's Royal Grant of Land" given to Abraham.

Page 120: Jon Crowdus' drawing of the western section of the Millennial City of Jerusalem.

Page 121: Used with the written approval of artist, Painting of Christ's Millennial Kingdom by; Artist Carlos Sandoval. Carlos.S "heavenstruth.blogspot.com"

Page 156: Voyage of Columbus, Dreamtime, Illustration "42958094 ©" Welburnstuart, PopTika, Royalty-Free stock photo, enhanced license, unlimited use. Dreamtime.com purchased unlimited rights to use illustration.

https://www.dreamstime.com/stock-illustration-santa-maria-arrival-map-flag-columbus-arriving-new-world-image42958094

Note: If above Link Fails enter in Browser

Page 157: Imagine, A Universe of Universes, by written approval from Terence Dickinson

Page 158: NASA *TESS SPACECRAFT DISCOVER'S NEW WORLD'S See additional credits on the page with illustration.

Page 184: Hubble Eyes an Emission Galaxy; Image credit: ESA/NASA/Hubble NASAID Rosario et al.

Page 248: Andromeda Galaxy; closest galaxy to our Milky Way Galaxy. Also known as Messier 31 (M31). Captured in a new image from NASA's Wide-field. Infrared Survey Explorer (WISE). See additional credits on page 174.

Page 296: The Known Universe, written approval received from Terence Dickinson

Page 297: The Universe: An Overview, written approval received from Terence Dickinson.

Page 319: New Jerusalem illustration at the beginning of the Age of Age's by Jon Crowdus

Page 332: Christ reaching into the water to save Peter. Credit, by Permission 'HavenLight,' Purchased unlimited use of illustration.

https://havenlight.com/collections/yongsung-kim

Page 341: Overlay of the footprint of New City of Jerusalem promised by God as the Age of Ages begins. Confirming that God's will is to create a new earth (habitation) for immortal humankind. The footprint of this new City will occupy 1,904,400 Sq. Miles of land.

Page 341: Authors salutations Credits are designated below the NASA & Goddard Space Flight Center photo.

Page 397: The Milky Way, Anatomy of our Galaxy.

REAR COVER: Shutterstock Inc., Copyright_© 2003-2020 Enhanced License, Unlimited use. See narrative description on page 401. Comment by Jon Crowdus:

My life has been filled with question's as long as I can remember; however, answers were far and few between! The various references identified throughout this book, Clarence Larkin's and Terence Dickinson's works, and especially the quoted versions of the Bible, "God's Holy Word," have opened my 'mind's eye' to the "Revelation Knowledge" of God's Long-Range Plan. I pray that your mind's eye will likewise be opened by the Holy Spirit.

ACKNOWLEDGEMENTS

DOUG & CYNTHIA SEAVER
FOR
ENCOURAGING ME TO ASK JESUS INTO MY HEART
ON JUNE 2, 1974

ALEX SWANSON
FOR
HELPING TO EDIT "OF HIS GLORY" FOR THE
FIRST OVERVIEW

TATUM BERND
FOR
PROVIDING FINAL EDIT "OF HIS GLORY"
PREPARING THE MANUSCRIPT FOR PUBLISHING.

TO PATSY BROWN
FOR
PROVIDING THE FINAL FORMAT "OF HIS GLORY"
PROVIDING MOCK-UPS FOR REVIEW'S AND HER
EXPERTISE
IN THE FINAL COMPILATION OF THIS WORK!

BLESSINGS TO ALL OF YOU, MY FRIEND'S!

And

To My Dear Wife Marlene
Thank you for your loving support and prayers!

Jon Crowdus

A TESTIMONY OF A SERVANT

"What *is your experience with the Lord?"* I was recently asked this same question myself. As I began recounting my life, I remembered all the marvelous experiences and blessings I received as a child. I was dedicated to God to be a priest before I was even born. I know this to be true because of conversations with my paternal grandmother. Due to familial tradition, the first-born son was expected to become a priest.

Looking back over the seasons of my life, I believe Satan set up a great many booby traps in my life's path to distract me, and throw me off course, and bring discouragement into my life. Having had the experiences that I've had, I am convinced one of his primary purposes is to prevent me and you from receiving all that God has planned for us to accomplish. In my opinion, He purposes to begin this scheme from the moment of our conception, our very first experience with the Lord.

I did become a priest, but not the white-collar variety as intended by my family when I was a young boy. However, I finally did become a priest of God when I was scripturally born again. Unfortunately, it took me thirty-three years to get there. I can very definitely say, without hesitation, that I was radically saved and delivered from the wilderness I had been wandering in and out of for most of my first thirty-three years.

Perfect American dream childhood? Well, I thought so, but looking back, I can see every step forward in faith and growth in the Lord was followed by attacks of the enemy. These attacks would many times push me two steps backward, and my life resembled a game of "Mother May I."

But Glory to God, His grace and love would appear right during the darkness and would fill the void that was causing me great distress and emptiness. I would be lifted to new spiritual heights and given the opportunity and ability to deal with and understand the evil things our common enemy, the devil attempted to seriously deceive me time and again. However, I would spend time talking, singing, and fellowshipping with the Lord, did experience a period of justification. I just didn't know or understand the 'Word of God' and fell again and again into a sinful nature from my lack of knowledge, as stated in Hosea 4:6. *My people* are destroyed *for lack of knowledge*! I still vividly remember the picture of the Guardian Angel that hung over my bed. It always reminded me that God loved me so much that He gave me my very own Angel to watch over me and protect me throughout my whole life. I can honestly say, my Guardian Angel really had his hands full over the years due to the wrong choices I unfortunately made. One day the Lord spoke to my heart as I daydreamed, sketched in my sketchbook, and just sat quietly daydreaming at the end of my third-grade year. I had just turned nine, and the Lord put in my heart that I was to become an architect.

I know you must be asking yourselves, why would this be such an unusual occurrence? Well, for one thing, I had no real knowledge of what becoming an architect meant, nor had I ever met one. All my friends were sure they were going to be baseball players, police officers, or Air Force pilots.

I believe the training and expertise God has provided me throughout my challenging personal life, my professional career as an architect, and as a volunteer in the ministry as a master teacher and children's pastor in the church for a tenure of sixteen years has been a prerequisite in God's plan for me to write this book and begin my full-time ministry. I have been waiting on the Lord for years to show me the next step that I should take to finish the journey He had me begin several years ago. He has now given me that direction, and today my hand is set to finish the race.

My fervent desire is that you will catch the vision of this work and follow the direction you receive in your spirit from the Holy Spirit. Where are you in your walk with the Lord? Are you ahead of

Him or following Him? If you don't really know or don't feel you now have a walk with the Lord, I believe you will soon have a vision of God's glorious, marvelous plan for the human-race and specifically His plan for you as a child of God, His heir to all that shall ever be forever.

In communities across our land, there is a problem with young people dropping out of the church. As a matter of fact, I have heard that three out of four Christian teens walk away from the church after they leave home. This book is written to all of today's generation to bring an expounded knowledge of God's long-range plan. I pray you will catch the vision and thus will bring glory to God the Father, Son, and Holy Spirit. God expects you to be exalted to the very highest honor of crowning achievement within the scheme of His Long-Range Plan, and He wants you to fully encounter the very literal essence.

OF HIS GLORY!

"If you are a stranger to prayer, you are a stranger to the greatest source of power known to human beings."

Billy Sunday

Note:

*e-book readers may 'Ctrl + Click' on the Links presented throughout this book for access to additional information/research on subjects

*e-book is an electronic version of a printed book that can be read on a computer or handheld device designed specifically for this purpose.

CHAPTER 1

God's plan is revealed

This generation is a generation being touched by the "Finger of God."

Jesus is coming, and He is coming in all 'of His glory'; the long-awaited Millennial Kingdom of Christ is very near! There is no mistaking the signs of this generation. Jesus Christ is coming soon!

You have no doubt heard this message from the pulpit of your local church, or soon will. It is based upon the following allegory that God has explained several places in the Bible with careful detail just for us.

> *"Then He spoke to them a parable: "Look at the fig tree, and all the trees. When they are already budding, you see and know for yourselves that summer is now near. So, you also, when you see these things happening, know that the kingdom of God is near."*
>
> *Luke 21: 29-31 (NKJV)*

> *"Assuredly, I say to you, this generation will by no means pass away till all things take place"*
>
> *Luke 21:32, (NKJV).*

God has used the symbol of the fig tree in many passages of scripture to describe the nation of Israel. A representative symbol that is as common to Israel as the eagle is to America. He likewise uses the trees in a general sense as a symbol to represent other nations. In the above passage, He is telling us that once we see Israel being regenerated as a nation, which until 1948 she had not been for almost 2000 years, that the time of harvest is near. He also tells us that in addition to this sign, we will concurrently see new nations coming into existence.

A phenomenon that we in this generation have witnessed is, as we search for this truth in the pages that follow, remember that the entire text of the Bible was written by ordinary men for ordinary people, not just for scholars and learned theologians. It was written just for you and just for me. It's ours—all ours!

> *In the beginning God created the heavens and the earth.*
>
> *Genesis 1:1, (NKJV)*

> *Then God said, "Let Us make man in Our image, according to Our likeness; let them have dominion over the fish of the sea, over the birds of the air, and over the cattle, over all the earth and over every creeping thing that creeps on the earth.*
>
> *So, God created man in His own image; in the image of God He created him; male and female, He created them.*
>
> *Then God blessed them, and God said to them, Be fruitful and multiply; fill the earth and subdue it; have dominion over the fish of the sea, over the birds of the air, and over every living thing that moves on the earth."*
>
> *Genesis 1:26-28 (NKJV)*

Did He say there was any limiting factor, a specific time frame in which mankind was to honor this command? No, He did not. Didn't He confirm this to Noah? Yes! Didn't He confirm this to Abraham, Isaac, and Jacob? Yes! Didn't Jesus confirm this by living and dying for all the human-race? Yes, God became man to offer Himself up for all of humanities sin.

When God uses words like 'forever' and 'evermore,' most ordinary people would take Him at His word and believe that He really meant what He said. Will you?

Let's take a quick look at an outline of God's long-range plan. Let's just see how humankind as a race of people and you as a saint of God might fit within His grand scheme of eternity. Since the sequence of end-time events began with the budding of the fig tree over seventy-two years ago, you should know:

1) Jesus is coming very soon for His Church.
2) Horrible wrath will be poured out upon the earth during The Great Tribulation.
3) Jesus is going to return to the earth with His saints in all His glory.
4) Jesus will destroy all wicked human-beings while preserving the lives of End-time believers.
5) Jesus will set up His 1000-year millennial kingdom on the earth with the end-time nations of believers.
6) The saints (you and me) will rule and reign over the nations with Jesus during His millennial reign.
7) Satan will fail in his attempt to defeat Jesus at the end of the 1000 years and will be thrown into hell for all eternity.
8) All of God's creation throughout the cosmos will be gloriously re-made and become heavenly perfect.
9) A sinless, holy race of God's elect people will continue to populate the whole of creation, forevermore.
10) The saints will live in the magnificently glorious city of New Jerusalem with God the Father, the Son, and the

Holy Spirit. This will be the city home of God's elite saints, where we the saints will continue to jointly serve our heavenly Father, Jesus the Son, the Holy Spirit and jointly rule and reign with our Lord Jesus Christ over all the righteous, holy nations throughout eternity.

11) As a supernatural child of the Most-High God, you, my dear saint, will become a most awesome and magnificent reflection "Of His Glory."
12) God will shower His Divine blessings upon all of creation beyond any human comprehension. There are no words in existence today on the Earth that can even begin to describe these blessings.

Seems simple enough, so why are there so many varying answers being given to the questions? Modernist theologians are saying one thing. Conservative theologians are saying still another. Popular teachers and preachers are holding that Jesus is returning soon, but they differ on the sequence of events that lead to the 1,000-year millennial reign of Christ.

Cultists are giving their different answers, but they are all still looking with great expectation for some great occurrence that they believe began around the year 2012.

Many of today's foremost theologians have unknowingly over-intellectualized the simple and ordinary interpretations of scripture beyond mankind's understanding. They have not only confused divine church doctrines but have successfully replaced simple child-like faith and obedience of God's word with a permissive and very worldly self-serving religion.

I believe the result of their work has even promoted a greater anti-Christ attitude among the younger generation today than the efforts of all 'new-agers' and other cultists combined. I believe this is the reason for young people staying away from the church and causing the exodus of three out of four Christian teens to walk away from the church after they leave home.

Together they are all unknowingly promoting Satan's plan for the advent of the False-Prophet and Anti-Christ's new world order! A plan that is leading an overwhelming number of people straight to Hell! Sad, but very true! But, I pray, not you, for you have in your hands, God's truth!

Had the people of Christ's day been knowledgeable of all the prophecy that is literally spelled out in scripture, they would have known with certainty that He was the Messiah. But they did not understand that God meant exactly what He said, and the learned men of the day either ignored or philosophized those scriptures conveniently away or totally misread the scriptures.

As a result, millions of people throughout the nations have since died and continue to die without Jesus Christ as their Savior, and many of God's elect will, as a terribly sad consequence, spend eternity in Hell.

I am sure that many of you readers can see the many similarities and parallel signs occurring in the world today that must have also occurred 2000 years ago. To the serious Bible student today, it is obvious that Jesus Christ is coming again very soon for His believers.

Unfortunately, millions of surprised people are going to miss the maiden flight (Rapture 1) and be tragically grounded. Millions and millions of people will die during the awful 7-year Tribulation period that follows without knowing Jesus Christ as their Lord and Savior, and the result for them may be eternal damnation.

Based upon all the arguments and debates between theological theory and opinion regarding God's divinity, His relationship to the world through His only begotten Son Jesus Christ and His indwelling Holy Spirit, plus the politically correct teachings of the organized religious community, it is no wonder we have apostasy within the major developed nations of the earth.

I have read and re-read the scriptures as I believe they relate to these questions. I have studied numerous books on the subject. I have listened to many teachers and preachers as they delved into the matter. I have had several informative debates with ministers, associates, friends, and family on these questions. But, more importantly, I have listened to the Spirit of God for the past several years concerning the knowledge I share with you.

These are eschatological questions. (Eschatology is the theology of the end time—and contrary to a popular opinion, Judeo-Christian thought is linear, not circular.) In the Judeo-Christian tradition, there was a beginning, and there will be an end. *In the beginning, God, and in the end, God!

Does this make me an expert? No! I'm nothing more than a born-again believer in God, who is revealed to me in Christ Jesus. I'm not anything more than one who listens as closely as I can to the Spirit of God, who is the Spirit of Christ, as He admonishes, exhorts, and reproves. I have sought to follow His guidance as I have sought out answers to these questions. What is God's plan? Where do we fit into His scheme of things?

By profession, I am an architect. I understand long-range planning, master planning, and strategic planning. I understand the synergism of building blocks and systems that will when they are combined, form a complete entity.

The following definitions fit well within our Master Planners model of which we are a very significant part:

1) The Long-range Plan assesses all pre-supposed conditions, projects trends and outlines future potentials regarding specific needs for a creative endeavor.

2) The Master Plan directs the long-range planning process and serves as a vehicle for active human participation within the planning process. In addition, it provides the following:
   - Assures a good fit between sets of diverse elements, activities and a pre-determined future accomplishment.
   - Promotes a thorough interactive response to the Needs identified in the plan.
   - Determines the eventual Quality and Scope of the total plan based upon its inherent limitations.
   - Functions as an Evaluative Tool for assessing all directional alternatives.
   - Results in a specific concept planned for Growth and Change
   - Targets' Perfection at the eventual completion of the plan.
3) The Strategic Plan identifies the overall Directions that most appropriately addresses the needs of the final planning concept as defined by its goals, facts, and precepts.
   - A specific Plan of Action and its timeline is then documented, and thus begins the process of implementation.

I see the scriptures as a collection of writings that contain scattered insights—like disassembled building blocks—into God's plan and Mankinds' place in it.

Taken together, these insights become, as the Holy Spirit reveals them, a whole entity. They reveal God's strategic, master, and long-range plans for His creation and for all of humanity.

In some instances, these building blocks or insights are in the literal meaning of the scripture—and these literal readings are of primary importance.

In other instances, these building blocks or insights are in symbolism and in typology—teaching us through parables and analogies that describe and define God's purpose, His goal for all human-beings.

Is this book the result of a private revelation from God just to me? No! Private revelations are always suspect—like discoveries by one scientist that cannot be verified by other scientists.

Have I received guidance and encouragement in its writing by the Spirit? Yes. This manuscript, which has been several years in its compilation, is largely an analysis and arrangement by me as I was guided and encouraged by the Holy Spirit. The underlying assumption is that God's long-range plan for creation and mankind is contained in the Bible and is knowable by the Spirit.

The Holy Spirit first spoke to me about developing this book several years ago, and I started researching scriptures in several versions of the Bible, looking for answers to questions that I have had most of my life. I spent time with the Lord to understand the purpose of this book, and why I would be encouraged to begin studying the scriptures and waking up in the middle of the night with an urging to read and take notes as I studied God's Word.

The first chapters were not immediately written for several reasons, for example, my doubts on whether this was the leading of the Holy Spirit or just my usual curiosity. It appeared to be the Holy Spirit encouraging me to write, but then the devil began telling me, "It's stupid to waste time on a subject you don't really know or understand, and besides, you are no writer." Well, I finally decided that if it's stupid according to 'Old Sluggo,' then it must be written.

So, I finally began, after much prayer and discussion with the Father and another confirmation from the Holy Spirit, I discovered the true meaning "Of His Glory."

This book has three purposes/objectives: First, it is written to satisfy what I believe is a God-given natural curiosity about His plan for creation and Man's place in it. Mankind receives this curiosity direct from God, and He wants us to satisfy it by obediently searching out His plan. Adam was the first to begin the search, but, through his disobedience, he rejected God's direction, took a shortcut without God, and discovered death, not life.

God wants us to satisfy this natural curiosity, but only through our obedience to His Word and the leading of the Spirit. Therefore, our obedience leads us to the knowledge of the Lord and perfects His wisdom in us. He wants to give us the knowledge and the wisdom necessary to satisfy our curiosity to discover His long-range plan to perfect our greatest love of Him and bring all the Glory to Him for eternity.

Second, it is written to give a confused and disillusioned generation of young men and women a sense of God's plan. With their sense of curiosity sparked, they will no doubt have an even greater desire to seek out the full knowledge and wisdom of God's long-range plan. A spark set upon tender souls that will ignite ablaze for the love of God, bringing purpose and direction to the lives of countless people everywhere.

Third, it is written to call the church to and strengthen the church in, a proclamation of the gospel of the Kingdom of God. To bring a renewed focus to the church and its responsibility for proclaiming the gospel of the Kingdom of Heaven to all the world. The following perfectly sums up the reason we, as Christians, must renew our intensity for the knowledge and wisdom of the Lord.

> *He shall be great, and shall be called the Son of the Highest: and the Lord God shall give unto Him the throne of His father David: and He shall reign over the house of Jacob forever; and of His kingdom there shall be no end.*
>
> *Luke 1:32-33 (KJV)*

> *"And this gospel of the Kingdom will be preached in all the world as a witness to all the nations, and then the end will come."*
>
> *Matthew 24:14 (NKJV)*

This gospel (good news) refers to the gospel that is to be preached again during the Tribulation by the 144,000. John the Baptist, Jesus, and His disciples all preached this "Gospel of the Kingdom," but after the cross, the "Gospel of Salvation" was preached almost exclusively.

But it once again has its time and place now that the time is at hand. Jesus is coming soon to set up the literal Kingdom as prophesied in Luke 1:32-33. This gospel should be shouted from the rooftops. It is a witness in these end times of the perfect love God wishes to share with all human-beings' through salvation in Jesus Christ. This same God is also calling many sons and daughters to their rightful inheritance of His Glory.

> *Looking for the blessed hope and glorious appearing of our great God and Savior Jesus Christ, who gave himself for us, that He might redeem us from every lawless deed and purify for Himself His own special people, zealous for good works.*
>
> *Titus 2:13-14 (NKJV)*

God's elite, His special people, the redeemed saints washed in the Blood of the Lamb, are called to a new and glorified heavenly life with their Father. We are called to have a unique relationship with God the Father, God the Son, and God the Holy Spirit.

As born-again Christians, we have a most unique part to play in our Father God's eternal Kingdom, as Jesus shares His sovereignty with each of us throughout the ages. God wishes to share this special glory with as many people as will accept Jesus as their Lord and Savior.

This book is intended to help you grasp the awesome Glory of God's long-range plan and effectively use your enhanced knowledge, with the Holy Spirit's leading, to bring the adoption of God's children to its fullest potential.

It has been said the youth of today's current generation has become the "Internet Generation." It is interesting to witness each succeeding generation inheriting and sometimes benefiting from each of the previous generations, with unique and distinct characteristics. They are open to change, more optimistic, and less religious. According to a study of the Pew Research Center a few years ago, only four percent of young adults (18-25 year-old's) view becoming more spiritual as their most important goal in life.

Maybe there has been no name available to really define them, but I believe they are a "Generation touched by the finger of God," the "Omega Generation," the last generation to know the love and grace of God through their redemption in Christ Jesus.

It appears that many people have just given up, throwing the baby out with the bathwater. Well, the unsaved youth of this generation may be going under for the third time, but we shouldn't just let them drown in their unfulfilled sphere of non-life. We should jump in after them, and by example, be a catalyst to help light the fuse to blow away the mountain of confusion surrounding their real purpose and God's intended vision for their lives.

Mining experts know that properly preparing an area with a well-placed charge will always explode and break away all the worthless burden to expose the payload, make it easily accessible and produce its reward, often with the ultimate fulfillment and enrichment of the mother-lode itself. I've been in the mines' hundreds of feet below the earth's surface and have seen the dynamite charges set and later witnessed the resultant payload that was obtained. I have seen this first-hand many times, and believe me, it is an awesome sight.

I was told my mother practically threatened bodily harm upon my grandfather when she found out he set the dynamite charges with me right at his side. I bet she would have too if she knew I even lit the fuse a few times myself.

"This Generation" has no real heroes, no one to show them the result of lighting the fuse, and no mentor to light the first fuse as an example or explain how to light one for themselves. What has happened to all the heroes, the good guys who taught by example?

Gene Autry and Roy Rogers were two of my heroes, and I didn't think I would ever forgive Mom and Dad for not allowing me to go live with Gene Autry on his ranch. You see, he really did invite me to go home with him one-night back-stage after his live stage show, and I really believed him.

Well, things do change with time, and forgiveness has a way of healing the hurts inflicted by adults on their kids. However, I sometimes thought about the grand time I might have had with Gene Autry on his ranch. I did have a grand time on a ranch. My very own personal hero's ranch, my grandfather's ranch, located within the *Ozark* Mountains. A blessing that I believe God certainly prearranged the opportunity for me to spend multiple summers with my grandparents on their 'Ozark Ranch'!

Then those good old teenage years brought on several new heroes and a new identity. These were wonderful years when everything was super cool, boys wore ducktails, girls wore short shorts, and a burger was only two bits. Rock'n'roll music, James Dean, Elvis Presley, Little Richard, Jerry Lee Lewis, Bo Diddley, and the list went on and on! Wow, did we have our share of heroes, and we really believed in "the American way."

We were a generation with a purpose, with a destiny to fulfill, and we moved through the 60's in swift pursuit of this life's best with our idealistic heritage and distinct identity on solid rock. But what happened during the next three decades and the cataclysmic event predicted for the year 2000? Why have things changed so much? Roy and Gene are still my original heroes, but none of the others remain, and the heroes we may have had when we were younger are now only memories of the past, except for my 'grandfather', an incredible hero I called 'Pop' who is now glorifying God our Father, our Lord Jesus, and the Holy Spirit.

Why doesn't the younger generation have their heroes like mine? Why do people have to call these young Americans from the teens to the mid-20s from decade to decade a fabricated name like "Generation X, Millennials or Post-Millennials"? In this new generation, is it true that today's youth have no heroes, no purpose, and no substance in their lives?

Well, after thinking about it, I must admit, this certainly does make sense for some of the present generations due to misinformation and lies being spread by some organizations to deceive, especially the younger generations. The so-called mainstream national media has violated their own creed, and instead of truthfully reporting the facts, they use their influence to attempt to increase their professional position in the industry.

The negative influences being promoted to the most recent generations are causing great challenges and are significantly misleading the moral fiber that once was inherent in people but is now considered to be a choice. Just look at the examples that their elders have set before them. In 1973 the Supreme Court legalized the disposal of unborn human life (a new name for murder). Over sixty-three million human lives have been terminated since Roe vs. Wade.

It would have taken over 275 Hiroshima and Nagasaki-type nuclear attacks to kill as many people as abortion has killed in the USA since Roe vs. Wade. In all the wars in the USA, from the Revolutionary War to the end of the Viet Nam war, the USA has had

1,048,659 deaths; abortions in the USA since 1973 have taken the lives of over 63,000,000 human beings.

At every turn of the dial, each new day brings examples of illicit sex, human trafficking, drugs, stealing, lying, cheating, killing, disowning anything of God, and basically abandoning all the principles upon which our nation was founded. These are just a few of the examples set by those in authority over us in the government.

In addition, this generation has received equal or worse examples from the entertainment world, the family, and even in some factions of the church. Human life has been shown to be something to scorn. Pleasure and sex have taken the place of love, and four-letter words that are repulsive to God make up most of the vocabulary used in the world today. Four letter words have replaced most of the verbs and adjectives in the English language and are permeating throughout the business, social, and family circles at alarming rates.

Sounds like a replay of life in Sodom and Gomorrah, the people of the earth at the time of Noah, and maybe, just maybe, the state of the earth between Genesis 1:1 and 1:2. Could it be that the moral condition of today's earth is giving us another clue of impending disaster? Of course, it is! Only a fool could not recognize the obvious and alarming similarities.

The USA always stood up to protect the innocent and came together when evil threatened our existence. We always knew what it took to defeat evil, and good always prevailed. If one doesn't have a hero, an example for guidance, and in addition has acquired little or no hope in anything with substance, then there is no purpose, no cause to champion. On a similar hand, if the wrong hero or an evil example are the ones most often being promoted, then the opposite result occurs, and evil will persist.

Before I formed thee in the belly, I knew thee; and before thou camest forth out of the womb, I sanctified thee

Jeremiah 1:5, (KJV).

He shall be filled with the Holy Ghost, even from his mother's womb.

Luke 1:15, (KJV).

And it came to pass, that, when Elisabeth heard the salutation of Mary, the babe leaped in her womb; and Elizabeth was filled with the Holy Ghost: And she spoke out with a loud voice, and said 'Blessed are thou among women, and blessed is the fruit of thy womb.'

Luke 1:41-42 (KJV)

This Generation may not know that they have a very special purpose and a cause to live for and even die for—God's vision. Recruiting the lost and directing them from darkness to the light through Christ's redemption, and promoting God's plan for His children, who are to become an eternal reflection 'Of His Glory.'

"So, the last will be first, and the first last. For many are called, but few are chosen."

Matthew 20:16, (KJV)

You and this Generation is being touched by the finger of God and are being called right now to be a king, a lord, a priest in the most unique, elite corps in all of God's creation—the 'Heir Corps.' This elite corps of God's children, His heirs, will receive the absolute highest and most prestigious glorious promotion in all of God's Kingdom as the saints of the Most High, the "sons of God."

In the order of hierarchy, there is God (Father, Son, Holy Spirit) and then the 'sons of God,' God's children (His godly heirs), and then all the other saints of the first resurrection, and the multitude of angels. Next is God's elect chosen people (Abraham's natural and spiritual decedents) and then last, but certainly not least, all the other holy people of the new earth who come out of the Millennial Kingdom of Christ.

Once you grasp the full meaning of this unique Godly promotion, you will begin to see and understand the awesome power and responsibility you are destined to receive from God.

His vision for you and me as the sons of God, His children, is for us to receive His eternal supernatural life; we are to become glorified like Christ and become a reflection 'Of His Glory.'

If this generation doesn't already have this Godly vision but a different purpose and cause to live and die for, they wouldn't be available as vessels to fulfill God's will for their destiny. He can't fill a vessel with any new substance (vision) if it's already filled with something else. And He certainly wouldn't pour anything new in with the old, or the new would become contaminated and completely lose its essence.

I believe God has a plan and a purpose for all of us, so let's encourage this generation to become a high-performance generation, a supercharged, *Omega generation. God's very own high-performance generation, racing against time to defeat Satan in the last race for all those lost souls before the natural human clock stops.

He wants to use this generation as an army of believers to carry His glorious banner and promote the good news of salvation and the Kingdom of Heaven. To capture back the hearts and souls of those lost to the new age and negate all of Satan's many deceptions that have enticed the world away from Christ, I believe it is now the time to once again shout the message.

> *Prepare ye the way of the Lord, make his paths straight. Every valley shall be filled, and every mountain and hill shall be brought low; and the crooked shall be made straight, and the rough ways shall be made smooth;*
>
> *Luke 3:4, 5 (KJV)*

> *"Repent, for the kingdom of heaven is at hand!"*
>
> Matthew 3:2, (NKJV)

Someone must get the message out to the people; the Kingdom of Heaven is glorious; your inheritance includes the stewardship of your very own personal kingdom as a joint heir with Jesus. You, too, can be adopted into the royal family of God and be promoted into everlasting kingship. Turn to Jesus and accept your Heavenly Father's glorious gift, get a wonderful life in Christ!

Is this a message of a literal kingdom and your inheritance just a theory, or is it speculation, conjecture, supposition, or fact? It's a fact, and it's from God!

Starting with a hypothesis that God does not lie, a demonstrative fact. (Meaning it is apparent, evident, real, true, capable of being demonstrated, and is proven by reasoning or evidence). The Holy Scriptures are, in totality, a revelation from our Father God of His glorious plan and purpose. He has promised this throughout all the ages of ages for all His creation and the whole human race.

The language throughout the scriptures is explained with three distinct meanings: the literal, figurative, and the symbolic, and we should read scripture as it is, without making something out of it that is not God's intended meaning. If in doubt as to God's true meaning, one has only to turn to the Holy Spirit for clarification.

In addition, there are some well-written commentaries available to help one better understand the scriptures. Some even have cross-references that provide additional support to the stated interpretation(s). God's plan is awesome, and so much so, I believe it would be impossible to write down everything that God has prepared for all human-beings.

If this book with all its words were used to represent natural Man's complete understanding of God's ultimate plan and purpose, it collectively wouldn't even be representative of a single comma in God's book. God has prepared such a grand eternal life for redeemed human-beings. He has prepared so many glorious unspeakable blessings for all of mankind, especially those whose names are written in the "Lambs Book of Life." It is impossible to even theorize their glory, for there are no words in any language today that could even begin to describe God's blessings.

> *For precept must be upon precept, precept upon precept, line upon line, line upon line, here a little, there a little.*
>
> *Isaiah 28:10 (NKJV)*

> *The works of His hands are truth and justice: all His precepts are sure"*
>
> *Psalm 111:7, (ASV)*

A precept is something authorized by God, over which Man is responsible. A direction intended as a rule of action to teach!

The chapters that follow include references to God's word that are the precepts upon which God's intended plan and purpose for mankind and all of creation are to be proven or theorized. They demonstrate, prove or make certain clear speculations through reasoning or evidence of apparent truths, providing a theory based upon a logical set of facts. Each precept is like a rung in a ladder that separately influences one's ability for an upward move, which, if taken one at a time, will accomplish the user's purpose. Taken together, they constitute the device that allows one to climb higher than natural man can attain by his own efforts.

This book has been prepared with a certain methodology: In the chapters that follow, rather than systematically making assertions and then arguing for them, I have presented certain facts and precepts to increase the knowledge of the reader as the plan and purpose of God's eternal kingdom unfolds.

So, 'happy trails, pardner!' The reading should prove to be exciting even though the trail may be a little rocky (controversial). Just remember, don't take my word for it, you talk to God about it.

> *Be diligent to present yourself approved to God, a worker who does not need to be ashamed, rightly dividing the word of truth.*
>
> *2 Timothy 2:15 (NKJV)*

This passage is telling us to be persistent in the study and in the application of God's word for our lives. It is telling us to be attentive and careful in choosing the direction we allow ourselves to follow.

A worker cannot intelligently do his or her work if they don't understand what is expected of them or does not have a clear picture in their mind of the resultant product that will be attained for their efforts. Just as a contractor must have drawings and specifications giving him a visual representation and description of the building he wishes to build, we as workers (believers) must also have a plan.

Therefore, we must diligently study our plan (God's word) to visualize in our 'mind's-eye'* the picture of God's kingdom—our inheritance! The pages that follow will help to unfold this glorious plan that God has for you and will challenge you to pass it on to others when you 'catch the vision'

OF HIS GLORY!

*visual memory or imagination of an image seen by the brain as a real vision.

MILKY WAY GALAXY—OUR LOCALITY

VIEW TOWARD OUR MILKY WAY GALAXY FROM THE VICINITY OF THE HERCULES CLUSTER. SPRAWLING SPIRAL ARMS REACHING OUT FROM A GLOWING YELLOW CORE WHERE 100 BILLION STARS RESIDE.

This artist's illustration gives an impression of how common planets are around the stars in the Milky Way. The planets, their orbits, and their host stars are all vastly magnified compared to their real separations. A six-year search that surveyed millions of stars using the microlensing technique concluded that planets around stars are the rule rather than the exception. The average number of planets per star is greater than one.

* *What does Omega mean spiritually?*

In spirituality, the symbolism of the 'Omega' is related to spiritual growth, evolution and enlightenment. It is the end of a cycle and the beginning of a new cycle. The symbol brings the human experience closer to the divine, because, according to traditions, from the spiritualities of the divine we leave and return to it.

Alpha (A) and Omega (Ω) are the first and last letters, respectively, of the classical (Ionic) Greek alphabet… This phrase is interpreted by many Christians to mean that Jesus has existed for all eternity or that God is Eternal and you have been appointed by our Father God to become a reflection…

OF HIS GLORY!

CHAPTER 2

God expects us to seek His knowledge

> *"In the beginning God created the heavens and earth" (Genesis 1:1, NKJV).*

This simple statement is perhaps the most divinely profound revelation of God's intended purpose and plan for people from the very beginning of time. The hope, the vision, and a promise for all the created universe brought into existence from nothing. The totality of God's created domain (estate) over which Man was and is to exercise sovereign dominion, as delegated to Man through Adam (Genesis 1:28). In so doing, God expected Man and all His creation to be reflections "Of His Glory."

Due to the consequential events that likely preceded Genesis 1:2 and the world's attempt to discredit any notion of a creator, Man has always wondered how the world and universe came into existence. Down through the ages, various secular groups and Christians alike have studied and struggled with the biblical view as well as the scientific view.

Man has for the past 6,000 years concerned himself with discovering and understanding the process of creation. Science has concluded from its study the worldwide belief that holds creation as a process of evolution, or the more scientific theory of the so-called "big bang" without a creator.

Sincere Christians have likewise concluded that one, or possibly both, the big bang and the process of evolution may have been used by God in His creation of the universe. It has even been theorized that the evolutionary process is continuing today in an ever-increasing and ever-expanding universe. See the photo of the front cover and its following description of the expansion occurring within the Constellation Orion.

To patronize the scientific community to reach a compromise that both groups will support is not necessary, and is it important. However, as a Christian, one should be careful not to make the Bible say something different than God intended. Genesis means "origin" or "beginnings," and when God revealed the "origin" of creation to Moses, He revealed that the universe (the whole cosmos) was created, not a product of blind chance and probability.

We don't know or understand the complexity of just how God did it, what process He used, or how long it may have taken by our measurement of mortal time. However, the Bible is very clear that God created the Heavens and the Earth. What was not, became something! And it became something gloriously astonishing! The Bible reveals that God's word went forth, and things with no prior existence came into being as God spoke His word (Psalm 33:6, 9) or even by the breath of His mouth. God created the Heavens and the Earth as a manifestation of His glory, majesty, and power. (Psalm 19:1) The Bible not only tells us about creation, it reveals who God is, His personality, His character, His image, and His marvelous plan; a plan for fulfilling His purpose and goal for people and all of His creation for eternity.

We can all know God in a very personal way and receive all the promises of God now and forevermore. We have before us as 'blood-bought' Christians, as God's children, as kings and priests and heirs of His glory—joint-heirs with Jesus Christ, the most exciting and rewarding eternal journey our heavenly Father God could prepare for us.

We are not even remotely capable of imagining the glory prepared specifically for us as God's children; this glory of which perfected mankind will enjoy cannot even be described. God's holy race of people during, and especially after, the climax of the wonderful millennial age of Christ's reign will extend beyond time into the "aeon's of the aeon's." Human-being's will then see the 'Kingdom of Heaven' as a full manifestation of His glory.

God created the heavens and the earth and then made all the enhancements, all the elements necessary to provide for a universe where His purpose and His goal for mankind would be fulfilled. He designed Man (male and female) in His very own image and likeness as a triune being (spirit, soul, and body) to worship and serve Him out of love, faith, loyalty, and gratitude. As God's people, we are to know Him, glorify Him, and live in righteousness and holiness before Him for all eternity. God made Man in His image and likeness without exalting one over the other. However, He did not make Man exactly like Himself because God has no physical mortal body. Man will never be totally like God because He is the Supreme Being, and we are made by Him. We do, however, become a reflection of Him and exhibit all His characteristics: His perfect love, compassion, forgiveness, patience, goodness, and faithfulness.

For the scientific world to say that the universe and all life "just happened" or "evolved" is incredulous. The very functions, remarkable organizational order and efficiency of the vast extraordinarily enormous universe points to one and only one logical and truly consistent possibility. God created it and made everything that is! Even those who subscribe to the Big Bang Theory recognize that an event had to take place for there to be a beginning.

The known universe or the universe identifiable by Man through his system of scientific identification and measurement of "the heavens" is incredibly vast. For example, it takes a beam of light (which travels at 700 million miles per hour) over 100,000 years just to cover the length of the milky way galaxy, in which planet earth's solar system is contained.

And this, our planet's galaxy, is only one among many *billions* of galaxies within the known universe, and this known universe is potentially only a part of God's entire celestial cosmos. It is important to understand the full and wondrously awesome magnitude of God's creation and see it in perspective to our own tiny speck of a planet called earth. To better understand, let us build a mental image of a scale model representing the distance to the edge of the 'known universe' from where you are sitting right now.

If the thickness of a single page of this book, which is actually about 0.005 of an inch thick, is used as a dimensional scale to represent the distance from the planet earth to the sun in our solar system (which is 93 million miles away) it would take a stack of these pages 31 million miles high just to represent the distance to the edge of what man knows today as the 'known universe.'

Another example of the magnitude of God's creation is the incredible size of most likely the largest star known to man, "VY Canis Majoris" Compared to our sun, which has a diameter of 870,000 miles, VY Canis Majoris has a diameter of 17.4 Billion miles. As a comparison, our planet earth has a diameter of 7,926 miles and our moon a diameter of 2,160 miles. VY Canis Majoris is so large 2,100 of our suns would fit inside of it, and 2.1 billion earths would fit inside this mammoth star. To help understand the order of magnitude of this comparison, there are many, many billions of enormously large stars in the universe larger than our sun. But even more significant than this known fact, astronomers have only just recently discovered about a dozen planets outside of our solar system, and these only since 1995. However, within the billions and billions of galaxies in the known universe, scientists believe they may have discovered just *one* in all of God's creations, like planet earth. Does this mean we live on the only one? Very doubtful based upon God's plan for eternity.

However, with approximately 200 billion galaxies in the part of the universe that we can see, even if there were only one planet per star, there would be around forty trillion billion planets in our observable universe. It is very likely that the number of planets in the universe is greater than all the grains of sand on this planet earth. How many of these might have been created by God to support life? Don't jump to any conclusions yet!

Even more spectacular and awesome than a view of the universe is God's magnificent order within this universe. Did you know that you and I travel twenty-one billion miles across empty space each year on this space-ship earth, and our whole milky way galaxy is spinning at the incredible speed of 490,000 miles an hour? But even at this incredible speed, it takes our Milky Way galaxy 200 million years to just make one complete rotation.

All this motion and speed like a busy intersection without traffic signals and we have never run into anything within this complex sea of billions and billions of spinning, speeding galaxy and solar systems. All of creation is functioning with remarkable order and efficiency, just as God chose to create it.

The creation story certainly teaches us the reality of the three attributes of God:

1) Omnipotence—His ability to do whatever He wills, limited by His nature of infinite love. Although the word "omnipotence" is not found in the Bible, the scriptures clearly teach us about God's omnipotence. (Job 42:2; Jeremiah 32:17; Matthew 19:26; Luke 1:37; Revelation 19:6)
2) Omnipresence—The virtue of God fills the universe in all its parts and is present everywhere at once. Not a part, but the whole of God is present in every place. The Bible teaches us the omnipresence of God the Father, Son, and Holy Spirit. (Psalm 139:7-12; Jeremiah 23:23-24; Acts 17:27-28; John 14:9-11)
3) Omniscience—God perfectly and eternally knows all things—past, present, and future. God knows how best to

> attain His desired objective. God's omniscience is clearly taught in scripture (Psalm 147:5; Proverbs 15:11; Isaiah 46:10)

Then why did God bother to start the clock again with Genesis 1:2? Well, God created the universe and Man as an expression of His love, and especially His deep love for all people. God chose to make us in His image and likeness, a little lower than Himself. He loves every one of us equally, and we are of the highest order of value in His kingdom.

God has revealed His love, His greatest desire is to relate to, and join in fellowship with the people He created. God took the ultimate step toward fellowship with us through His supernatural conception and birth as a mortal human child, becoming the "Son of God," named Jesus Christ, the Savior of His own people to deliver Man from sin's bondage and Satan's power. (Acts 26:18; Colossians 2:15; Hebrews 2:14, 7:25)

Has the world, with all its scholars of the Bible and of science, overlooked the incredible importance of God's plan due to its very humble beginning? A small garden between the Tigris and Euphrates Rivers on a small planet called Earth and a naked gardener named Adam who, by his own will and choice disobeyed God. Then because of his disobedience, he lost the title to God's creation and gave it over to the enemy of God, Satan.

Then 4,000 years later, in a dirty little stable, in a cave located in a small town called Bethlehem, God Himself became a man. He was born of a virgin as a 'god-man' for the purpose of taking back the title from Satan and again giving it to Man, so God's long-range plan would be fulfilled. God's purpose, as always, is focused upon His plan of peopling the earth with a holy race of men and women, boys and girls. Giving mankind His eternal love and abiding fellowship throughout all of eternity and forevermore. What makes the purpose of His human birth such an unbelievable event is the fact that Man alone cannot believe any further than the knowledge he has acquired. So, without the Spirit of God, Man has no discernment of God's plan.

> *"God's people are destroyed for lack of knowledge" (Hosea 4:6, NKJV).*

> *"For thou hast made him a little lower than "ELOHIM," and hast crowned him with glory and honor" (Psalm 8:5, KJV).*

Note: ELOHIM (Is a plural noun belonging to the three persons who are the Elohim) is the Hebrew word translated in the Bible that is plural for God. Thus, Adam was created a little lower than God. Jesus knew that Man was created a little lower than God, not angels. This is the reason He stated in John 10:35, *"I said, ye are gods… unto whom the word of God came"* (in His reference to Psalm 82). We should always remember that any time the spirit of God desires to do something, the devil will try to counterfeit it or negate its credibility. As heirs of salvation, having been redeemed by the blood of Jesus and being heirs of God and joint-heirs with Jesus Christ, I have great news pilgrim—your destiny is to become one of God's most 'elite', glorified, Christ-like, sovereign heirs "Of His Glory."

As one of God's elite heirs, you dear saint, will be ruling and reigning in glory forevermore over all of God's peopled universe. A member of Christ's heavenly governmental body, higher than the angels, and in perfect harmony with God's very own nature and will. Oh! My friend, we have no conception of all that has been prepared for us. But this we do know, *"we shall be like Him,"* and if that doesn't give you goosebumps, contemplate on the following scripture.

> *[8] The LORD's instruction is right; it makes our hearts glad. His commands shine brightly, and they give us light.[9] Worshiping the LORD is sacred; He will*

always be worshiped. All of His decisions are correct and fair.

(Psalm 19:8-9 (CEV) Contemporary English Version)

Don't change yourselves to be like the people of this world, but let God change you inside with a new way of thinking. Then you will be able to understand and accept what God wants for you. You will be able to know what is good and pleasing to Him and what is perfect.

Romans 12:2 (ERV)

AUGUSTE RODIN'S "THINKER"

Conceived in 1880 to be the crowning element for Dante's "The Gates of Hell." He may have been thinking of mortal humans who have rejected God and received their ultimate fate of passing into an eternity separated from God?

CHAPTER 3

"I have said you are gods."

It has been said, 'He is a fool who gives up what he can never lose to gain what he can never keep.' The truly wise person knows the value of eternal life and is willing to do whatever is necessary to obtain it. I am convinced that there are people in this world who wouldn't believe the scriptures, or accept the notion of eternal life, even if Jesus Christ in all His glory walked up to tell them of the unimaginable glory of God's plan.

Sadly, there would almost be as many excuses for not listening as there were people approached. 'Don't have time,' 'not now,' 'come back later,' 'what's the trick,' 'don't bother me,' 'gotta go,' 'Oh! That's just your interpretation,' etc., etc. Or they might just tune out completely, not listen to a single word, and walk away.

Some people will just never have the time or inclination to accept or receive any of Christ's truth or life. They will go to hell faster than a speeding bullet, piercing the darkness with a loud shrill as the unspeakable reality of "pain eternal" enters their very being and consumes every bit of their joy and peace. Oh, how tragic and how sad! But this is not for you or me, because we are informed and full of knowledge, or soon will be.

> *"Come to me all of you who are tired from the heavy burden you have been forced to carry. I will give you rest. Accept my teaching Learn from me. I am gentle and humble in spirit. And you will be able to get*

some rest. Yes, the teaching that I ask you to accept is easy. The load I give you to carry is light."

Matthew 11:28-30 (ERV) Easy-to-Read Version

I pray wonderful Lord God Almighty, in Jesus' most precious, blessed name that not a single person who will read this book shall ever grieve your Holy Spirit; but will hear and receive from this same Spirit, the knowledge of God's agenda and rejoice before God's throne as an heir of His glory.

Together, we thank you for your riches, your wealth, your love. Lord Jesus, you are our great Redeemer, our Lord, our King. Let your presence come upon all these, my brothers and sisters, and fill your church with a mighty harvest of saints and then come, Lord Jesus, come!

The Enemy always returns to deceive Man:

You have probably noticed or are acutely aware that there is a resurgence today, a growing interest in and practice of occult beliefs, such as astrology, fortune-telling, witchcraft, psychic phenomena, and sadly that the Arabic Allāh ("God") is the one and only God in Islam and anyone who does not profess this must be killed especially all of the entire Jewish nation.

A few years ago, a Christian man was forced to confess this on a video and, after doing so, was savagely beheaded because he was a non-Muslim. Just another example from the Bible is telling us of things that will happen during the end times. The true nature of all these false beliefs is shrouded by various forms of deceitfulness (Revelation 18:23), and through it, a great many people are being cleverly deceived and will never find the Door to eternal life. In John 10:9-10, Jesus said, *"I am the door. If anyone enters by me, he will be saved, and will go in and out and find pasture."* (He is telling us He will provide us with abundant life and provision.)

In verse 10, He tells us, *"the thief does not come except to steal, and to kill, and to destroy. I have come that they may have life, and that they may have it more abundantly"* He is telling us that the enemy (Satan) comes to prevent us from receiving all that God has planned for us. He comes to rob us of the prosperous, abundant life that is full of God's blessings, to oppress our bodies through disease, accidents and to destroy everything that we love and hold dear.

Occult practices were common among the pagan nations of the ancient world, and in these last days, the Bible tells us to expect a resurgence of these practices and warns us not to become involved. These practices are called *"an abomination to the Lord,"* and as such, we are forbidden to respond to these practices.

Today, we are told in fine print at the bottom of the television screen that it is for entertainment only as we are bombarded with advertisements to call our own personal psychic. These programs promoting the psychics and their many enticements are transmitted to our homes by the numerous satellites traversing our planet in the heavens above (a form of spiritual wickedness in high places). Some of these programs are being promoted by some very worldly, successful celebrities, providing an air of tremendous credibility and shrouding the true nature and purpose of the program—which is to promote and carry out Satan's hidden agenda.

Advertisements, programs, testimonials, and various worldly temptations are being used to snare unsuspecting souls and reel them into the soulish realm of sense consciousness appealing to the emotions, the intellect, and the appetite of the will; especially those of human-beings passions, their deepest wishes.

Mankind's soul consists of the mind (intellect), will (desires), and emotion (feelings). When one enters the soulish realm, their soul becomes a playground and practice field for evil spirits and demons. They are expressly charged by Satan to delude all humans into carelessness, greed, self-centeredness, and ultimately into total ruin.

When God made "Man" (men and women) in His image and likeness, He made Man a spirit, soul, and body. He placed Man's spirit in the highest order of hierarchy to maintain an open, uncluttered line of communication between Himself and Man. In addition, all three of Mans' attributes were set in total complete harmony with God's will. When Mans' soul is elevated to a dominant position above the spirit, the here and now becomes of greatest importance, and a man loses sight of eternal life along with all the supernatural rewards, promotions, and benefits that God has prepared for those whose names are written in the Lambs Book of Life.

1 John 3:1 gives us a glimpse of God's love and the call to participate in the blessings of the Kingdom. *"Behold what manner of love the Father has bestowed on us, that we should be called children of God!"* The next verse, 1 John 3:2, tells us *"Now we are children of God"* (upon accepting Jesus as Lord—i.e., Born again) *"and it has not yet been revealed what we shall be, but we know that when He is revealed, we shall be like Him, for we shall see Him AS HE IS."*

This verse is telling us that we will be transformed into the real, the actual supernatural godly image and likeness of Christ. So, besides being God's children today and knowing that we will become glorified, supernatural beings like Christ, God has reserved something very special for His children that has not yet been fully revealed.

God does give Man the promise of eternal life for all those who put their faith in Jesus Christ and remain His obedient children. This eternal life is not just a long life, but is a god-life, like God's, that will last forever, without end. A life that is in total complete harmony and balance with the perfect will of God the Almighty, "I AM!"

Then why do so many people fall prey to the tricks of the enemy, and why don't they just as easily see the wondrous glory of God's plan unfolding and accept the gift being offered to them? Why would anyone ever spend $3 to $5 or more per minute to call a total stranger seeking the answers to their future life, liberty, and pursuit of happiness? Remember Hosea 4:6 tells us, *"My people are destroyed for lack of knowledge."*

I said, you are gods

In the world of business, Man has an agenda, understands and completely embraces that agenda. He has developed it through much strategic planning, goal setting, and a well-defined long-range plan, a master plan for worldly success, great fame, and lots and lots of money. What about "The Master's Plan?" His agenda? Could it be you might just have the opportunity of a lifetime to become a member of one of the biggest and most elite groups of supernatural beings ever fulfilled in God's eternal long-range plan for His peopled universe?

Suppose the Prime Minister of England wrote you a letter and advised that Parliament had conducted a genealogical search of their royal records and discovered you are the rightful heir to the throne. You are advised that to receive your rightful position as King or Queen, you must give up your citizenship in America and leave for England. The letter also advises you to pack your bags because very soon, the royal delegation will arrive to escort you to your Kingly inheritance. Would you prepare yourself for the journey to receive your Kingship, or just ignore the letter?

Well, pilgrim, this is your wake-up call—your Heavenly Father wants you to know He is looking to fill numerous supernatural divine positions. He wants a billion or so men and women to be the kings (gods) in His government for the duration of eternity.

Are you interested? Are you available? Then prepare yourself for this incredible journey. The Royal Delegation with Jesus Christ in the lead will be announcing His arrival soon!

For Jesus said: *"Is it not written in your Law, I have said you are gods?"*

John 10:34, (NIV)

I said, "You are gods, and all of you are children of the Most-High"

Psalm 82:6, (NKJ)

"If he called them 'gods,' to whom the word of God came—and the Scripture cannot be broken—what about the one whom the Father set apart as His very own and sent into the world?"

John 10:35-36 (NIV)

9 I am the Door; anyone who enters through Me will be saved [and will live forever], and will go in and out [freely], and find pasture (spiritual security). 10 The thief comes only in order to steal and kill and destroy. I came that they may have and enjoy life, and have it in abundance [to the full, till it overflows].

John 10:9-16 (AMP) Amplified Bible

I am the door!

AD·WWW.HAVENLIGHT.COM/YONGSUNG-KIM
PAINTING BY YONGSUNG

CHAPTER 4

It's Time to Take a Stand

God really wants mankind to have a perfect, sinless soul, to be a Holy person, a whole person with mind, emotion, and will in perfect fellowship and communion with Him through the Spirit and in service to Him through the body. He desires Man to be gloriously alive with the very life of God! Perfect expressions of love with the very nature of God's goodness and totally God-centered. A reflection "Of His Glory."

Has God changed His mind? Has He changed His plan? Has Satan's interference caused God to take a different position? Of course not! God has told us, in Malachi 3:6, *"For I am the Lord, I change not."*

But how do we know the Bible is the truth? How do we know that the Bible hasn't been changed or the actual meanings of its statements haven't changed?

It is sometimes just as difficult to accept the Bible as literal truth for the Christian as it is for the unsaved. There are more people today than ever before who would argue its validity and claim the scriptures are open for interpretation and that parts of it are not meant for today's world. What do you believe?

'The Book,' 'The Bible,' 'Holy Bible,' 'Scripture,' 'God's Word,' 'The Word,'—a collection of work with many names, one message. It is a very special message to us from our God, and although it may have many names, it is all the same "Good News." All 66 separate parts combined into one magnificent road map for humanity. "The original Route 66!"

> *All scripture is given by inspiration of God, and is profitable for doctrine, for reproof, for correction, for instruction in righteousness: that the man of God may be perfect, thoroughly furnished unto all good works.*
>
> *2 Timothy 3:16-17 (KJV)*

So, God tells us that all scripture—the entire 66 parts were "given by inspiration of God." The scriptures were given for the perfection of Man that he might be fully prepared to glorify God and serve in His kingdom.

The literal Greek translation reads, "The scriptures are God-breathed." If anyone reading this disagrees or just doesn't know, I encourage you to visit a good Christian bookstore, ask for selections that will increase your knowledge and help you prove this truth—then study it for yourself.

You will then know and appreciate Holy scripture as the voice of God reduced to writing, the "Word of God," and will see that all parts of the Bible have God as their author. It is God's instruction book for Mans' redemption and eternal life. It has been said that ignorance of the Bible means ignorance of Christ.

You simply must trust God's word because "It is impossible for God to lie." And His promises to Abraham are just as true as His Word in all of Scripture.

> *Because God wanted to make the unchanging nature of His purpose very clear to the heirs of what was promised, He confirmed it with an oath. God did this so that, by two unchangeable things in which it is impossible for God to lie.*
>
> *Hebrews 6:17-18 (NIV)*

> 2 Peter 1:20-21 tells us: *Knowing this first, that no prophecy of scripture is of any private interpretation, for prophecy never came by the will of man, but holy men of God spoke as they were moved by the Holy Ghost.*

God gave mankind the Bible to guide the human-nature of Man to fulfill His long-range plan. He inspired men to write it exactly as they received it from God's divine revelation. Apart from errors in transcription when rightly interpreted together, all the books of the Bible, from Genesis to the Revelation of Jesus Christ, constitute an infallible rule of faith and practice.

The Bible was written by more than 40 different authors over a period of 1,600 years, and all were divinely inspired because the Holy Spirit guided each writer. The things that were written the first year agree perfectly with those things that were written last.

There are many books written on the authenticity of the Bible and the evidence of its divine inspiration, so if you really have a problem accepting this, you are again encouraged to please search out the truth for yourself. Don't be deceived by the lies of the evil one who would like nothing better than for you to continue in your present state of unbelief. Jesus not only believed in the scriptures, He divinely inspired and guided the compilation of our new testament canon and sanctioned the validity of the old testament as written in *Matthew 5:18 (KJV):*

> *"For verily I say unto you, till heaven and earth pass, one jot or one tittle shall in no wise pass from the law, till all be fulfilled."*

A jot in the Hebrew alphabet is the smallest letter and almost identical to our apostrophe sign ('). Likewise, a tittle is a small mark used to indicate an accent in Hebrew.

It is also good to study different translations for comparison. The Bible teaches that we are to *"rightly divide the word of truth"* (2 Timothy

2:15) and you can be assured the Holy Spirit can and will use more than one translation to enlighten and confirm God's word to a believer.

In this present age, Satan uses the world's ideas, morality, philosophies, desires, governments, culture, education, science, art, medicine, music, economic systems, entertainment, mass media, sports, agriculture, and even religion to oppose God, His people, His Word, and His righteous standards.

Satan uses all the resources and imaginations he can and makes every unceasing effort to destroy Man's rightful place with God through Jesus. He continues today to lead unsuspecting people to spiritual destruction with some of the cleverest and most deceptive thoughts ever planted in the human mind. And he cleverly uses those who reject Christ to unwittingly snare other family members and friends away from Christ and into eternal damnation.

The most deceptive of all is the spirit of apathy or just plain indifference to everything except the here and now. Some people have even become totally indifferent to everything except a man's worldly pleasures and promises. They put all their hope in things or themselves and just live day to day without any concern for tomorrow, living futureless lives of hopeless despair.

Well, turn on the power button to your soul, tune-up your intellect, get control of your emotions, and continue reading with a desire to gain the knowledge of God. He intends for you to have this knowledge so you will understand your rightful inheritance.

God has given you and me a divine right to receive the title and take possession of our 'royal crown' and 'sovereign rights' as an heir and joint heir of God's eternal glorious 'Kingdom of Heaven.'

This Kingdom of Heaven, contrary to popular belief, is not the one pictured in various movies or television shows or the one so often mentioned by those deceived by the devil's many tricks and lies.

The Kingdom of Heaven we are going to discuss right now, and unless otherwise mentioned, is the literal future Kingdom of Heaven, not the kingdom of heaven or kingdom of God that is spiritually available to the believer today.

The Bible has much to say about the kingdom in the present and if you are not a citizen of heaven today, read on, for you will be soon. The Gospels of Matthew, Mark, Luke, and John focus on the present aspect of the Kingdom of God and clearly show that 'The Kingdom' will be realized perfectly only at the second coming.

The future Kingdom will close the present age and usher in the perfect age promised by God. A careful study of the Gospels shows the two phrases "Kingdom of Heaven" and "Kingdom of God" are sometimes used interchangeably, so do not let this confuse you in your study of the gospels. Because of the work of Jesus Christ on the cross, Heaven is, in part, present today with believers on earth as they obey God. (John 14:2, 23).

Over the past few years, it has become quite evident to me that most Christian's do not know their place in God's Kingdom, now or in the future. Many Christians have not even tried to comprehend the greatness and magnificence of our Heavenly Father, nor all that He has prepared for us, His children, and heirs. I discussed Heaven with a young lukewarm Christian couple not long ago and was told they were not ready to play the harp and float on the clouds with the angels. They first wanted to live out all that this life had to offer.

They thought perhaps when they were old and grey, and their children were grown, they would be ready for the rest. Then and only then would they look forward to Heaven. Is this deception, or what? Imagine anyone thinking that the joy of life on today's earth could supersede Heaven's joy.

Others I have talked with have been romanced by the new-age trivial pursuit of universal peace, evolutionary utopia, and the belief that Mans' inner being can be perfected through prayer directed to various heavenly resources. Mankind has a need to overcome the deception being espoused by these anti-Christ groups. And it would certainly appear that with a fuller comprehension of God's master plan for eternity, Man might be better equipped to dispel Satan's many lies.

By increasing mankinds knowledge of those things to hope for, he will have more strength and persistence to overcome the temptations of today's earthly romance of the 'new-age' peace and humanism movement that is being perpetrated by the great deceiver. Jesus Christ is the way, the truth, and the life. He became flesh to redeem mankind from the dominion of death and the sinful nature of Satan. He has led the way for the people of earth to receive the everlasting covenant that God promised to Abraham, Isaac, and Jacob. A sinless universe with man's total being in complete harmony with God's will.

I believe it is time for you to take a stand, believe all of God's word, hope believing in hope and obtain the resolve to go forth as Abraham in faith, and "claim your inheritance." To effectively claim your inheritance, it is important to know and understand that two things happened to Man when he sinned in the garden: First: Man's divine image was marred and lost. Second: Man became devil-centered instead of God-centered. He gave up his godliness (Holiness) and handed the power and authority (dominion) he had received from God over to the devil.

Jesus came and gave these two things back to mankind. Mans' spirit was revived, and he again received the originally created potential for glorious Eternal life, 'the God kind of life.' Have you accepted? Well, it's time for you to 'take a stand' and focus your life on the things of your Heavenly Father, for you have been appointed to become a reflection…

OF HIS GLORY!

CHAPTER 5

Are you not the Seed of Abraham?

As stated earlier, the truly wise person knows the value of eternal life and is willing to do whatever is necessary to obtain it. Such a person was Abraham, a man considered to be the second of the seven greatest men who ever lived.

Aside from Jesus Christ, who was God/man, these seven are Adam, Abraham (Abram before God Himself changed his name), Moses, David, John the Baptist, Peter, and Paul.

The importance of Abraham's life cannot be underestimated, for he is known as the "friend of God." His name is mentioned in the Bible 234 times in the Old Testament and 74 times in the New Testament.

The first of three great biblical covenants are the Abrahamic covenant, an everlasting covenant. The keyword here is everlasting, which means eternal, without end.

> *And I will establish my covenant between Me and thee (Abraham) and thy seed after thee in their generations for an everlasting covenant, to be a God unto thee, and to thy seed after thee.*
>
> *Genesis 17:7 (KJV)*

> *"And if ye be Christ's, then are ye Abraham's seed, and heirs according to the promise" (Galatians 3:29, KJV).*

God's promise to Abraham is extremely important to Man's discovery of God's purpose for our personal lives, as well as God's purpose for all of creation. God not only gave a world-changing eternal promise to Abraham, but He then confirmed it over and over throughout the scriptures. He confirmed it many times, providing mankind conclusive proof of His far-reaching promise to emphasize the purpose of His long-range plan. The plan that He established and put into motion for all of creation from the beginning of time.

God's purpose has always been the peopling of earth (the entire sphere of natural human life as distinguished from spheres of supernatural life or spirit life), with a sinless holy race of people possessing the nature of God and the very essence of His glory.

God formed Man in his own image, a being without sin, higher than the angels, and gifted with the powers of procreation, that man might by "Him," populate the universe. Man was made to be a picture of the triune Godhead, a reflection of His glory.

Don't be confused by the statement 'higher than the angels', because this is not a contradiction with scripture, as you might think.

> *When I consider thy heavens, the work of thy fingers, the moon and the stars, which thou hast ordained; What is man that thou art mindful of him? And the son of Man, that thou visiteth him?*
>
> *For thou hast made him a little lower than the angels, and hast crowned him with glory and honor.*
>
> *Thou madest him to have dominion over the works of thy hands; and thou hast put all things under his feet.*
>
> *Psalms 8:3-6 (KJV)*

"The angels" in Verse 5 is translated from the Hebrew word 'ELOHIM.' And the correct translation of the word Elohim is 'GOD.' This means what it says, Man was made a little lower than God Almighty Himself.

Man was created in the image and likeness of God. Man was sinless and perfect. Man was created by God to be 'gods' over all creation. God created Man to have fellowship with Him; therefore, Man was created to be as much like God as possible.

The occupation of the earth (land habitable for Man) has always been an important part of God's plan for humanity. God has always wanted to extend the blessings He promised to Abraham to all his descendants. This desire of God will be met when the new heavens and new earth are made for Man after the 1,000 years Millennial Reign of Christ. Introducing the glorious Age of Ages, which simply means "forever" or "continuously."

The book of Isaiah 66:22 sums up God's eternal promise:

> *As the new heavens and the new earth that I make will endure before me, declares the Lord, so will your name and descendants endure.*

To fully understand the awesome magnitude and magnificence of God's future society we must look back to the life of God's friend Abraham to form an image of God's plan in our mind's eye.

God said to Adam in Genesis 1:28, *"Be fruitful and multiply, and replenish (fill) the earth."* If Adam had chosen the 'tree of life' and rejected the 'tree of the knowledge of good and evil,' God's plan would have progressed much farther than it has today, and every natural human born since Adam would still be alive today.

Additionally, if Man's adversary Satan had been rejected and expelled from mankind's sphere of existence, all things would be different. Planet earth would have been totally filled to capacity long ago and God would have had to either remove the procreation power from mankind, or mankind would have had to find additional habitable earths. If you think about it, God is much too perfect and orderly to allow His people to progress to such a state of insufficiency in His plan.

But Man thinks so small, and he overlooks the obvious. God is not limited by anything, and the universe, or possibly even universes', is a vast creation by Almighty God beyond human comprehension. Furthermore, all of God's creation plays a major part in God's eternal long-range plan, as does our own tiny planet we call Earth.

God authored the concept of the organization, and He has shown down through the ages that good organization is essential to maintain effectiveness. Additionally, it helps people work or exist in harmony and ensures that a specific desired goal will be reached.

We see pictures of God's bias for organization in the Bible from Genesis to Revelation. I Kings 4 shows us how well-organized Solomon was with his eleven chief officials, twelve district governors, and managers of the district officers.

In Luke 9:14 and Mark 6:39, we witness God's organizational tendency through Jesus' instructions to His disciples to have the multitude (5000 men plus women and children) sit in groups of 50. If the organization of such a small group as this is so important, wouldn't you think the organization of 40, 60 or 100 billion of God's people would require some special accommodation?

Well, let's go back and find out how Abraham fits into this picture: Abraham (Abram before God changed his name) was from Mesopotamia and the city of Ur of the Chaldeans. Ur was a seaport on the Persian Gulf at the mouth of the Euphrates River some 12 miles from the traditional site of the Garden of Eden. Ur was also one of the most magnificent cities in all the world.

Abraham was called by God to give up the world he knew and embrace a promise he would not see fulfilled in his lifetime. So…

> *By faith Abraham, when called to go to a place he would later receive as his inheritance, obeyed and went, even though he did not know where he was going.*
>
> *Hebrews 11:8 (NIV)*

> *"For he was looking forward to the City with foundations, whose architect and builder is God" (Hebrews 11:10, NIV).*

He had hope for something better and obeyed without knowing where, how, when, or why, before there was any precedent for physical resurrection either by promise or example. The book of Genesis spans a period of around 2,350 years. The first 11 chapters describe the creation, fall, flood, and the tower of Babel. The last 39 chapters concern themselves with Abraham, his seed, and God's promises. In other words, God gave us more detail about Abraham and His covenant with Abraham than about the origin of the universe!

The following scriptures outline the eternal promises God made to Abraham, Isaac and Jacob, written in the book of *Galatians.*

> *"Just as Abraham believed God, and it was accounted to him for righteousness." Therefore, know that only those who are of faith are sons of Abraham. And the Scripture, foreseeing that God would justify the Gentiles by faith, preached the gospel to Abraham beforehand, saying, "In you all the nations shall be blessed." So then those who are of faith are blessed with believing Abraham.*
>
> *Galatians 3:6-9 (NKJV)*

> [14] *that the blessing of Abraham might come upon the Gentiles in Christ Jesus, that we might receive the promise of the Spirit through faith.* [15] *Brethren, I speak in the manner of men: Though it is only a man's covenant, yet if it is confirmed, no one annuls or adds to it.* [16] *Now to Abraham and his Seed were the promises made. He does not say, "And to seeds," as of many, but as of one, "And to your Seed," who is Christ.* [17] *And this I say that the law, which was four hundred and thirty years later, cannot annul the covenant that was confirmed before by God in Christ, that it should make the promise of no effect.*
>
> *Galatians 3:13-17 (NKJV)*

Matthew 1:1 shows us that if anyone is in Christ, he is the seed of Abraham, and the blessings promised by God are as real today and tomorrow as they were to Abraham. *"The book of the genealogy of Jesus Christ, the Son of David, the Son of Abraham."*

Now, don't get the idea from all this that Abraham was any better a person than you, for he was not. If you sometimes feel it takes too long for God to move in your life, if you think your life has been too self-centered and it's embarrassing to ask God for another chance to get it right.

Or if you believe there is too much sin and not enough faith—you've just messed up your life so much it has caused others to get hurt and mess up their lives. If you have been bogged down so long and delayed making that commitment, because you don't believe there is any hope left for your recovery. Then as it is often stated—'you ought to see the other guy.'

Talk about messing up, read about Abraham's life and see how he messed things up. There is no sadder situation in the world today than the agony being lived out in one of the world's most troubled spots, the Middle East. Abraham's sin 39 centuries ago is the cause of this problem through Ishmael, his son, and the father of the modern Arab Nations.

But you know even with all this mess, God still blessed Abraham, and still blesses his descendants today, and will continue to bless his descendants forevermore.

So stop kicking yourself in the head and know this—God's plan includes you in a big way and in spite of everything you or I may have done, our gracious Heavenly Father God forgives, forgets and restores us all back into divine fellowship with Himself through Jesus Christ His Son.

Romans 10:9 tells us to *"confess (say it) with your mouth that Jesus is Lord and believe (trust) God raised Him from the dead, and you will be saved."*

By praying this prayer, you're not only saved but you're redeemed from the curse of the law. You are made an heir of God and have received legal title to all of God's promises.

How all this fits into God's plan is the subject of the next chapter and is outlined in the Abrahamic Covenant. This covenant was announced in Genesis 12:1-4, confirmed in Genesis 13:14-17, Genesis 15:1-7, officially and legally ratified in Genesis 15:8-18.

Just as God has promised, mankind and especially those redeemed of Christ will live victoriously in the promised land for all of eternity, and the Heirs of God through Christ Jesus will become the heavenly reflections…

OF HIS GLORY!

CHAPTER 6

A man of dust to A nation, As the dust!

God called out Abraham and made a special covenant with him, known as the "Abrahamic" covenant.

> *I will make your offspring like the dust of the earth, so that if anyone could count the dust, then your offspring could be counted.*
>
> *Genesis 13:16 (NIV)*

God then repeated His covenant to Abraham's son Isaac (Genesis 26:3-5), and again to his grandson Jacob (Genesis 28:13-15). God repeated it to no one else, although this covenant is re-affirmed repeatedly throughout the Bible in both the Old and New Testament.

A few of these affirmations are: Genesis 15:5, 22:17, 32:12; Psalm 72:17; Acts 3:25-26; Galatians 3:6-9; Hebrews 6:13-18; Galatians 3:26; and Galatians 4:6.

These three Patriarchs are therefore known throughout history as the covenant fathers and affirm mankind's eternal inheritance.

> *"I am the God of your ancestors, of Abraham, Isaac and Jacob" (Acts 7:32, GNT).*
>
> *"We are Abraham's offspring and heirs according to promise" (Galatians 3:29, BSB).*

Why do you suppose God was so adamant about this covenant that He repeated His promise to Abraham twice, then repeated it again to Isaac and then again to Jacob?

He was most assuredly confirming that this covenant was for all generations down through time to the new generation and even beyond into the eons and eons of eternity.

Romans 4:18-19 says, *"Who against hope believed in hope, that he might become the father of many nations."* God has affirmed many times throughout the Bible that Abraham, a believer in Him, would be the father of God's peopled earth throughout the universe.

He affirmed to Abraham that his descendants would fill the earth, then based upon a comparison of his descendants to the sand, stars, and dust, He inferred that Abraham's descendants would continue to expand forever.

By expanding to the numbers indicated, they surely become God's sinless, holy race of mankind that will continue to multiply and fill His entire creation throughout eternity. Now don't go throw any stones just yet, first look at the evidence and rationale for this statement.

God promised Abraham that his descendants would be as numerous as the stars in the heavens and the sands of the seashore or even the dust of the earth. He also inferred that His covenant would continue forever.

> *Know therefore that the Lord your God is God; He is the faithful God, keeping His covenant of love to a thousand generations of those who love Him and keep His commands.*
>
> *Deuteronomy 7:9 (NIV)*

Because God has the foreknowledge of all things, the death of Christ was always a part of His long-range plan. It was carried out by Man under the influence of unsuspecting Satan to redeem the earth and the entire human race itself from the very cause of sin and the domination of the father of Sin himself, Satan.

The result of which will be as planned, a universe that is populated with sinless mankind and specifically the heirs of the covenant, Jews and Gentiles without sin in complete harmony and agreement with the perfect nature and will of our Triune God. A society in God's holy universe based solely on righteousness and love.

God did not give his Son on cavalry only to redeem a few billion of mankind out of the total human race and then call it quits for the rest of eternity. No, and God will not permit Satan to block His plan for peopling the earth and, more specifically, the entire sphere of His habitable creation.

The plan is set and now awaits the actual physical occupation of all habitable land by mankind throughout the total created universe. His plan calls for a sinless, holy race of people in the very image and nature of God to glorify His eternal sovereignty and love.

This never-ending fulfillment of His original long-range plan is on such a wondrously grand scale that no one can even begin to imagine the majestic abundance of His Glory prepared for Man.

According to the Godless culture of our worldly society today we are approaching the so-called new age, golden age, and the age of universal peace. Whatever newly coined word or phrase may be used to describe the condition of life being given to our future society, it is painfully evident that the most important person on the agenda is oneself.

I have been told that literally tens and possibly hundreds of millions of dollars are spent each month by people who are being enticed through various television and radio programs promoting psychic phenomena.

People are being deceived into believing they will receive a positive influence in their lives through metaphysical thought, astrological divination, sorcery, and other forms of irresistible appeals and fascinations commonly known as witchery.

All these diversions are being promoted for the sole purpose of satisfying the countless inner needs of people, their curiosities, their fantasies, and their fetishes. An intense pursuit of pleasure, knowledge, wealth, power, or just the simple acceptance of self and the satisfaction of a multitude of human desires.

The persons who are the most vulnerable to these influences are the young, the inexperienced, the misinformed, and the lost. But no one is exempt from the lure of temptation, for just recently, I have known professing Christians to get caught up in the deception and appeal of one or more of these deadly influences quite unsuspectingly. Satan can certainly be one tricky dude!

What do you suppose an intelligent person could be searching for that would allow himself or herself to get involved in this sort of thing? Could it be they are searching for the meaning of life, and the easiest, most available vision of this is the image being painted by these godless groups?

What can the church do to combat this? Well, for starters, we need to better understand the long-range goals God is intending for humankind to gloriously achieve in the future. How do the men and women, teens, youth and children of today fit into God's plan, and what about all those righteous dead of the past from Adam until now? How do the millions and millions of infants, children and aborted babies throughout history fit into Almighty God, our Father's plan?

To completely understand God's plan, we will have to wait until we are called into His presence. When we receive our eternal inheritance from the King of kings and Lord of lords, He will reveal the Master's plan and His most glorious eternal strategy will then be known by us, the saints.

Until then, however, we can see a silhouette of His glorious plan through God's word and from the types and shadows of the things to come that are so masterfully presented in the Word. We can even see a glimpse of the new heaven and new earth in several chapters of God's written plan, the Bible.

With a little divine reasoning and logic, we can see further into the future today than any of our forefathers because we have a far greater knowledge and understanding of today's end-time events as they are unfolding before our very lives.

Although all we have is a glimpse of God's vision, it is more than sufficient to show us a glorious eternal life with our Triune God; a life that is more than enough to negate Satan's many deceptive programs and practices with the enticements of worldly promises.

The book of Hebrews assures us that God is unchanging and His promises remain steadfast, forever:

> *Because God wanted to make the unchanging nature of His purpose very clear to the heirs of what was promised, He confirmed it with an oath.*
>
> *Hebrews 6:17 (NIV)*

God can not lie. His promises to Abraham are true. God's truthfulness applies not only to His word to Abraham, but also to His word throughout and in all scripture. Because all scripture is the inspired word of God, it is completely true and trustworthy.

What would you do if you were to discover a document that stated you were an heir of the richest, most powerful man in all the world, and your inheritance would make you a virtual king with a kingdom greater than Solomon's; a kingdom over which you would rule and reign as the sovereign lord?

If this inheritance to which you were entitled was an enormous estate that included vast land areas including cities with millions of people, and all you had to do to receive it was to walk to the courthouse and file your birth certificate as proof you were the heir, wouldn't you run to receive your rightful inheritance?

I don't know of any person who would reject their inheritance, or not cash in on a winning entry, turn away the prize patrol with a $10 million giveaway, or even walk past a one hundred dollar bill laying on the sidewalk in front of them! Do you? I think not! I know what some of you are thinking. "Okay, sure, I've heard that before. I'm a king through Christ Jesus, but that is for the here and now and is only figurative."

> *"You have made us kings and priests to our God; and we shall reign on the earth" (Revelation 5:10, NKJV).*

As Christ's redeemed, we, through His sacrifice and glorious resurrection, have been made "kings and priests" to God as shown in the scriptures.

> *"And has made us kings and priests to His God and Father, to Him be glory and dominion forever and ever, Amen" (Revelation 1:6, NKJV).*

It is so obvious that the sacrifice Jesus has given to all believers, Jews or Gentiles, the honor and privileges that God promised ancient Israel; we, His people, have a present calling to advance the Kingdom of God today in the here and now, in witness and in worship. As priests and kings under Christ, we are the new breed, the reborn, the children of God, to whom God our Father has delegated His own authority to extend and administrate the powers of His Kingdom. As 1 Peter 2:9 NIV so aptly puts it:

> *But you are a chosen people, a royal priesthood, a holy nation, God's special possession, that you may declare the praises of him who called you out of darkness into his wonderful light.*

We are a chosen generation, a special people began with Jesus' choice of the first twelve, who became 120, who became thousands on that day of Pentecost and millions today. We are a unique part of this continually expanding "chosen" generation when we accept Christ as our Lord and Savior, our King.

We are a royal priesthood, a worshipping army walking and living for Him in the light and standing with Him against Satan and all his followers. We are a holy nation (a community of people) composed of Jews and Gentiles, under the blood, from every nation under heaven.

We are a very special people, His own special people, *"chosen by God and precious to Him" (1 Peter 2:4, NIV).*

God's intention, as a part of His eternal plan from the very foundation of the earth as defined from the time of Abraham, has been to call forth a people with a special mission, a special purpose. A goal to extend His heavenly blessings to all of mankind throughout the whole of creation through His glorified children who are to become the realized reflection, "Of His Glory."

> *"Ask of Me, and I will give you the nations for your inheritance, and the ends of the earth for your possession" (Psalm 2:8, NKJV)*

This Psalm wonderfully proclaims that all the nations of creation are intended to come under the protection of Jesus' rule, and we, as joint heirs of Jesus (Romans 8:17), likewise receive this inheritance of the nations as God has promised.

> *And if children, then heirs—heirs of God and joint-heirs with Christ, if indeed we suffer with Him, that we may also be glorified together.*
>
> *Romans 8:17 (NKJV)*

Revelation 22:5 tells us that *"the inhabitants of the New Jerusalem will reign forever and ever."*

To reign forever and ever would imply someone or something to reign over. At the end of the 1000 years (millennium), once Satan is cast into the lake of fire forever, the earth is renovated by fire and made perfect, perhaps like the original Garden of Eden. The oceans are gone, and a perfect human race now begins to live in the fullness of the covenant God made with Abraham.

This human race is sinless, in perfect alignment and in complete harmony with God's very own nature, in the very image and likeness of our Triune God. A human race with a pure nature of God-like perfect love incapable of sin. But you and me, dear brother and sister in Christ Jesus, we are not in this group, we have previously been promoted! Glory to God!

Abraham's seed continues to populate the vast new earth, the new habitable universe, to fulfill God's glorious promise that Abraham's descendants would be as numerous as the *"dust of the earth"*.

Thus, the descendants of Abraham populate the universe and the body of Christ (the glorified church), the transfigured saints, the righteous children of God, rule, and reign forever along with Jesus as kings, lords, and priests over all of God's creation and the inhabited universe as it populates forever, and ever—for evermore.

Just imagine how large the new earth might be if God's holy city is 1,380 miles high. Astronauts today just happen to float around in an orbit +/- 200 miles above the earth.

"For of the increase of His government (Jesus) there will be no end" (Isaiah 9:7). Thus, a continually expanding universe! The body of Christ must therefore have a heavenly home in the new Jerusalem and a second home in the new earth (God's sphere of mankind's eternal life).

> *"In my Father house are many mansions: I will come again and receive you unto Myself; that where I am, ye may be also."*
>
> *John 14:2, 3 (KJV)*

Let us now go to the next chapter and see what God told Abraham and get a glimpse of His glory, and what it means to you as His heir.

EARTH TODAY

Our earth, as wonderful as humankind might believe, is the most incredible and beautiful place that God ever created. Just imagine what will be the most awesome and beautiful creation God has planned for "Himself" and His Saints?

Just imagine God's long-range plan for you and all His children. A NASA summer intern in 2019, a 17-year-old high school student from Scarsdale high in New York discovered its first world with two suns. A world 6.9 times larger than our present earth - 7,926 mi x 6.9 = 54,689.4 mile-diameter.

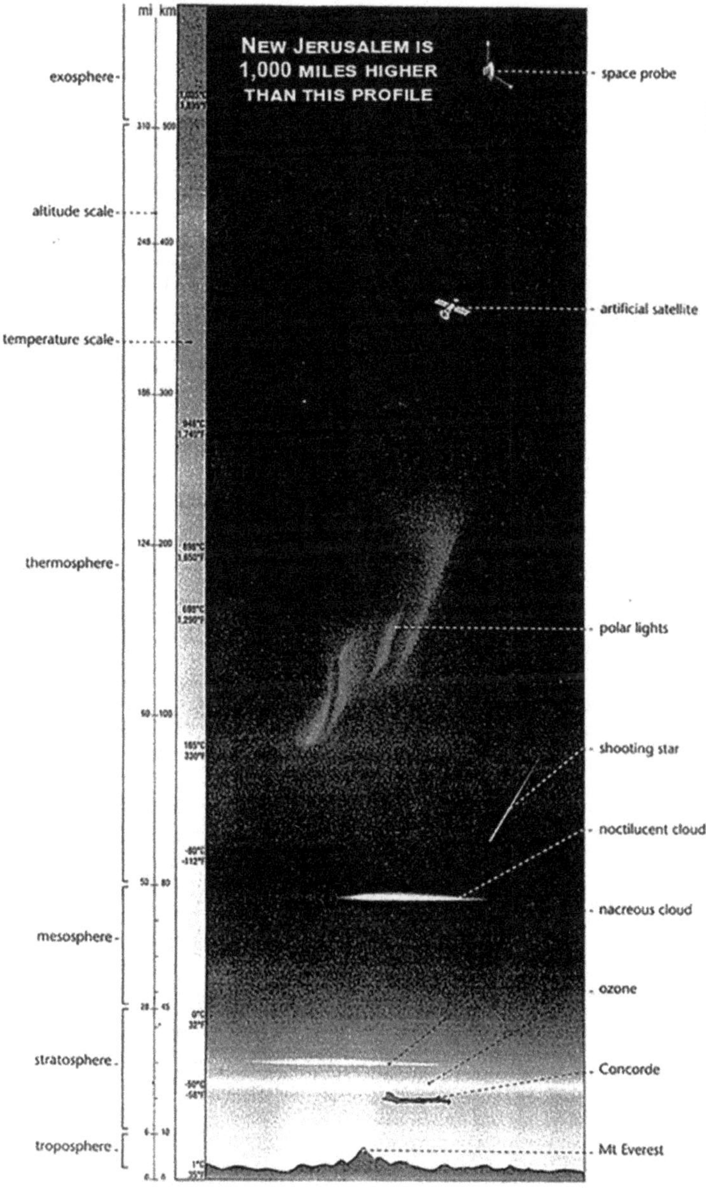

PROFILE OF EARTHS'S ATSMOSPHERE COMPARED TO THE HEIGHT OF NEW JERUSALEM

GOD GAVE MAN THE DIMENSIONS OF THE NEW CITY OF JERUSALEM W/ THE THICKNESS & HEIGHT OF THE FOUNDATION WALL THAT WILL CONTAIN 12 GATES NAMED AFTER EACH OF THE 12 TRIBES OF ISRAEL.

This should confirm that the New Jerusalem is to be located on the New Earth's surface not in the new heavens of the new earth, which is 4 times the height of this profile.

SPACE STATION ORBITING EARTH AT APPROXIMATELY 230 MILES FROM EARTH. FINLAND IN MIDDLE LEFT OF PHOTO.

FROM 310MILES ABOVE THE SURFACE OF THE EARTH BEGINS THE EXOSPHERE, WHICH HAS NO DEFINITE OUTER BOUNDARY . FROM 400 MILES' SPACE IS AN EVEN GREATER HOSTILE ENVIRONMENT FOR MAN. THE HUBBLE SPACE TELESCOPE ORBITS AT ABOUT 375 MILES WITHIN THE EXOSPHERE.

THE KNOWN "LAW OF PHYSICS OF THE UNIVERSE" MAY ALSO BE REMADE BY 'GOD' BEFORE THE PERFECT KINGDOM OF HEAVEN, THE PERFECT AGE OF AGES' BEGINS.

CHAPTER 7

His kingdom shall stand forever

"For the Lord will not cast off his people, neither will he forsake his inheritance." (Psalm 94:14, KJV).

God promised that He would create a new heaven and new earth (Isaiah 65:17; 66:22). And that promise will be fulfilled when the events foretold in Revelation 21-22 occur.

The occupation of the *Land* has always been, and it remains an important part of, God's plan for mankind. Abraham and all his descendants were promised land, but Israel only enjoyed a partial blessing of that land.

But was its God's ultimate plan just to include the tiny area of real estate known as Canaan? Or has God always planned to extend His many blessings into all habitable lands? Will this covenant plan of God be met when a new heaven and a new earth are created? Will the new earth be re-made to a size of greatly increased dimensions compared to our existing tiny planet earth? Yes! Our existing earth is just a baby planet in a relatively small galaxy compared to others throughout the known universe.

For the present, our planet earth remains under God's curse, and because of Adam's sin, Satan the Prince of this world has introduced much pain and suffering upon the earth (Romans 8:19-22). But hallelujah, God's Spirit also groans in supportive prayer for the weakness of God's people until the new earth appears (Romans 8:26-27).

Man remains the only creature in the universe that can tell God no, and from history, we can see that a Man has told God no many times. However, there have been, and still are, many men and women who said yes, allowing God to further demonstrate His grace and His purpose for all of creation. Abraham was just such a man.

Hebrews 11:8, 10 (NIV) shows us the obedience and faith of Abraham:

> *"By faith Abraham, when called to go to a place he would later receive as his inheritance, obeyed and went, even though he did not know where he was going" (Hebrews 11:8).*
>
> *"For he was looking forward to the city with foundations, whose architect and builder is God" (Hebrews 11:10).*

He had hope for something better and obeyed without knowing "where," "how," "when," or "why" before there was any precedent for physical resurrection either by promise or by example.

When God called out Abraham, He made a promise, a binding agreement, a sovereign pledge, an oath:

> *For when God made promise to Abraham, because he could swear by no greater, he sware by himself, saying, "Surely blessing I will bless thee, and multiplying I will multiply thee."*
>
> *Hebrews 6:13 (KJV)*

Genesis 12:1-3 says that God promised Abraham, a believer in Him, that he and his descendants would:

1) *be blessed*

2) *become a great nation*
3) *be used to bless all nations*

God even repeated these promises to him two more times in Genesis 18:18 and Genesis 22:15-18. God knows how stubborn and unbelieving Man can be, so he gave great emphasis to His Word by mentioning His promise so many times to Abraham, Isaac, and Jacob. He then re-affirmed it throughout the Bible, including the New Testament, to be certain we really hear it for ourselves today. (See Chapter 5 for God's affirmations.)

Abraham believed God, although, in the natural, he knew there was no hope because both he and Sarah were so old and had long passed their reproductive period of life.

Romans 4:18-19 tells us, *"Abraham against hope believed in hope."* His focus was more on the here and now, just like people today, for he desired above all things to have a son, a bouncing baby boy, all his own.

Can any of you relate to the feelings he must have had? Can any of you who have desired a child but haven't received the fulfillment of your desire related to Abraham's yearning?

Hearing the words spoken by God and knowing the importance of a family's genealogy (Asian cultures place great importance on bloodlines), Abraham believed in his heart (spirit) he would receive his son from God. He knew that he knew!

God revealed His long-range plan for all of creation to Abraham to confirm and continue to build up Abraham's faith for a son. He promised Abraham that his descendants would be as numerous as the stars in the sky and the sand of the sea or even the dust of the earth. (Genesis 22:17 (28:14, 32:12,)

> *But you have said, "I will surely make you prosper and will make your descendants like the sand of the sea, which cannot be counted."*
>
> *Genesis 22:17 (NIV)*

> *And thy seed shall be as the dust of the earth, and thou shalt spread abroad to the west, and to the east, and to the north, and to the south: and in thee and in thy seed shall all the families of the earth be blessed.*
>
> *Genesis 28:14 (KJV)*

> *I will surely bless you and make your descendants as numerous as the stars in the sky and as the sand on the seashore. Your descendants will take possession of the cities of their enemies.*
>
> *Genesis 32:12 (NIV)*

Just as God himself tells us that doctrine should not be built on just one Scripture. Statements of faith should be supported by more than one Scripture.

> *"…in the mouth of two or three witnesses shall every word be established"*
>
> *2 Corinthians 13:1, (KJV).*

> *"He determines the number of stars and calls them each by name"*
>
> *Psalm 147:4, (NIV).*

What an incredible magnitude of greatness God has revealed to us! Our frail underdeveloped human minds can't even begin to conceive the awesome magnitude of blessing our Heavenly Father has prepared for us, His heirs and joint heirs with Jesus, for all of eternity. As pointed out in Chapter 1, God's total universe is so vast that Man can't even begin to determine how large a universe our galaxy is inhabiting. If it takes a beam of light over 100,000 years just to cover the length of our Milky Way galaxy, which is only one among the many billions and billions of galaxies in the known universe, it is hard to even imagine the enormity of the universe.

Some of the billions of galaxies within the known universe are so vastly enormous they significantly dwarf our own Milky Way Galaxy. It appears that today we are not only on a very small planet in a very small solar system, but we are the only occupants in this tiny galaxy. However, even more, significant than the magnitude of the universe, we appear to be the only occupants throughout all the billions and billions of galaxies God has created.

Recently two different scientists said that there are 10^{28} (ten to the 28th power) stars in the sky and 10^{28} grains of sand on the Seashore. Based upon God's promise to Abraham, Isaac and Jacob, this would make the number of Abraham's descendants 2 x 10^{28} (the number 2 with 28 zeros' after it).

The entire population of the world since Adam has numbered 40 billion people (the number 4 with 10 zeros' after it), with the estimated number of believers out of these to only be in a range of about 1 in 40. Therefore, the sum of all names written in the Book of Life over the past 6,000 years would only represent about 1 billion people. Not a very significant number in comparison.

The dust of the earth is probably equivalent to the sum of the stars and grains of sand on the seashore, if not greater, but who wants to split hairs over a number this large. However, it is interesting that the numerical name for this number (2×10^{28}) is 20 Octillions.

Octavo meaning eighth, and the number 8 meaning new birth or new beginning. Like with Adam!

20 OCTILLIONS (2 x 10^{28})

20,000,000,000,000,000,000,000,000,000 (Dust of the Earth)
-40,000,000,000 (Mankind since Adam)
19,999,999,999,999,999,960,000,000,000 (More than all of humanity)

The number 20 meaning redemption. (It is noteworthy that in Hebrew society, any forfeited land could be redeemed by the nearest of kin.)

The actual count is of little concern since the number could be off by +/- 1 billion times. Besides, the comparison used by God and His own statement of qualification infers that the number is infinite. *"I will make your descendants like the sand of the sea, which cannot be counted"* (Genesis 32:12).

However, the real significance of this is the implication of mankind populating the immense universe because our present tiny island earth couldn't even begin to hold a fraction of this number. If the new earth, even without the oceans, is not increased in size by immense proportions, the planet earth at its current size would be incapable of supporting even 122 billion people. This would equate to an allotment of land the size of a football field for each person.

To just contain the estimated number of descendants of Abraham promised by God, 2 x 10^{28} would require 164 quadrillion earths based upon the above allotment. (The number 164 with 15 zeros' after it.) Impossible you say? At least not very probable in our limited human understanding.

"Is anything too hard for the Lord?"

(Genesis 18:14, NKJV).

Although there is no conclusive proof that there are any life-supporting planets within the billions and billions of galaxies in the known universe, astronomers have recently discovered what might be a planet the size of our sun. And our sun could hold 1.3 million planets the size of our tiny planet earth.

If we just study a few astronomical facts that are worthy of being mentioned, you might be amazed at the comparison of our suns physical size related to others. The star Antares could hold 64 million of our suns. In the constellation of Hercules, there is a star that could hold 100 million Antares or 6.4 quadrillion earths (the number 64 with 14 zeros' after it).

*I have often wondered if the apostle Paul when he was caught up into the third level of heaven, could have imagined the probability of its total magnitude since it is beyond our own universe (the second level of heaven as stated in the scriptures).

There are numerous scriptures related to God's promise to Abraham that are critical to our understanding of God's total purpose for mankind, and for us to get a clear perspective view of Revelation 21 and 22.

Prior to the flood, the number of man's years was 120 (Genesis 6:3) but according to Psalm 90:10 *"the days of a man's years are 70, or 80 if we have the strength."* Based on God's promises to Abraham, Isaac and Jacob, Abraham's descendants will span a time of 1,000 generations or 70,000 years—perhaps 80,000 years with God's strength. (Eighty means millennial rest.) But the inference here is that the 1000 generations spoken of by God implies infinity.

> *Therefore, know that the LORD your God, He is God, the faithful God who keeps covenant and mercy for a thousand generations with those who love Him and keep His commandments;*
>
> *Deuteronomy 7:9 (NKJ)*

It certainly appears from the scriptures that the perfect age includes "aeon's of the aeons" or many ages within the age of eternity. One aeon is potentially one billion years. If the 1,000 generations described above are just representative of a literal age within eternity, then this 70,000 or 80,000-year period is just one of the glorious ages we will enjoy with our Lord and God.

> *He remembers his covenant forever, the word he commanded, for a thousand generations…to Israel as an everlasting covenant.*
>
> *1 Chronicles 16:15, 17 (NIV)*

> *He remembers His covenant forever, the word He commanded, for a thousand generations, the covenant He made with Abraham, the oath He swore to Isaac.*
>
> *Psalm 105:8-9 (NIV)*

> *And they shall dwell in the land that I have given to Jacob my servant, FOREVER: and my servant David shall be their Prince forever, and I will place them, and multiply them, and will set my sanctuary in the midst of them for evermore."*
>
> *Ezekiel 37:25, 26 (KJV)*

For as the new heavens and the new earth, which I will make, shall remain before me, says the Lord, so shall your seed (Israel's) and your name remain.

Isaiah 66:22 (KJV)

Today we are only in the beginning stages of mankind's development, and by comparison to God's glorious promises for our eternal lives, it is obvious that we the people are still in the un-germinated seed stage of His long-range plan. The seed is no doubt ready to sprout, but it is a long way from the fruit producing stage.

Of the increase of His government and peace there will be no end. He will reign on David's throne and over His kingdom, establishing and upholding it with justice and righteousness from that time on and forever.

Isaiah 9:7 (NIV)

This implies that the body of people that will constitute the governing authority and those of the new earth will populate the universe without end!

James 1:18 tells us we are only the first fruits of His creatures, and Jesus was the first fruits of these.

Amos 9:14-15 states that Israel, God's people, will be restored and re-build their ruined cities, never again to be plucked from the land.

Zechariah 8:8 states they will dwell in the midst of Jerusalem in truth and righteousness. Revelation 22:5 tells us that *"the inhabitants of the new Jerusalem will reign forever and ever."* To reign forever and ever would imply someone or something to reign over.

Now, don't misunderstand what our responsibility for reigning means to a sovereign God. It is giving, mentoring, loving, guiding and serving as an extension of God's very essence.

What does this mean to the church? As kings, lords, and joint heirs with Jesus, each of the saints whose names are written in the Lambs Book of Life will be receiving an inheritance as God's holy stewards.

These heirs will reign over a very large measure of Abraham's descendants alongside of our sovereign Lord and King Jesus Christ, all in the presence of our Father and Triune God. "I AM."

To continue with our glimpse of God's eternal plan, we need to back up just a little and investigate the 1000-year millennial reign of Christ (a period of great happiness and human perfection).

Enter the following link in your browser or if you are reading the e-book, continue your personal study of Paul's revelation and follow the additional links on Biblia for more information.

https://biblia.com/Bible/esv/2-corinthians/12/2

*The three "*heavens" implied in 2 Corinthians 12:2* and on a previous page this was mentioned as three different realms that we call "the sky," "outer space," and the "spiritual heaven."

Graphic illustrations describe the physical land God promised Abraham but has not yet been attained, plus an artist's rendition of the new city.

I BELIEVE YOU MIGHT AGREE THAT THIS STORY IS BEGINNING TO GET REALLY INTERESTING. WE UNDERSTAND THAT A MAN NAMED ABRAM TOOK HIS WHOLE FAMILY AND ALL HIS ASSETS AND LEFT A CITY NAMED "UR" IN OBEDIENCE TO GOD'S INSTRUCTIONS.

Around 2000 B.C. "UR" was in Mesopotamia, a sinful place which is now called Iraq. Tragically UR practiced the ritual of child sacrifice to appease the top seven or ten of their false gods. Horrible? Right!

The only god being honored by the *majority* of the 61 million babies sacrificed from 1973 up to the year 2020 was a means of personal self-forgiveness or justification. Not a sacrifice to any false gods but mostly as a mere convenience in one's life. Obviously, when Abraham was asked by God to sacrifice his son Isaac, it was not a complete shock to him having grown up in UR himself, but there was one great difference.

Abraham knew that by his obedience to God, Isaac would be spared. Likewise, Isaac knew in his heart that he was to continue the lineage of Abraham's descendants and by faith knew he would not die. Yes, God provided the substitute!

UR was a very wealthy city in an Empire that developed into a major center for trade that brought people from many great distances from the Mediterranean Sea.

Abram obeyed God even though he didn't know where God was sending him. Of course, he ended up in Canaan, the Promised Land and God called him His friend. God also changed his name to Abraham, which means "Father of many nations" or "Father of mankind throughout eternity"...

God's Promise to Abraham, not yet Realized

NeXT

The Scriptural Division of the Land for Holy Use

The following three illustrations identify 1) the boundaries of the land God promised to Abraham, 2) the area apportioned to the 12 tribes of Israel probably exceeded 60,000 square miles, 3) The assignment of the specific parcels as directed by God. The fourth illustration is an artist's depiction of the City as seen in the artist's mind's eye. I seriously doubt Man is capable of visioning Christ's Millennial City, but Carlos' work is very impressive.

God's people will occupy all the land God promised Abraham and his sons. Not just the small section they have occupied, but the entire area represented in the following illustrations. Jesus will reign as king over Israel as well as all the nations of the world *(Isaiah 2:4; 42:1)*. The entire earth will live in peace *(Isaiah 11:6–9; 32:18)*. This millennial period under Jesus' rule will allow mankind to live free of any political party and serve only Jesus Christ.

> *You will divide the land for the Israelite tribes by throwing lots. At that time, you will separate out a part of the land. It will be a holy part for the LORD. The land will be 25,000 cubits long and 20,000 cubits wide. All this land will be holy. A square area that is 500 cubits long on each side will be for the Temple. There will be an open space around the Temple that is 50 cubits wide. In the holy area you will measure 25,000 cubits long and 10,000 cubits*

wide. The Temple will be in this area. The Temple area will be the Most Holy Place.

This holy part of the land will be for the priests, the servants of the Temple. This is where they approach the Lord *to serve him. It will be a place for the priests' houses and a place for the Temple. Another area, 25,000 cubits long and 10,000 cubits wide, will be for the Levites who serve in the Temple. This land will also become cities for the Levites.*

And you will give the city an area that is 5000 cubits wide and 25,000 cubits long. It will be along the side of the holy area. It will be for all the family of Israel. The ruler will have land on both sides of the holy area and the land belonging to the city. It will be next to the holy area and the area belonging to the city. It will be the same width as the land that belongs to a tribe. It will go all the way from the west border to the east border.

This land will be the ruler's property in Israel. So, he will not need to make life hard for my people anymore. But they will give the land to the Israelites for their tribes.

Ezekiel 45:1-8 (ERV)

Note:

The phrase "from the Nile to the Euphrates includes a much larger area than Dan to Be'er Sheva (highlighted in pink on the following map). These two rivers mark the limits of the potential expansion of the original borders of the Land of Israel. By saying that the land in between these two bodies of water is set aside for the Children of Israel, God is implying that it is Israel's destiny to become a blessing to all mankind by declaring His name "at the crossroads of the two great centers of civilization."

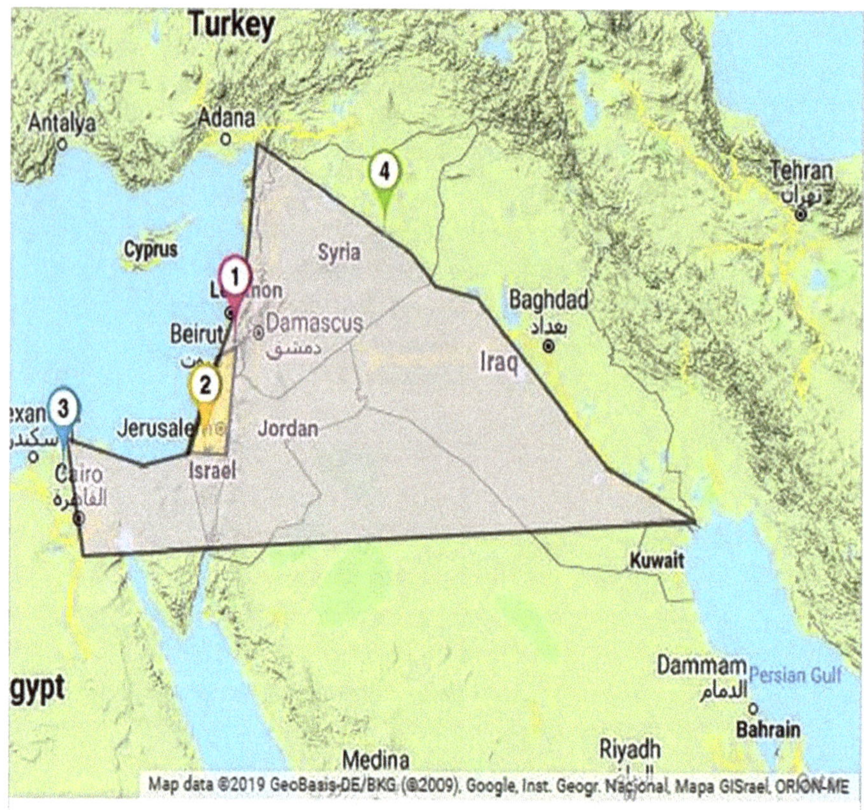

Boundaries of the Land of Israel as described in Genesis 15:18 and Genesis 17:8

1) Dan is described in the Bible as the northernmost city of the kingdom of Israel.
2) Be'er Sheva is described as the southernmost city settled by the Israelites.
3) The Nile River is Egypt's primary source of water. At the beginning of the Israelite's slavery in Egypt. The first two plagues that God brought upon the Egyptians also began in the Nile (Exodus 7:14-24, Exodus 7:26-8:11).
4) The Euphrates River is the longest river of Western Asia and one of the two defining rivers of Mesopotamia. According to the Bible, the Euphrates was one of four rivers whose source was a river flowing from the Garden of Eden (Genesis 2:14).

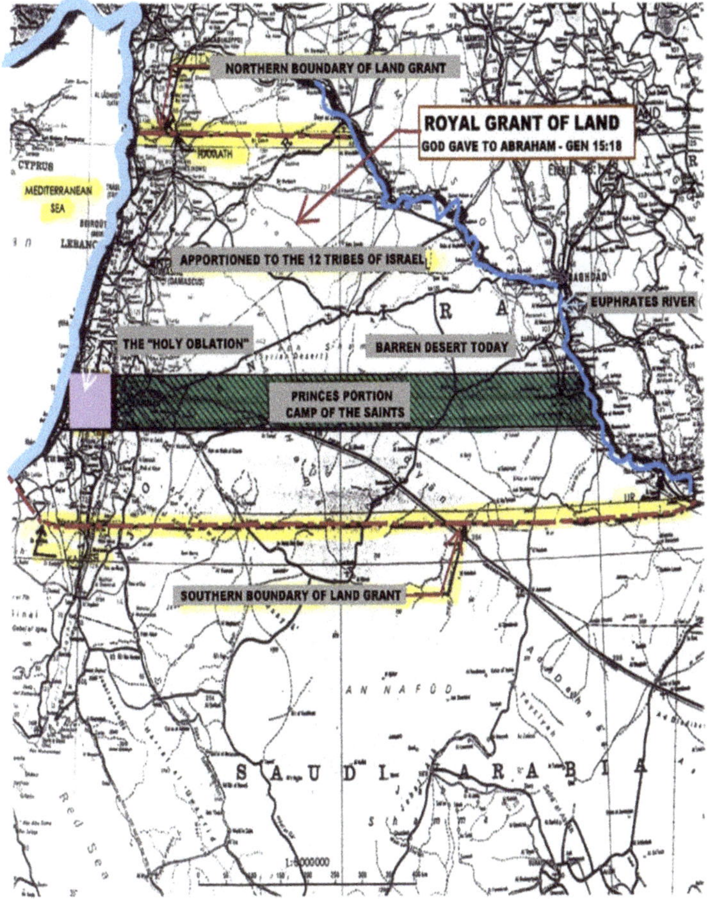

THE 1,000 YEAR MILLENNIAL REIGN OF CHRIST:

There will be two distinct groups occupying the Earth during the Millennial kingdom—those with glorified bodies and those with earthly bodies who lived through the tribulation and on into the millennial kingdom. Those with glorified bodies consist of the Church, receiving glorified bodies at the rapture (1 Thessalonians 4:13-18; 1 Corinthians 15:21-23, 51-53), and those who are resurrected after Christ returns to Earth (Revelation 20:4-6). Those who have earthly bodies can be subdivided into two groups: believing Gentiles and believing Jews (Israel).

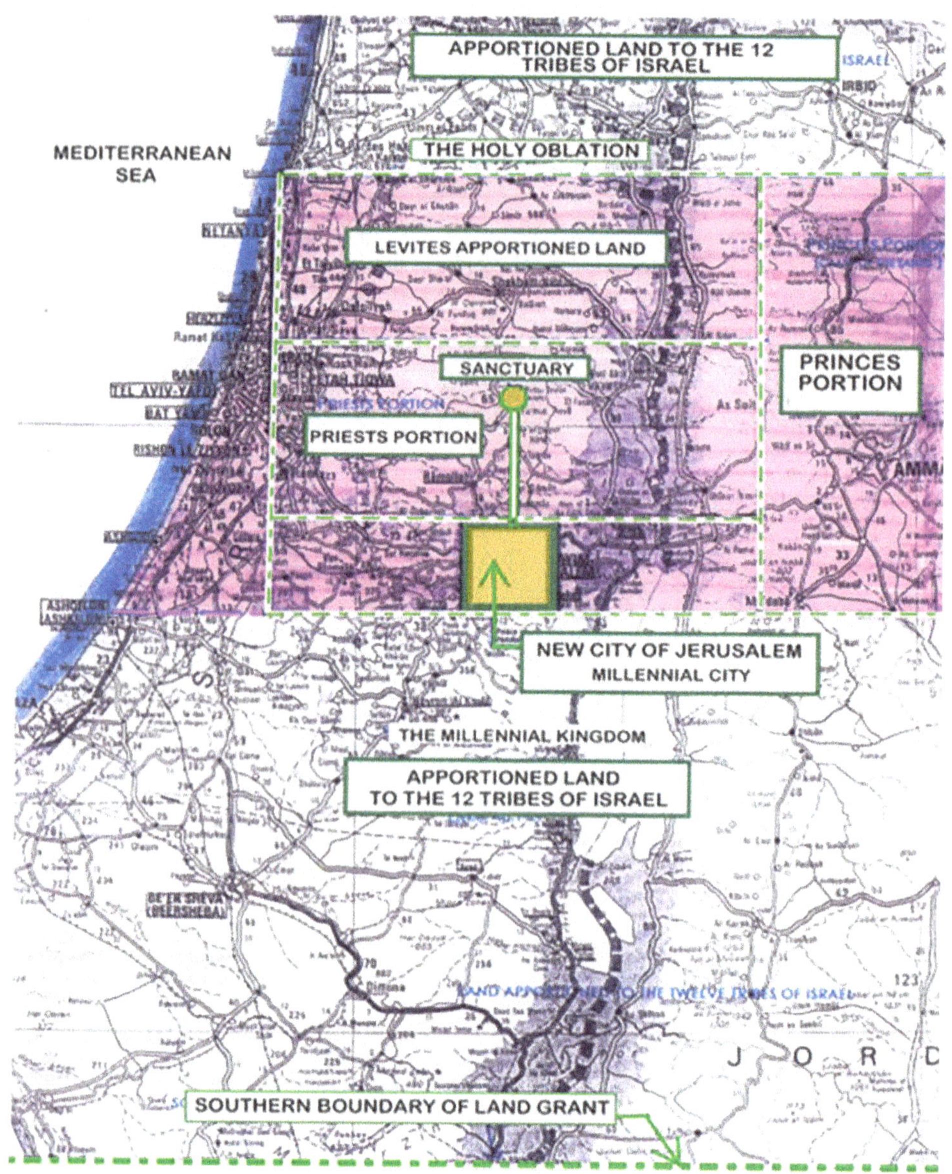

THE MILLENNIUM KINGDOM OF CHRIST
THE "HOLY OBLATION"

Enter: ***Christ's*** Millennial Kingdom in browser for more detail.

CHRIST'S MILLENNIAL CITY OF JERUSALEM:

Ezekiel 48 defines the City as an area that is approximately 8 miles in length on each side or 64 square miles of land within 56,000 square miles of the land promised to Abraham from God. About the size of the State of Iowa. See below the link for more descriptive information.

The above artist's depiction of the City during the 1,000-year reign of Jesus is a good representation of an awe-inspiring built environment. As an architect who has been directly involved in contributing over 45 years of my career involved with the built environment, I have to say the description of materials and finishes in the design is awesome, but only God can actually visualize this marvelous future 'City of Jerusalem.'

CHAPTER 8

The success model—Jesus!

> *Beloved, now we are children of God; and it has not yet been revealed what we shall be, but we know that when He is revealed, we shall be like him, for we shall see Him as He is.*
>
> *1 John 3:2 (NKJV)*

> *And we know that all things work together for good to those who love God, to those who are called ACCORDING to his purpose.*
>
> *Romans 8:28 (NKJV)*

> *For whom He foreknew, He also predestined to be conformed to the image of His son, that He might be the firstborn among many brethren.*
>
> *Romans 8:29 (NKJV)*

The above passages show that God's purpose for His called and justified people has always been to glorify believers and give them a resurrection body just like Christ's. He is telling us that as Children of God, we can be certain that God will fulfill His plan in His children, and we will ultimately be like Christ, "conformed to the image of His Son."

We are a very special, super victorious people who win more than just an ordinary victory—we receive the grand prize, as "heirs of God and joint-heirs with Christ."

We, the righteous sons and daughters of Almighty God, attain the highest position of honor and Glory possible in the Kingdom of Heaven. We become eternal reflections "Of His Glory," the status, the power, the love, and the very nature of Christ, forevermore.

> *"When the son of man comes in His glory, and all the holy angels with him, then He will sit on the throne of His glory.*
>
> *All the nations will be gathered before Him, and He will separate them one from another, as a shepherd divides his sheep from the goats.*
>
> *And He will set the sheep on His right hand, but the goats on the left."*

Matthew 25:31-33 (NKJV)

This judgment occurs after the tribulation and Christ's return, but before He begins His reign on earth. The wicked will not be allowed to enter Christ's kingdom but will go into eternal punishment. The righteous will inherit eternal life and the literal kingdom of God.

> *"Then the King will say to those on his right hand, come, you blessed of my Father, inherit the kingdom prepared for you from the foundation of the world."*

Matthew 25:34 (NKJV)

These "blessed of my Father" people are not the righteous 'saints' of faith, the church, or any of the ones whose names are written in the Lambs Book of Life. They are the living, breathing human beings that lived through the great tribulation, the remnant of God's people left on the earth after Satan's great defeat.

At the end of the great tribulation, Christ returns to the earth to defeat the armies gathered outside of Jerusalem and ushers in a judgment based on moral character revealed by charitable deeds.

The Millennial Reign of Christ

The above tribulation period is a two-phase event just preceding Jesus beginning his earthly reign for 1,000 years with the royal priesthood of righteous saints reigning with Christ. This royal priesthood is the 'elite' of Christ and is an assembly of the church and all the faithful of the Old Testament, who have already been in heaven and delivered from all impurity.

These are the blessed, who were invited to the glorious wedding supper of the Lamb, and who have their names written in the Lambs Book of Life.

There have been a great many books and articles written on the rapture of the church, the tribulation, and the great tribulation. A few books have also included informational writings and overviews of the millennium, the new heavens, and the new earth.

Whatever your belief of the rapture of the church might be, and whether your theology or doctrine allows the use of this word or not, the fact remains that the scriptures have informed us of an impending wonderful reunion with our risen Lord.

> *Then we which are alive and remain shall be caught up together with them in the clouds to meet the Lord in the air. And thus, we shall ALWAYS be with the Lord.*
>
> *1 Thessalonians 4:17 (NKJV)*

Call it what you will, but in the Hebrew language, the word used for "catching away" is "Raptu" from which Christian writers have coined the word "rapture" to represent the event spoken of in 1 Thessalonians, 4:17 (NKJV).

The reason that this is so important to present-day Christians is due to the impending ushering in of Christ's day, and the first resurrection of the saints.

It's like the chairman of the board calling all the board members to order to begin the annual meeting. A meeting at which all the business of the previous year is ended and the business strategies for the New Year are revealed and entrusted to the board members, the officers, and the leadership hierarchy of the whole organization.

This occurrence is the *"blessed hope"* spoken of in the scriptures, the close of the church age and the grand opening of the doors to the wedding supper of the Lamb.

It's wonderful that so many people have accepted Jesus as their Lord and have perfected their faith to the level of Abraham's faith. Christians today believe in hope for eternal life with God without fully knowing what it really means or what we are to receive as our inheritance on that glorious day when we see Him as He is.

But there are still millions and millions of people out there that don't have the faith or who are just lukewarm believers who need revelation knowledge to overcome Satan's many deceptions. These people need to turn their back on the things of the world, take a stand for Jesus, and commit their lives 100 percent.

From a very early age, we are taught to be competitive and aspire to win, win, win. Then all through school, we strive for acceptance and success. Once we complete school, acceptance becomes less of a factor in our lives, and success becomes paramount.

No matter where the strata of our lives might be, we strive for our own special level of success. We work for a level of success that is based upon some internal or external pressure. We work to acquire the image of success we developed and nurtured from the world's various models and standards of success.

Money is usually the measuring stick of one's success, but positions of authority and power are the most sought-after goals because reaching one's desired power level will ensure the money, thus, success.

Just think about your own life's trade, profession, vocation, or calling. What is the position you most desire(d)? Manager, supervisor, officer, president, or chairman of the board might be the level you established as your goal.

Still again, it may have been president, chief of staff, prima ballerina, top gun, star quarterback, head chef, chief mechanic, famous artist, etc., etc.

One thing all these positions of accomplishment, power, or authority provided was a model, an example, a picture of what the position offered the one seeking the position. There is always an image, a recognizable objective that could be hoped for and sought after with clearly defined lifestyles accompanying the attainment of the position.

Most of the professional staff and many employees in my own business wanted promotions to become managers, directors, associates, vice-presidents, and even presidents. They knew the measurement of success, money, would be a by-product of the position. So, when they aspired to a higher level of power and authority, they visualized themselves in that position and looked at the representative model(s) of that position. They pictured themselves in that role. They played dress-up.

It is sad but true. People spend the better part of their lives striving for the level of success they have set for themselves as a goal.

Unfortunately, many people reach their goal only to discover they still have an emptiness that their success didn't satisfy. They are not any happier than they were before and discover that their success just wasn't worth the price they had to pay.

What is wrong here is the equation for success they use for themselves doesn't include God. Oh, He might be allowed into the background of their lives and occasionally allowed to visit, but generally, God is placed in a secondary role to the attainment of their desired goal to achieve success.

Many children are taught at an early age to set goals and strive for the attainment of these goals above everything. The priorities set for these children are all geared to the satisfaction of the flesh and to worldly successes. Even their toys and recreation are usually enhancements and motivators to support and promote the whole program, often established for the child by one or both parents.

Unknowingly, some parents are sponsoring the devil's plan for their children and, sadly, assisting in the brain washing and programming of their children for spiritual death. Worldly success, yes! But without Jesus at the center of their lives and successes, what have they gained? With hard work and much of their time spent on attaining their goals, they often become like so many others before them and wake up one morning only to discover, "lordy, lordy," they just turned forty.

Half of their lives will have been spent fighting for the top, and by this time, a good percentage may have even reached their goals. They are now the "swells," living for the god of this world, and if they have children, they are passing down the same need for goals based on the same set of standards and starting the process all over, in the next generation.

But now, they must also maintain their acquired lifestyle to have at least another 25 or 30 years of life enjoying their fame and fortune (provided all goes well). But what about the next 30 years, 100 years, 600 years, 6,000 years? Chances are pretty good; they won't be with Jesus.

Satan has used many counterfeit replications of God's creation and distorted the true picture of God's ultimate plan for mankind. Past, present, and future elements of God's eternal plan have been singled out and distorted by Satan to mock God and conceal the truth from "would be" believers and believers alike.

He is a master at taking God's word, twisting it to his advantage, and then deceiving people with his own version to prevent them from ever knowing the truth. Some religious cults have masterfully added to and/or taken away from God's word to keep people in bondage and separated from Christ. Sadly, most of these never read anything but organizationally correct or even cult published materials.

The information that is presented usually instills a belief in their followers that the Bible is open for many interpretations because it is written in very confusing language. Or it includes much symbolism and mystery that cannot be understood by man in this life, but only in the hereafter.

Well, bless God, nothing could be further from the truth. What good is it going to do Man in the hereafter? It is meant for Man in the here and now, and with the Holy Spirit's help, it is very definitely understood by God's children.

> *These things I have written to you concerning those who try to deceive you. But the anointing which you have received from Him abides in you, and you do not need that anyone teach you.*
>
> *1 John 2:26, 27 (NKJV)*

> *"Behold what manner of love the Father has bestowed on us, that we should be called children of God!"*
>
> *1 John 3:1, (NKJV)*

If Man's equation for success includes God and obedience to His word then the Holy Spirit guides and directs his steps throughout this life, and right into the glorious eternal life to come.

> *"The steps of a good man are ordered by the LORD, and He delights in his way"*
>
> *(Psalm 37:23, NKJV).*

> *Beloved, I pray that you may prosper in every way and (that your body) may keep well, even as (I know) your soul keeps well and prospers.*
>
> *3 John 1:2 (AMPC)*

What better model could we ask for than the one provided by our Lord and Savior who came in the flesh to redeem us from the curse and bring us into everlasting life? And what a life it will be as a holy reflection…

OF HIS GLORY!

CHAPTER 9

You are a Unique Citizen!

Have you ever thought about what it will mean to you in your future life, after the first resurrection, to be a child of God? To be like Jesus and to have the actualized likeness of God's eternal divine nature, with the full manifestation of His glory being reflected through His Holy Spirit who lives within you! Personal study on the first resurrection is available by entering the following link in your browser:

https://www.gotquestions.org/

The full manifestation of God living within and through us, His children *"the sons of God,"* will most definitely become an actualized reality. When our Lord Jesus calls us home and we *"see Him as He is,"* we instantly become like Him, a reflection of His glory, the wonderful fullness of God living in and through us. Can you even begin to imagine the awesome power that will accompany the perfect eternal love of God Almighty residing in you, one of God's children, ruling and reigning with Jesus, "the King"!

Today, the Holy Spirit who lives in and through redeemed Man (the church) is only like a down payment, a deposit. It is only a small measure of God's earnest promise of the total fulfillment of all He has prepared for His children who participate in the first resurrection.

His power works in us and transforms us in the here and now to live as God's children. However, what we experience now is just a microscopic amount of the total magnanimous glory we will experience throughout eternity at the side of our Father and Triune God.

Having believed, you were marked in HIM with a seal, the promised Holy Spirit, who is a deposit guaranteeing our inheritance until the redemption of those who are God's possession—to the praise, ***Of His Glory.*** *Ephesians 1:13-14 (NIV)*

> *Now it is God who has made us for this purpose and has given us the spirit as a deposit, guaranteeing what is to come.*
>
> *2 Corinthians 5:5 (NIV 1983 V)*

This is God's promise to all believers, His guarantee that we will receive everlasting glorified bodies. However, as believers, we have our eternal life living within us right now through the Holy Spirit's indwelling presence, and our citizenship is already in the heaven of heavens.

It is like the financial instrument, a "bond," that you may purchase and have in your possession today, with the guarantee that upon reaching maturity, it will provide you with its full value. But, until it has reached complete maturity, you won't receive the fullness of its total value.

> *Then I saw thrones, and sitting on them were those to whom authority to act as judges and pass sentence was entrusted. Also, I saw the souls of those who had been slain and they lived, (came to life again) and ruled with Christ, the Messiah, a thousand years.*
>
> *Revelation 20:4 (AMP)*

> *Then the kingdom and dominion, and the greatness of the kingdoms under the whole heaven, shall be given to the people, the saints of the Most-High. His*

kingdom is an everlasting kingdom, and all dominions shall serve and obey Him.

Daniel 7:27 (NKJV)

The book of Revelation covers these 1,000 years referred to as the Millennium in the first six verses of Chapter 20. It is a glorious period of peace, love, and perfection when all that God has created lives in complete harmony, just as God had intended in the Garden of Eden.

"For the earth shall be full of the knowledge of the Lord as the waters cover the sea" (Isaiah 11:9, KJV)

All mankind will know of God and of Christ's redemptive work and His love for Man. During the Millennium, the sacrifices offered up in the new temple will provide Man with a remembrance of Christ's suffering and death for all of mankind's redemption.

This millennial kingdom of Christ is a transition period of final perfection for mankind's righteousness before God prior to the beginning of the final age of ages, the "perfect age." It is the age of an unimaginable glorious future kingdom that our Father God has reserved for His own special children, "the sons of God." It is also the age in which "the land" will be possessed by all the sinless, perfect human race, who will people the universe, just as God originally planned in fulfillment of God's covenant with Abraham.

Christ's "Millennial Kingdom" will not be perfect even with His physical presence, and sin will still exist in the hearts of Man. However, not all of mankind will yield to sins destructive forces but will purge it from their hearts as they serve their Lord.

Jesus, their Christ, will reign as Lord and King, and the "kingdom of God" will be eternally established within the lives of His subjects, both Jew and Gentile—preparing the way for the perfect age to come where sin will not exist, nor even come to mind.

"For indeed, the kingdom of God is within you"

Luke 17:21, (NKJV)

The kingdom spoken of in this passage is the internal and spiritual one that is now within each believer. When the actual literal "kingdom of God" is fully come upon the earth, Man will have received the fully realized actual image, likeness, and nature of God's very essence embodied within them. Man's will shall then be in perfect alignment and harmony with God's will, not as a clone or like a robot, but perfected to be of like nature.

With the rule of the earth under Jesus, God will deal with all of mankind as a whole, but they will be made up of many separate groups 'nations' with the Jewish people (God's "elect") as the head of the nations. The principle under which God will deal with Man will be righteousness, and Jesus will rule with a *"rod of iron"* based on love. (Isaiah 11:1, 4; Revelation 2:27, 19:15; Psalm 2:9)

At the end of Christ's 1,000 year "millennial" rule, good and evil mankind will be separated into two entirely identifiable and distinct factions of humankind. Then, after Satan is loosed from his chains, he will go out into the nations of the world and gather rebellious Man. When this happens, all those with an evil nature who have rejected God's righteousness will come to an end in apostasy.

At the end of the Millennium, Satan and his army of all wicked, evil mankind shall be destroyed by God and doomed to the "second death" to spend all of eternity in the *lake of fire,* "forever and ever!"

Evil will now become completely conquered by righteousness, and within all remaining people, mankind's sinful nature will be forever purged from their nature and replaced with God's holy nature.

> *"Holy, holy, holy is the Lord of hosts; the whole earth is full of His glory!" (Isaiah 6:3, NKJV).*

The above passage of scripture is a praise to God for revealing His innermost nature and character that emphasizes His wonderful greatness, divine authority, and His unending love for all of mankind.

> *He who is unjust, let him be unjust still; he who is filthy, let him be filthy still; he who is righteous, let him be righteous still; he who is holy, let him be holy still.*
>
> *Revelation 22:11 (NKJV)*

This passage shows that the deliberate choice that Man makes fixes his unalterable fate, but God, in His infinite greatness and love, will always allow Man the opportunity to freely make that choice by himself. Remember, mankind is to become perfected and be in harmony with God's holy will, not a robot or a God-controlled and directed creature.

Not only will each one of us, as the "sons of God," have a new and glorified existence in the millennial kingdom and the eternal kingdom to come, but we will each have an extremely unique relationship to Jesus. We will all have a very distinct and unique part to play in God's eternal kingdom.

From the rapture of the church, up until Christ's second coming, the Jewish people across the whole earth will experience the most terrible and awful judgments of all mankind remaining on the earth.

Those who do not die for Christ but come out of the "Great Tribulation," the remnant of God's chosen people, will be gathered as a new nation, finally recognizing Jesus as their Messiah. This new nation will form the nucleus of a natural earthly people who will be fruitful and multiply to replenish the earth. The Jews, as a nation, will then become the head of the nations and will govern the earth under Christ's Kingship.

Jesus Christ will rule over the whole earth with a "rod of iron" based upon an autocratic form of government with unlimited, absolute power and authority over all the nations of the earth. (Remember that a nation is defined as a community of people possessing a defined territory of independent status.)

These will not be like the nations as we know today that each has individual autonomous governments because there will be, but one government, one autonomous rule, and that is the rule of Jesus Christ, the Lord.

Let's digress just a moment to get a real perspective on Christ's millennial reign so you'll understand the Master's plan and how you may fit in His plan.

As just mentioned above, Christ will rule (exercise control over), and the new Jewish nation will govern (organize and direct the common activities of society). But you dear overcomer, child of God, heir, and joint heir of Christ, as one of God's children, the "sons of God," you will reign with Christ. You will receive from Christ the royal authority and sovereignty like that of a monarch and will be a representative of Jesus and a reflection of His glory to all the people.

So, the order of His government is:

1) Jesus, the Lord of lords and King of kings, ruling over the whole earth.
2) The glorified righteous saints, God's adopted heavenly children, the "sons of God," ruling and reigning with Christ as lords and kings.
3) The new Jewish nation (God's 'elect'—His chosen people) as the head of the nations of an earthly people.

4) The earthly people of all "sheep nations" were rewarded by Jesus with entrance into the "millennial kingdom."

"And He will set the sheep on His right hand, but the goats on the left. Then the King will say to those on His right hand, come, you blessed of My Father, inherit the kingdom prepared for you from the foundation of the world."

Matthew 25:33, 34 (NKJV)

The Bible tells us that only those who have a part in the "first resurrection" become the children of God (i.e., the "sons of God," both men and women), which include all the glorified righteous saints throughout history. These alone are God's adopted heavenly children who are set apart from all of God's creation for all of eternity to rule and reign with Him over the peopled universe forever.

Those included in the first resurrection are:

1) Jesus Christ.
2) The dead saints of Old Testament times.
3) The dead saints of the church.
4) The living raptured saints.
5) Those who are martyred for their testimony during the Tribulation.

Those *"blessed of My Father,"* the sheep nations, enter the 'millennial age' in their natural bodies. They are not a part of the 'elite' group of glorified righteous saints that enter the "millennial age" with Christ as the "sons of God." Neither are they His heirs and joint heirs with Christ, who rule and reign with Jesus and are reflections of His glory.

So, upon entering this age, God will deal once again with mankind. However, the church is not a part of this age and is no longer on the earth, except as it is represented by those in the elite group of Christ's heavenly bride. For these are the ones who rule and reign with Jesus and who were a part of the "first resurrection."

Whether you have been saved and redeemed by the blood of Jesus for 5, 50, or 100 years or even just one minute, you have the distinct privilege of acceptance into His kingdom as a dear child of God, our heavenly Father. So, don't discount the wonderful blessing you have received and miss the awesome reality of being a participant with this unique, very "elite" church of heavenly saints.

This group, including you and me, is a very special group of righteous people who will enter the "millennial age" in magnificent glorified heavenly bodies just like our Lord and Savior Jesus Christ's with all the attributes of His glory.

I pray that I am rightly referring to you, dear brother or sister, and to your future promotion from this earthly body to the eternal heavenly body God has prepared for you. If you have any doubts this could really be your inheritance, read on—believe God, it is!

You are unique, and you have a unique part to play in God's eternal kingdom as Christ shares His sovereignty with you, providing you have accepted Him as your Lord and Savior.

> *For our citizenship is in heaven, from which we also eagerly wait for the Savior, the Lord Jesus Christ, who will transform our lowly body that it may be conformed to His glorious body.*
>
> *Philippians 3:20, 21 (NKJV)*

As you should recall from a quotation previously stated, "The truly wise person knows the value of eternal life and is willing to do whatever is necessary to obtain it. "Believing that Jesus is the embodiment of God in human form and the personification of God's perfect love, what value do you place on the incarnate Christ that is to become manifested in you?

The earth has been for ages past, and more than ever before, today is the home of so many unwise spiritually blind people. People are blinded to the truth primarily because there is such a tremendous flood of confusing messages being propagated by both the factions of good and evil.

Yes, even good, well-meaning men and women of God are contributing to the confusion by promoting new priorities and professing doctrines that are false and out of order. A truly unwise direction for themselves, their families, and those they lead astray. Some have even gotten to the point of rejecting the virgin birth and divinity of our Lord Jesus Christ.

Just as Jesus sent the disciples out into the world, He is likewise sending us, and we should all go forth now in faith and preach the "good news "of the gospel. To all who will hear, let them hear, the real fullness of their inheritance from God is to become the *"sons of God"* and joint-heirs with Jesus as kings, lords, and priests, forever, and evermore to the eternal glory of God.

The devil, God's enemy, and our enemy have repeatedly tried to delude the truth about Man's inheritance from God—to lead Man down the wrong path and confuse his way. This is especially true today as we, the church, look up with the expectation of His glorious coming.

I believe it's time to stand and shout with joy—God's got a plan, and you're in it! Do you know, really know your destiny? Imagine the thought of it—God the Son sharing His sovereignty with Man!

> *"I am the resurrection and the life, he that believeth in Me, though he were dead yet shall he (LIVE*

> *Saints) and whosoever LIVETH (is alive when I come back) and believeth in Me shall NEVER die."*
>
> *John 11:25, 26 (KJV)*

You have an opportunity to accept or reject being born into God's sovereign royal family. You do not have to just accept the position and status you've acquired through happenstance. You do not have to settle for the belief that you may be destined to receive nothing more than mortal life from your natural birth.

Through God's word, we can peer into the everlasting future. We can see our potential destiny and choose to be born unto God, a new creature in Christ Jesus, and a child in the royal family of "I AM." What natural mortal person today wouldn't want an opportunity to select the position, status, and quality of their life instead of just accepting what comes by taking a chance? There is a coexisting or corresponding sphere of existence in which the supernatural, the spiritual dimension of eternal life, is located. This dimension is not subject to the physical laws of mortal space, time and distance, but has its own heavenly existence outside the natural forces of Man's temporal sphere.

Since it is impossible for Man to know or even comprehend the actual reality of God's realm beyond the mortal dimension of natural human understanding, Man generally chooses to ignore its existence. Just because Man doesn't know, and it is beyond human comprehension doesn't mean it isn't there. However, it will in the very near future be totally actualized and become a realized sphere of existence for God's royal family throughout timeless eternity.

It is a very special part of God's creation and a part of God's greatly diversified domain and its omnipresence (the created and the always forever present realm of God). There is neither word nor thought in human existence that can identify or defining this glorious realm of our Heavenly Father God. It is totally unspeakable because Man has no words in his earthly vocabulary or the mental comprehension to communicate its awesome beauty and incomprehensible attributes. Are you ready for the grand "prize," the "event" of the ages? Well, I would suggest that you "watch and pray," for it's not far away!

CHAPTER 10

What matters in our Life is Christ!

Spiritually, each believer is with Christ now and shall be always, but to be with Christ bodily can only be attained through one's resurrection or translation at His coming.

> *"If anyone loves Me, he will keep My word; and My Father will love him, and We will come to him, and make Our home with him."*
>
> *John 14:23 (NKJV)*

In this fast-moving, worldly society we live in today, there just never seems to be enough time for family, friends, or self, at least not with any real quality time.

Just ask this simple question to the typical man or woman on the street, providing they will even stop long enough for you to ask a question—'do you know the promises in God's word for your life?'

Most people would immediately say, "I don't know much about the Bible because it is too hard to understand!" Or, "The Bible is all Greek to me, you know, with all those begets and all!"

This could very possibly be your own answer, dear reader, or maybe you just haven't had that real quality time set aside for yourself to really get into the word.

But, do most people really want to understand? If they do really have the desire to know, then God's word will open up to them, the

Holy Spirit will guide them, teach them, and He will most assuredly show them the things to come and bring life to the words they read.

God doesn't just drop total revelation knowledge upon a natural person so that one day He knows not and the next He *knows all.* Knowledge of God's Word is revealed one step at a time, much the same way as one climbs a ladder to reach a plane higher than naturally able, one rung at a time.

Just as it takes an effort on man's part to climb a ladder to reach the top, he first must have the desire to begin the climb. He also must know that the climb will produce a given result and must have a vision of that result in his mind's-eye.

> *"But the Helper, the Holy Spirit, whom the Father will send in My name, He will teach you all things, and bring to your remembrance all things that I said to you."*
>
> *John 14:26 (NKJV)*

To obtain real understanding and have God speak clearly to your heart, you must diligently study God's word! You must search out truths for yourself and find those passages that apply to the specific subject of your study.

Once you find them, you must read them, think about them, and pray over them until the Holy Spirit guides you into the truth, and the Word comes alive in your spirit.

Did you know that the early Christian church, the early fathers of our faith, looked for "That Blessed Hope?" It was a universal (catholic) belief that Jesus was going to be coming again in glory to reign with His saints over the whole earth during the 1,000-year period that came to be called the Millennium.

The whole notion was later spiritualized away by the newly organized Roman Church but praise God, it eventually came to life once again along with the doctrine of salvation by simple faith in a crucified Savior. Those over-spiritualized religious Christian leaders could justly be called the "Pharisees" of the early church, causing as much confusion and disbelief in the church as did the Jewish Pharisees with the Jews over Christ.

Their actions not only caused a negative effect to domino through the church, but they caused many people to put aside any belief in a literal millennial reign with Jesus. However, the Holy Spirit worked through those dark ages and once again brought light to the godly men and women who studied God's word.

Afterward, with their knowledge restored by the Holy Spirit, the church once again with the same prominence as the early church proclaimed the promise of "That Blessed Hope."

The truth is that when one becomes a child of God, it is the absolute highest honor and most glorious privilege bestowed in the whole eternal realm of our Heavenly Father. It is also one of the greatest revelations in the New Testament that God has given to us for identifying mankind's potential glorious future.

Our eternal life can only be attained by willingly accepting Christ's redemption and faithfully committing our lives to Him. Upon acceptance, our commitment to His vision for mankind should be our greatest hope for glory in the future age of ages. God expects this, our hope for the future, to cause us to seek Him and His kingdom with much greater intensity and zeal.

> *For our citizenship is in heaven, from which we also eagerly wait for the Savior, the Lord Jesus Christ,*

who will transform our lowly body that it may be conformed to His glorious body.

Philippians 3:20, 21 (NKJV)

We also who have the first fruits of the Spirit, even we ourselves groan within ourselves, eagerly waiting for the adoption, the redemption of our body.

Romans 8:23 (NKJV)

You received the Spirit of adoption by whom we cry out 'ABBA, FATHER' the Spirit Himself bears witness with our spirit that we are children of God.

Romans 8:15, 16 (NKJV)

The Holy Spirit is the pledge of our literal full adoption as God's children when our bodies are redeemed by Christ and our transformation of becoming like He is completed.

The resurrection body and the transformed body will be perfect in every way and beautiful beyond description. It will have such unlimited capabilities that no one today could even imagine what it will be like to have a spiritual body like Christ's. It will be a glorious body that is in every way fully adapted to the heavenly sphere of our Father's Kingdom and unquestionably beyond mortal comprehension.

Although we cannot fully know or understand the characteristics of the spiritual body believers shall receive as a participant in the First Resurrection, we do know that it will not be an immaterial body or a ghost-like body.

Jesus' resurrected body was that of the man Jesus. He ate and drank, He could materialize and pass through locked doors at will, and He had complete dominion over all of creation. He was and is the Fountainhead of the new creation, and "we will be like Him."

Being the children of God, the children of the first resurrection, we transcend beyond a state of immortality; clothed in immortality, yes, but wonderfully changed to be like Him, a reflection "of His glory."

The Bible speaks very clearly to us about the first resurrection (the first to life and the second to death) as the resurrection of all the saints who will participate in the resurrection to eternal spiritual life.

This first resurrection has several different stages within it and includes all the numerous faithful servants throughout all of mankind's history. It includes the very elite group of saints (the church) at the glorious future event that has been named the "Rapture," and it likewise includes all the future Jewish and Gentile tribulation saints who accept Jesus as their Lord.

> *"Two men will be in the field; one will be taken and the other left" (Matthew 24:40).*

The second resurrection is for sinners who reject God's calling and will experience spiritual death for eternity, "the second death" (Revelation 20:14).

This "Blessed Hope," our glorious hope, has been ever-present before the church to keep all believers in a proper attitude of expectancy and longing, a longing to see the Lord as He is! To become like Him, a glorious reflection of our Father God's eternal love.

Just like Israel in the wilderness, we should recognize our earthly position in God's long-range plan as pilgrims disembarking from the world looking for a land, a city not made with human hands. We should be looking forward to being received by a king who is the manifestation of God to mankind throughout the age of the ages.

He who raised up Christ from the dead, and who has given us the spirit of adoption as the "sons of God," will by His Spirit that dwells in us, also quicken (make eternally alive) our mortal bodies. Then, we can inherit the fullness of the kingdom prepared for us from the foundation of the world. With Jesus as the rightful heir of all things, we will become the heirs of God and joint heirs with Christ and shall reign with Him, forever.

God has created a natural desire in the heart of mankind to know the future, to explore the unknown, to reach out beyond the limits of previous experience, and even to challenge himself. But, for every truth of God's eternal plan, Satan has fabricated and supplied Man with a counterfeit substitute for each reality of purposeful life that God has prepared for mankind. Satan has taken the truth, twisted it, and made it into a lie to deceive the nations through various religious cults, organizations, and numerous errant doctrines.

This book is not written to spark controversy but to only bring to light, state the convictions, and acknowledge the scriptural importance of Jesus Christ's return to earth to set up the literal kingdom of Christ. Truth is spoken of in the scriptures by the early disciples who repeatedly encouraged us to look for Jesus' return (Philippians 3:20; Titus 2:13; Hebrews 9:28; 2 Peter 3:14).

This hope, "The Blessed Hope," spoken of in Titus 2:13, causes a purifying separating power in the heart, sanctifying and bringing believers into a state of holiness, love, and godly service.

We are admonished to watch for His coming just as Jesus told His disciples' time and again to watch!

> *"Watch therefore, for you do not know what hour your Lord is coming"*
>
> *Matthew 24:42, (NKJV)*

"Take heed, watch and pray"

Mark 13:33, (NKJV)

"And what I say to you, I say to all: WATCH!"

Mark 13:37, (NKJV)

Man is a spirit, he has a soul, and he lives in a body. We know that the 'spirits' of the Christian souls living in heaven with Christ will come with Him when He descends in the air to "catch up" the church. We also know that "the dead in Christ will rise first," as they (the descending spirits) will receive their new transformed bodies, which have been raised to meet the Lord in the air. And, in just a moment of time, they will all be joined in their new glorified bodies, their new supernatural spiritual bodies, just like Christ's.

> *Then, we who are mortally alive, and still on the planet Earth will be "caught up together with them in the air. And thus, we shall always be with the Lord.*
>
> *1 Thessalonians 4:17 (NIV-1983 Revision)*

Although the early church believers didn't use the word "rapture" to describe the future "catching up" of the body of believers (the church), they understood and awaited the coming translation of their bodies. They waited with an expectancy just as the early saints who had reported seeing Jesus caught up into the air, into the clouds, and heard the Angels say He would someday return in like manner.

The saints who participate in the rapture, who have accepted Jesus as Lord and Savior, will receive transformed glorious bodies, bodies made in heaven. They will be made by God the Father just for His very special 'children.'

They will be fashioned like the body He made for Himself and received unto Himself as Jesus Christ, that we believe will likewise receive as His heirs. We will then appear before Him at the judgment seat of Christ to receive our crowns and rewards.

> *"That each one may receive the things done in the body, according to what he has done" (2 Corinthians 5:10, NKJV).*

The Bible very clearly tells us that this new body we are to receive will be spiritual, but it will be "real" flesh and bone body like the one Christ received and showed to His disciples after His resurrection.

However, this body He showed the disciples did not have the same shining characteristics of heavenly glory that His body now has in heaven, or that we will have when we *"see Him as He is."* When He met with His disciples, He had to dim the heavenly radiance of His glory. For no mortal Man can look upon Him and live!

When we become incorruptible, as the scriptures describe, our body will not flow with mortal blood, the life-giving substance of corruptible Man, but will instead flow with the water of life. It will flow with the actual realized substance of God's Spirit, the very quintessence of His glory, and the pure, absolute essence of God's Supreme Being. After receiving our new bodies, the Bible tells us we will shine with God's glorious radiance.

> *Those who are wise shall shine like the brightness of the firmament, and those who turn many to righteousness like the stars forever and ever.*
>
> *Daniel 12:3 (NKJV)*

"Then the righteous will shine forth as the sun in the kingdom of their Father. He who has ears to hear, let him hear!"

Matthew 13:43 (NKJV)

"This little light of mine" is not really a little light, as the children's song indicates, but it has the radiance of the Son—Praise God! Even with the radiance of His Glory, our spiritual body will not be unrecognizable but will be characteristically very similar to our earthly image and certainly identifiable by our family and friends. We will also have inborn wisdom of knowing and recognizing everyone, just as our Father can. We will also possess the essence of God's fundamental knowledge and wisdom, and the total potential of our brainpower will be enhanced and tuned to its absolute infinite maximum perfection.

"Thanks be to God for His indescribable gift!"

(2 Corinthians 9:15, NKJV).

But our citizenship is in heaven and we eagerly await a Savior from there, the Lord Jesus Christ, who by the power that enables Him to bring everything under His control, will transform our lowly bodies so that they will be like His glorious body.

Philippians 3:20, 21 (NIV)

We will be easily recognized in our new glorified bodies, yet they will be better than we can even imagine. But they will still have our own special personalities, our wonderful individualities, besides being perfect in all respects.

Our translated bodies will be very different in many ways, but very individualistic, just as our earthly bodies. And we are assured that when Christ returns to take us into His eternal kingdom, we will be glorified and made completely perfect.

> *For we know that if our earthly house, this tent, (we live in) is destroyed, we have a building from God, a house not made with hands, eternal in the heavens.*
>
> *2 Corinthians 5:1 (NKJV)*
>
> *"When Christ who is our life appears, then you also will appear with Him in glory." (Colossians 3:4, NKJV)*

Our glorified transformed body will be perfect in every detail and beautiful in totally unimaginable terms. It will also have unlimited capabilities that are beyond natural Man's comprehension on this earth. However, it will be adapted for eternal life in the spiritual realm, God's realm.

Our spiritual body will not be an immaterial body like the ghostly images Man has portrayed in his attempts to define this mysterious existence. Quite the contrary, our spiritual body, will be of the highest order attainable in the heavenly sphere of God's glory.

Our spiritual body will be a supernatural body, one adapted to the actualized realities of the age to come. This body is to be "celestial." It will be capable of transcending (passing beyond human limitations) the material existence of the universe.

Superior to, and independent of, the material universe, our spiritual body is one that will be exalted to a position of eternal glory and honor in God's heavenly realm and a magnificent reflection OF HIS GLORY.

Just as Paul has said in Colossians 3:1-4, we should focus on the "things above" rather than the "things on the earth." He very clearly tells us to *"set your mind on the things above,"* put Christ first in your lives and make Him the center or hub of your existence.

He tells us this because Jesus Christ is what really matters and should most certainly take precedence over anything this world has to offer. Besides, what on Earth could even begin to compare with the rewards of God's kingdom? The things on the earth are only temporary, and as such, we should handle them with careful consideration and not place greater emphasis on them than on Christ.

During all our worldly pursuits and interests—our family, our careers, and the many pleasures offered by the world, we believers must remind ourselves that this mortal life is simply a temporary assignment. It is only a testing ground, a place of training, a preparatory life for our eternal inheritance.

> *The Spirit Himself bears witness with our spirit that we are children of God, and if children, then heirs—heirs of God and joint heirs with Christ, if indeed we suffer with Him, that we may also be glorified together.*
>
> *Romans 8:16–17 (NKJV)*

Since we will not be governed by space, time, or age in our glorified eternal bodies, our own unique personality will distinguish us one from another, as will our own special physical appearance that will be fashioned by God.

Paul defines the difference by comparing the seed to the mature plant. The seed and the plant are the same, but the actual plant grows to a very different physical appearance than the seed because God gives it a new, distinctly unique body. Our earthly natural bodies are like the seed, and although age is a very distinguishable characteristic of this seed when God transforms us from seed to beautiful plant, age will not be a recognizable trait.

So, whether you are 18 or 88 when you die or are blessed with life until being caught up alive to meet the Lord, your new glorified body will be like the beautiful plant and forever ageless. God will, in the twinkling of an eye, change the seed no matter what the size, shape, or its condition and will transform it into a manifestation of His glory.

Anyone, man or woman, boy or girl, of any age who has accepted Jesus Christ as Lord and Savior are immediately counted worthy, and their names are written in the Lambs Book of Life. By having their names written in the Lambs Book of Life, they are promoted into the membership of the body of Christ (the church) and will be later joined to the Lamb as the bride of Christ.

Although God has called us to believe and walk in faith, He has supplied more than enough proof and support in the scriptures confirming our Christian beliefs that Jesus died to redeem Man from sin and death. And that He is raised from the dead to bring eternal life to all who will answer the call.

Numerous writers, many of whom were personally very close to Jesus, recorded the many miraculous events that occurred immediately after Jesus arose from the dead. He arose during the Jewish "Feast of the First fruits," from which the word "First fruits" was used to describe "The First Resurrection."

> *And the graves were opened; and many bodies of the saints (over 12,000) who had fallen asleep were raised; and coming out of the graves after His resurrection, they went into the city and appeared to many.*
>
> *Matthew 27:52, 53 (NKJV)*

The First fruits of this the first of the first resurrection included Jesus Christ and all the 12,000 plus Old Testament Saints that were raised from the grave who walked and talked throughout the streets and alleyways of Jerusalem for forty days.

These Saints of Old appeared to many of the 'cities' 250,000 residents and the out-of-town visitors (probably over a million) that came to Jerusalem during the Feast of Passover. They not only identified themselves but told of the glorious event that just had occurred in fulfillment of the recorded prophesies of the scriptures.

As these visitors later returned to their own countries, cities, towns, and villages, the message of salvation and the promise of eternal life through Jesus Christ began to spread throughout the nations.

The early church, until sometime around the years 250 AD to 300 AD, taught the prophetic truths about the pre-millennial reign of Christ and the Translation or "catching-up" of the church, actually describing the fact that Christians would meet Christ in the air. (I Thessalonians 4:13-20).

To conclude our discussion of the "catching-up" of the church, let's focus our attention on children for just a moment and answer a vital question many parents have in their hearts about the future of their little ones.

Any believer's unsaved children who are below the age of accountability (probably their 13th birthday) will go with their parent(s) in the rapture of the church. These children are made holy and righteous because the believing parent(s) faith has sanctified them.

> *For the unbelieving husband is sanctified by the wife, and the unbelieving wife is sanctified by the husband; otherwise your children would be unclean, but now they are holy.*
>
> *1 Corinthians 7:14 (NKJV)*

Any unsaved children below the age of accountability of any unbelieving parent(s), when neither parent is saved and redeemed in the Blood of the Lamb, will remain on the earth, is not raptured, and must face the tribulation just the same as the parent(s).

But those unsaved living children still below the age of accountability upon Christ's return at the end of the great tribulation will enter Christ's millennial kingdom with the sheep nations.

Unsaved children over the age of accountability from the teen years and older will not go with the saved parent(s) in the rapture of the church and are abandoned along with all the other unsaved people to face the tribulation. But they do still have a choice to choose Christ and eternal life.

From conception, everyone's name is written in God's "Book Of Life," and when a child reaches the age of accountability, if they haven't accepted Christ as Lord and Savior and they sin thereafter, their name is blotted out of the "Book Of Life" (Psalm 69:28, Exodus 32:31-43, Daniel 12:1-3, Revelation 3:5, Revelation 20:12).

But during the church age (before the rapture), if they receive Jesus as their Lord and Savior, then their name is written in the "Lambs Book of Life (Revelation 21:27)

What future awaits all those people whose names are in the Book of Life but not in the "Lambs Book of Life?" The answer to this question and many other vital issues remains to be answered in the following chapters. *Maranatha*! (The Lord Cometh!)

> *"For many deceivers have entered into the world, who confess not that Jesus Christ is coming in the flesh" (2 John 1:7, KJV).* The Greek word 'Erkomenon' is used in this scripture passage, and it means "coming."

John knew that not all of those who would claim Christ would be true followers, but deceivers who would distort the truth about Christ. As believers, we are admonished to know the basics of what the Bible teaches, so we will be able to detect an error in the statements of others.

> *"In My Father's house are many dwelling places; if it were not so, I would have told you; for I go to prepare a place for you."*
>
> *John 14:2 (NASB)*

So, believers, you must develop spiritual discernment if you are to remain loyal 'to truth' and reap the wonderful benefits...

OF HIS GLORY!

COLUMBUS SAILING TO THE EDGE OF EARTH
Was this trip a surprise to Columbus? No, he had a vision!

Christopher Columbus had three ships on his first voyage, the Niña, the Pinta, and the Santa Maria. Columbus sailed from Palos de la Frontera on 3 August 1492. His flagship, the Santa Maria, had 52 men aboard while his other two ships, the Nina and Pinta, were each crewed by 18 men.

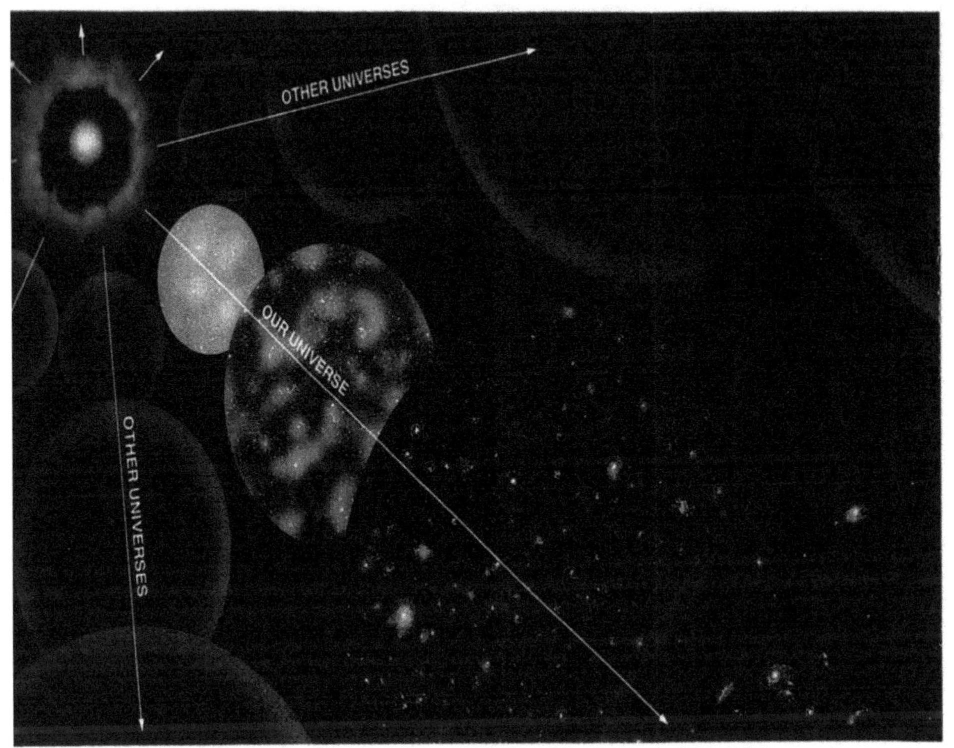

IMAGINE A UNIVERSE OF UNIVERSE'S
Is this just another foolish idea like Columbus?

THE EXPANDING UNIVERSE AND STARS WITHIN OUR SIGHT TODAY MAY BE JUST A TINY SEGMENT OF GOD'S CREATION. REMEMBER THE YEAR OF 1492? THE GREAT SCIENTISTS OF THE DAY KNEW THE EARTH WAS FLAT AND IF ONE TRAVELED TOO FAR THEY MIGHT FALL OFF THE EARTH.

IMAGINE A CHILDLIKE FEAR THAT MIGHT HAVE OCCURRED IN THE HEARTS OF THE MEN ON THE JOURNEY WITH COLUMBUS. PARTICULARLY SINCE MANY OF THESE MEN WERE PRISONERS PARDONED BY THE GOVERNMENT TO HELP ENCOURAGE MEN TO GO WITH COLUMBUS.

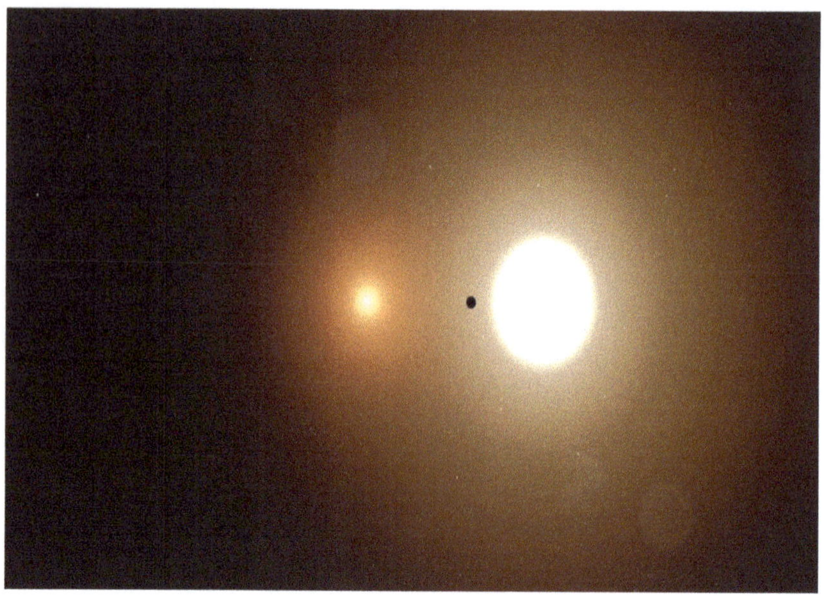

NASA'S TESS SPACECRAFT DISCOVER'S NEW WORLD'S

NASA'S TRANSITING EXOPLANET SURVEY SATELLITE (TESS) SENT A SIGNAL FROM A SYSTEM CALLED TOI 1338 THAT TURNED OUT TO BE A PLANET WITH TWO SUNS. A POSSIBLE NEW WORLD ORBITING TWO STARS. TESS IS EXPECTED TO OBSERVE HUNDREDS OF THOUSANDS OF ECLIPSING BINARIES DURING ITS INITIAL TWO-YEAR MISSION.[5]

https://svs.gsfc.nasa.gov/13510

https://www.cnbc.com/2020/01/10/17-year-old-discovers-planet-on-third-day-of-internship-with-nasa.html

https://www.nasa.gov/feature/goddard/2020/nasa-s-tess-mission-uncovers-its-1st-world-with-two-stars

* Tess is a NASA Astrophysics Explorer mission operated by MIT in Cambridge, MS., and managed by NASA's Goddard Space Flight Center.

CHAPTER 11

Develop a Desire to Win

The Bible promises us a productive and blessed life in the present, but a glorious *eternal life* in our future life with God. A life with a very special position—as God's heirs, we receive an abundance of blessings, wonderful challenges, dominion over all His creation, and totally awesome experiences beyond anything we have ever dreamed or imagined.

> *Eye has not seen, nor ear heard, nor have entered the heart of man the things which God has prepared for those who love him. But God has revealed them to us through His Spirit.*
>
> *For the Spirit searches all things, yes, and the deep things of God. Now we have received, not the spirit of the world, but the Spirit who is from God, that we might know the things that have been freely given to us by God.*
>
> *1 Corinthians 2:9, 10, 12 (NKJV)*

Have you ever seen a movie or read a book in which two bad guys (one may even be the hero) peer into each other's eyes and say, 'see ya in hell!' Or maybe you've heard the quotation 'better to *reign in hell* than serve in heaven.' Well, this is what Hollywood sometimes considers as 'macho.' But I have news for them, it's far better to reign in heaven than burn in hell—wouldn't you agree?

Jesus says, *"To him that overcomes, I will grant to sit with Me on My throne."* Worldly Man says, 'it's better to reign in hell, than to serve in heaven.' Well, the world had better wake up, because there is no reigning in hell neither is there any rain—only eternal pain.

> *And it shall come to pass in all the land, says the Lord that two-thirds in it shall be cut off and die, but one-third shall be left in it:*
>
> *I will bring the one-third through the fire, will refine them as silver is refined, and test them as gold is tested. They will call on My name, and I will answer them. I will say, this is My people; and each one will say, the Lord is my God.*
>
> *Zechariah 13:8, 9 (NKJV)*

A remnant of God's chosen people (the elect) who are protected in exile will survive the great tribulation. But tragically, millions and millions of people of all Nations and ages die horrible deaths and eternally gain only the pain—no reign!

The subject of the tribulation period (the two three-and-a-half-year eras), the last of which is called The Great Tribulation, has been the focus in the ministry of many great men of God. Because so much has already been written on this subject, you are encouraged to seek out and diligently study this topic for yourself. However, for a small sampling of its devastating impact on the world, the following should provide a quick thumb-nail illustration of its horror!

> *And there was a great earthquake, such as was not since men were upon the earth, so mighty an earthquake, and so great. And the great city (Jerusalem) was divided into three parts, and the cities of the nation's fell. And every island fled away, and the mountains were not found.*
>
> Revelation 16:18-20 (KJV)

Every city on the earth is leveled by this great world quake and then bombarded by a terrible hailstorm with giant hailstones that will weigh about 100 pounds each. Hailstones of this magnitude will measure over two and a half feet (approximately 32 inches) in diameter, and each one made up of almost twelve gallons of water. (Have you ever seen a wrecking ball?)

> *And great hail from heaven fell upon men, each hailstone about the weight of a talent. Men blasphemed God because of the plague of the hail, since that plague was exceedingly great.*
>
> *Revelation 16:21 (NKJV)*

Every island of the world sinks into the oceans, and all the mountains of the whole world are leveled. The entire geography of the earth is changed, and the actual continents and oceans of the world as we know them today are significantly re-configured from their present massive areas, shapes, and coastlines.

This will not just be an isolated earthquake on one continent, but a major quake throughout the whole earth—an enormously great earthquake from extensive volcanic eruptions from the very core (bowels) of the earth. There are those who would have you believe that this is only fiction, nothing more than a symbolic representation of what could occur if Man does not take better care of mother earth.

Hundreds of fulfilled prophecies in the scriptures conclusively prove that God has revealed Himself and His plan for the future of mankind in His Word, the Bible. The actual literal meaning of its sentences and paragraphs is the normal approach of communicating in all languages, with any secondary meanings depending upon cross-references from some previous literal meaning.

So, unless the scriptures are specifically identified as having a different meaning than inferred in the text or indicated by the context in which it is presented, we should hold only to the literal interpretation.

Spiritualizing away the literal meaning of plain texts of scripture has the effect of undermining the very foundation of Christian doctrine and will lead us into infidelity. The purpose of language is to convey definite ideas, so surely, the Holy Spirit Himself chose words to convey God's thoughts correctly.

If Jesus didn't mean what He said, why didn't He say what He meant? He did mean what He said, and His words will "not pass away "(Matthew 24:35).

If He came and literally fulfilled the prophecies of a suffering Messiah, will He not as surely come and likewise fulfill the prophecies of a glorified Messiah reigning in victory and majesty?

Mankind desperately needs to understand God's plan and the importance of not rejecting the literal fulfillment of these many wonderful prophecies that describe His future coming, and His glorious reign upon the earth.

There is no symbolism in the plain prophecies that give anyone authority to 'spiritualize' them. Let us then expect that He will literally fulfill these prophecies as He did the others at His first coming. Satan would like nothing better today than the continued propagation of the spiritualized confusion that entered the early church. Politics, spiritualism and intellectualism crept into biblical interpretation and many of the truths of the Bible were 'spiritualized' and 'allegorized' to the point of tragically denying the early truths, even to the point of denying that Jesus was the Son of God.

This denial of the scriptures supported the political aspirations of the empire (government) and led to the suppression of divine knowledge. A suppression that has permeated religious doctrines throughout the centuries and is still ever-present today.

Satan has cleverly used Man's own selfishness, greed, and intellectualized spiritualism to promote the lies he introduced, almost two thousand years ago, into Biblical interpretation through teachers such as 'Origen' of Alexandria, Egypt. He also promoted these lies through political leaders like 'Constantine' and even church leaders and influential theologians like 'Augustine.'

It was also very convenient for the reigning few to control the flow of knowledge within the church and the nations—manipulating the very will, emotions, and beliefs of the people whose very behavior became unknowingly like puppets. Unfortunately, these unsuspecting people spent their whole lives believing falsehoods due to the deception of their leaders. Sadly, they were deceived into believing that their leadership was infallible and specially designated to lead them to God.

Tragically, people have believed more in the story of 'The Holy Grail' as the literal truth than they have in Jesus Christ as the Son of God. His resurrection, second coming, and His millennial kingdom, for many people, are not even seriously considered as topics for discussion.

For mankind to properly understand God's long-range plan, the subject of Jesus' return for the church, the revelation of His second coming, and His actual literal reign on the earth is of vital importance. It is so largely interwoven within the entire body of scripture that it provides a boundless field of investigation and an exhaustless mine of scriptural truth. A prospector's dream, the mother lode of mother lodes.

The one generation today which will undoubtedly realize the coming of our Lord without death; the one generation who can light the fuse to blow away the worthless burden from the priceless ore of truth; the one generation who is unjaded and chaste, is none other than today's high performance, supercharged Generation 'Z.'

A 'saved' *generation* made up of all those who choose to pull out of the vogue generations of the past and are part of a new more inquisitive, education-seeking young people identifying themselves as Post-Millennial or Gen 'Z' millennials with a purpose.

The recent Barna release found that, despite some resistance from some Gen 'Z' young people who oppose evangelizing, the new Christian millennials consider themselves good evangelists and still see themselves as representatives for their faith. Nearly all practicing Christian millennials (96%) said witnessing for Jesus is part of being a Christian, and they were more likely than any other generation to say they were gifted at sharing their faith (73%). I believe this generation has *"caught the vision"* and is ready to spread the gospel.

We all need to focus on the prize, the award, and the reward for all the effort given to minister blessings to those we are led to by the Lord. The awesome Glory that will accompany these rewards will be enjoyed by our new brothers and sisters forever and throughout Eternity by all believers who accept and follow the Lord in obedience and holiness.

All the scriptures that give us the descriptions of heaven and our eternal life with Christ tell us that our eternal destiny will provide us a Godly hierarchy of rewards. The scriptures describe the many promises that believers will receive at the judgment seat of Christ. Paul used the Greek word "bema" to describe the event that will take place in heaven when "every knee shall bow, every tongue confess" to God, and every believer will give a full accounting of themselves to God.

He used this word because in Greece, this was a raised platform of honor where prizes and awards were given out—much like the example we see today at the Olympic games. This judgment will take place in heaven after the Rapture and before the glorious marriage and wedding feast of the Lamb. It is the time and place when eternal rewards are given out to all the righteous saints for their obedient service to God during their lives here on earth.

Besides the eternal rewards, there are also five crowns that are given to believers at this glorious event:

The *CROWN OF LIFE* is given to all those who love Jesus and who have been faithful to death, including all those martyrs who chose death rather than renounce their faith in Christ.

The *CROWN OF GLORY* is given to all those who have served Jesus Christ in the capacity of elders and pastors in the church. Those who freely gave of themselves and their time willingly serving as shepherds and overseers of the church—the Body of Christ.

The *CROWN OF REJOICING* is awarded to all those soul-winning saints who have led others to faith in Jesus Christ as their Lord and Savior. A special honor from God for all those who have faithfully witnessed to others about salvation through Jesus Christ.

The *CROWN OF RIGHTEOUSNESS* is given to all "who have loved His appearing" and have longed for the return of Christ and watch for His Kingdom.

The *INCORRUPTIBLE CROWN* is a victor's crown for not yielding to fleshly lusts and is awarded to all those who have "fought the good fight," "put on the whole armor of God," and found victory in their daily spiritual struggle in life.

> *"Behold, I am coming quickly! Hold fast what you have, that no one may take your CROWN.*
>
> *He who overcomes, I will make him a pillar in the temple of My God, and he shall go out no more! (Will dwell in the house of the Lord forever.)"*
>
> *Revelation 3:11, 12 (NKJV)*

> *By faith Moses, when he became of age, refused to be called the son of pharaoh's daughter, choosing rather to suffer affliction with the people of God than to enjoy the passing pleasures of sin, esteeming the reproach of Christ greater riches than the treasures in Egypt; for he looked to the reward.*
>
> *Hebrews 11:24-26 (NKJV)*

This is a wonderful example given to us by Moses. It is proof that he understood the tremendous eternal rewards which God offers to all believers who reject the false riches, glory, and promises of the world.

As a disciple of Jesus Christ who subscribes to the teachings and doctrines set out in the Word of God, the Bible, don't ever discount the truth of His glorious legacy. The rewards of God are an "indescribable gift" to all those who minister and those to whom are ministered, too, and accept Christ.

The righteous saints will have their lives judged by Jesus based on their works (service to God in holiness and obedience to His commands) and whose lives have revealed true spiritual honor and love. These 'saints will receive the many eternal rewards and *crowns of glory* in heaven.

One of the greatest rewards the righteous saints of all ages will receive as the children of God is their 'inheritance as an heir of God' and joint heir with Jesus Christ. They receive a calling to kingship, to rule and reign with Christ over the peopled universe forever and ever, beginning during the millennial reign of Christ and extending on into the future age of the ages (Aeons of the Aeons).

Every believer that has accepted Christ, or will accept Christ, can share in Christ's sovereignty and receive their promotions to various positions of leadership in God's future eternal world.

A promotion is determined by their obedience to God's word and the fruit they produce for the Kingdom of God. These positions of authority will be given to the 'saints' based upon their spiritual lives and the manifestation of one's works.

The church (body of Christ) will be taken to heaven in their glorious resurrection bodies and receive their rewards at the "bema" judgment seat of Christ that involves believers giving an account of their lives to Christ.

After participating in the marriage supper of the Lamb, the saints (church) will live in heaven with Christ and enjoy all the heavenly hosts and our Father God.

We (the 'Saints') remain with God until that time when we will return with Christ on the "Day of the Lord" and are seen with Christ as the clouds of Glory descending from the heavens. An event that will usher in the 'Millennial Reign of Christ.'

Since we shall be appointed to rule and reign with Christ, we will have a permanent home in the New Jerusalem—our city home (described in a later chapter), and we will also have a second home in the earth—like having a country home.

We will possess a supernatural ability that will allow us to transcend the limits of mortal existence and the material universe. Although it is beyond the grasp of human understanding, we will exist above and be totally unconstrained from physical space and time.

Our knowledge will be expanded beyond the limit of human potential; it will be pure, holy intuitive knowledge inherited from our Father and Triune God.

Our inherent abilities as the "sons of God" are only limited by the love of our Father—almost, but not quite unlimited, for we are not Supreme, but we do gloriously share in His sovereignty over all of creation.

And we have access to and the privilege of enjoyment and use of all God's sphere of existence, even that which was before the beginning of time.

This is truly an unspeakable joy, for there are no words in existence, since time began, to describe the glorious, magnificent sphere of existence of our God, "I AM."

As the children of God, our inheritance provides supernatural power, allowing our will to be done in the 'twinkling of an eye.' Our mental, physical and spiritual power, under God, will greatly transcend beyond anything within the sphere of creations' physical existence.

We discussed previously that the first resurrection began with Jesus as the first of the first resurrection and that the church was a major participant. But also included in the first resurrection are all those saints who:

> *Died in faith, not having received the promises, but having seen them afar off were assured of them, embraced them and confessed that they were strangers and pilgrims on the earth.*
>
> *But now they desire a better, THAT IS, a heavenly country. Therefore, God is not ashamed to be called their God, for He has prepared a city for them.*
>
> *Hebrews 11:13, 16 (NKJV)*

In our Christian walk with God in Christ, it is often that Christians forget the deceptions perpetrated by Satan that can unknowingly prevent Man from understanding the truth. Then in ignorance, Man will reject the wisdom and knowledge of the scriptures.

We should learn from the example we often cite and sometimes shake our heads over in disbelief. However, we should always be extremely careful not to condemn the Jews for rejecting Christ, for this was a major deception of Satan.

Although Jesus came in the literal fulfillment of prophecy, and it appears to be such an obvious error of the Jews as one studies the scriptures, look at the error being made today. Jesus is coming soon, so why doesn't the world rejoice? Christians should take note of this example and not allow Satan to deceive the nations by ignoring the 'obvious signs' that are now pointing to the literal fulfillment of prophecy regarding Christ's second coming and all the events preceding "His glorious appearing."

CHAPTER 12

"Will it seem Marvelous to Me?"

There are three books kept by God. The first is the Book of Remembrance, in which it appears that the names of the exceptionally faithful throughout human history are kept.

> *Then those who feared the Lord spoke to one another, and the Lord listened and heard them; so, a book of remembrance was written before Him for those who fear the Lord and who meditate on His name.*
>
> *Malachi 3:16-18 (NKJV)*

"Those who feared" refer to those who love, honor, and obey the Lord. Those who live faithfully before Him and are committed to His word. This passage assures the faithful throughout the ages that God observes and records the names of those who love Him.

The second book is the Book of Life, in which the names of all those who have ever received life on this earth are written. It occurs at the very moment of conception when life is breathed into each new human child by the Holy Spirit, and a spiritual person with a soul is created that will live forever.

> *"He who overcomes shall be clothed in white garments, and I will not blot out his name from the Book of Life; but I will confess his name before My Father and before His angels".*
>
> *Revelation 3:5 (NKJV)*

These white garments are the robes of the righteousness of Jesus Christ that assures all the faithful righteous of the earth are redeemed and will not have their names blotted out of the Book of Life.

> *"And anyone not found written in the book of life was cast into the lake of fire" (Revelation 20:15, NKJV).*

This event occurs at the final judgment (the great white throne judgment) at the end of the millennial kingdom and the end of the first history of mankind living under the sin of Adam.

The book of life is opened, and the names of the spiritually dead do not appear in it. All the wicked from the beginning of Man's history have had their names blotted out of the book. Their doom is the second death!

> *...and at that time your people shall be delivered, everyone who is found written in the book and many of those who sleep in the dust of the earth shall awake, some to everlasting life, some to shame and everlasting contempt.*
>
> *Daniel 12:1, 2 (NKJV)*

The third book is the Lambs Book of Life, in which are written the names of all those who have accepted the blood of Jesus for their sins and who are called the bride of Christ.

> *Let us be glad and rejoice and give Him glory, for the marriage of the Lamb has come, and His wife has made herself ready.*
>
> *Revelation 19:7 (NKJV)*

In the old testament, Israel was called God's wife, but in the new testament, the church takes this honored position of restored intimacy with God through Christ, an intimacy that will be a more glorious and loving relationship than God has ordained since the creation of the world.

There is a clear distinction between the old testament saints and the new testament saints, the church, the body of Christ—the future bride of Christ. The old testament saints, from Adam to Jesus, by faith are made holy and righteous and participate in the first resurrection. But God has provided something better for us.

> *And all these, having obtained a good testimony through faith, did not receive the promise, God having provided something better for us, that they should not be made perfect apart from us.*
>
> *Hebrews 11:39, 40 (NKJV)*

All the old testament saints died without receiving all the promises of God, but through their faith in a savior not yet seen, they received perfect salvation at Christ's death and resurrection. In addition, they will receive their full inheritance with us, the new testament blood-bought believers, the church! Together, we, the chosen heavenly bride of Christ, become a reflection of His glory, not to be reigned over but to reign forever with our Lord, Jesus Christ.

> *"For if we died with Him, we shall also live with Him. If we endure, we shall also reign with Him"*
>
> *(2 Timothy 2:11, 12, NKJV).*

> *For You were slain and have redeemed us to God by Your blood. Out of every tribe and tongue and people and nation and have made us kings and priests to our God; and we shall reign on the earth.*
>
> *Revelation 5:9, 10 (NKJV)*

We win! This passage assures us that all the people of the earth will have the opportunity to be redeemed by the blood of Christ. And all will have authority as believers to function as kings and priests in Christ, even while on this present earth.

As a royal priesthood, the saints spiritually reign now with Christ on the earth and will continue this spiritual reign until the kingdoms of this earth literally become the kingdoms of our Lord and of Christ. When this occurs, He will then rule and reign over His kingdom forever and ever, and we shall also reign with Him.

There are several questions that are not clearly answered in the scriptures. These questions, left unanswered, will many times form a mental block in people's minds preventing a more in-depth understanding of the pertinent issues regarding God's plan. Diligently seeking the answers to a few of these questions together will prove interesting and allow us to proceed unhindered into God's long-range plan.

In native America, many Indian families may question the fate of their beloved ancestors, who obviously were not Jews, nor did they have any knowledge of Abraham's God or the scriptures. Likewise, there have also been countless other people on this earth, in a very similar isolated situation, without any knowledge whatsoever of God or of Jesus Christ.

The scriptures are very clear about those who never had an opportunity to know the God of Abraham but are a law unto themselves, and as God judges their hearts, they too may be justified if they honored and obeyed their law.

> *For there is no partiality with God. For as many as have sinned without law will also perish without law, and as many as have sinned in the law will be judged by the law. For not the hearers of the law are*

just in the sight of god, but the doers of the law will be "justified." *

Romans 2:11-13 (NKJV)

*justified—a legal term signifying to acquit, declare righteous, show to be righteous. (To be declared righteous in God's sight.)

For when Gentiles, who do not have the law, by nature do the things in the law, these, although not having the law, are a law to themselves.

Who show the work of the law written in their hearts, their conscience also bearing witness, and between themselves their thoughts accusing or else excusing them?

Romans 2:14, 15 (NKJV)

God is telling us in this passage that on the day of judgment, Jesus will determine people's condemnation or justification based on their heart's response to the Spirit. All people of the earth differ from one another and, by human nature, do similar things because God has given them all a moral instinct at creation.

Therefore, God will judge all people according to the basis of revelation knowledge they possess. The basis of judgment for the Jews will be the written law. The basis of judgment for the Gentiles (Pagans, Africans, Indians, Orientals, etc.) will be the unwritten law of conscience and nature.

The first resurrection, as stated earlier, includes "all righteous saints of old testament times," and this means all! So, these spirits of *all* the righteous are now with God the Father and Jesus in heaven with all the other saints, awaiting the glorious reunion with their resurrected bodies.

Can't you just imagine the glorious time of celebration in Heaven, when the spirits of all the righteous Indian saints meet with the Great Spirit, their heavenly Father, God Almighty?

Have you ever stopped to consider what future awaits the children of the many old testament Jewish and Gentile generations throughout history who died before the age of accountability? What is the fate of these children?

Any unsaved child below the age of accountability of a believing parent is sanctified and made 'holy' by the believing parent(s) faith. Therefore, the children of any righteous parent are saved according to the scriptures. In 1 Corinthians 7:14, it tells us, *"But now they are holy."*

The unsaved, unrighteous children over the age of accountability of a believing parent will be given the opportunity to choose life and receive justification by their own free will—just like their parent(s) and others were also given.

The unsaved, unjustified, unrighteous children down through the ages from Adam to the second coming of Christ, who have had no righteous parent(s) and who have died before the age of accountability, still have their names written in the Book of Life.

These children undoubtedly will awake from their sleep in the earth and enter the literal kingdom of Christ at the beginning of the millennium. (As previously mentioned, the age of accountability is probably the 13th birthday based upon Jewish tradition when a boy became a man.)

Even though some children may be below the age of accountability, they are very capable of accepting Jesus Christ as their Lord and Savior prior to attaining this designated age. Likewise, it is possible that a child below the age of accountability could also willfully reject Jesus and salvation.

These unsaved children do not receive the glorified bodies of the saints but are transformed from death to life (similar to Lazarus) into the millennial kingdom from their sleep in the dust of the earth to live out the lives they have been cheated out of by Satan's evil influences.

In addition to these, there are millions and millions of unborn children and stillborn children throughout history who were conceived, received the 'spirit of life' from the Holy Spirit, and have a living soul.

However, due to the circumstances of mortal life, including intentional abortion, they were never born into the world as God had intended. These little living souls that were formed in God's image had their house (body) destroyed before it was completely ready for occupancy.

These unjustified little unborn children have similarly all been cheated out of their natural lives on the earth. They, too, will be transformed from death to life into the millennial kingdom from their sleep in the dust of the earth to also live out the lives God has fully intended for them from the very foundation of the world.

All these little ones' (including the abortion babies throughout history) will miraculously enter the millennial kingdom of Christ and live in righteousness for God. If this were not so, it could be implied that aborted babies are not a part of humanity, and the pro-choice group follows the correct doctrine.

All these unjustified children are raised to life and transformed into the millennial kingdom with their God-given souls (sin nature still intact) in a flawless natural mortal human body. Any unjustified child who died imperfect with any defect whatsoever, whether physical or mental, will be transformed into their God intended natural mortal life. Their new lease on life will be in a fully functioning, flawless human body. These children enter the kingdom as aliens (strangers) and as orphans' who will be adopted into the Jewish nation and Christ's millennial kingdom. They will be raised by God's 'elect,' the living remnant who enter the millennial kingdom from the great tribulation.

It is important to note here that many unjustified children throughout the ages have lived and died with all manner of physical and mental defects due to Satan's persecution of mankind. Some of these unjustified children lived many years beyond the age of thirteen. However, they never reached an age of accountability. They, too, will be included with the group that will be transformed and enter Christ's Millennial Kingdom in their flawless human body as described above.

Let me reiterate once again that any child of a believer (a born-again Christian) from conception, whether born alive into the world or not, has been sanctified by the parent(s). These children are made righteous in the sight of God and will inherit all the promises of eternal life as a child of God just as their parent(s).

There are many examples in the scriptures where little children were raised up from death (sleep) by Jesus and by His disciples. These examples show us that our life-giving resurrected Lord has the power and the desire to give mortal life back to all the little ones who die prematurely before their appointed time.

There have been some who have said that these little children are taken to heaven and remain with God for all eternity. While others have said that these children return to the new earth to either rule and reign with Christ or to help populate the new earth.

Unfortunately, neither scenario considers the prerequisite of justification that must first be attained for the grace of God to follow this order and sequence of events. These little children range in age from conception through gestation to birth and extend up to the age of reason.

Those children who came from the corrupt seed of the fallen angels never received the breath of life from our God and are not included. However, a great number of God's little children are the 'mongrel' offspring of atrocious sinful nations, and we should consider the disposition of these little souls.

These 'mongrel' children that came from many of the world's deprived people and nations had no chance for a full, meaningful life as God intended. From the time they were conceived until they died, many of these poor little children fully died after being exploited possible in all manner of horrible and unspeakable acts of depravity. Pagan practices were so despicable I can't even mention any example in this book.

These little ones never consciously recognized or believed they were involved in anything that was wrong. To them, this was just life, and they became what they were taught. To them, there was no right or wrong. In many cases, they perhaps even became pawns of Satan and were possessed by evil spirits.

Would these, could these, children upon death go directly to heaven to be with a God they didn't know existed or never even imagined? Could they similarly be permitted to enter the glorious, perfect age with perfected mankind after sin has been finally eradicated from natural Man's nature?

It is reasonable to assume that they first need to be sanctified, and can only receive this through justification by faith, or by receiving their redemption living under the righteousness of Christ's kingdom. Living under the righteousness of the King of kings and Lord of lords, substituting God's loving nature for Satan's sin nature would provide this sanctification.

It has been 2,000 years since Christ walked the earth, and many in a depraved human society has spawned "mongrel" children, as mentioned above. However, there was also a period of 4,000 years before Christ in which pagan mankind also spawned millions of "mongrel" children, who were dearly loved by God but totally corrupted by the evil of Satan.

These children need another time, another place to fulfill the destiny God planned for them before the foundation of the world. Our just and loving God is faithful and true, and all these children shall become a marvelous sign of God's glory.

> *Thus, says the LORD of hosts: 'If it is marvelous in the eyes of the remnant of this people in these days, will it also be marvelous in My eyes?' Says the LORD of hosts.*
>
> *Zechariah 8:6 (NKJV)*

> *They shall be to you as native-born among the children of Israel; they shall have an inheritance with you among the tribes of Israel. And it shall be that in whatever tribe the stranger sojourns, there you shall give him his inheritance, says the Lord GOD.*
>
> *Ezekiel 47:22-23 (NKJV)*

First, mankind from Adam's fall until the dawn of the perfect age to come will be born with a sinful nature. Immediately after the millennial age, Satan is delivered into the lake of fire, and a Perfect Age without sin begins.

After Christ's death and resurrection, to rid oneself of this sinful nature, there is but one requirement for justification. By God's grace through faith, accepting Jesus Christ as Lord and Savior, thereby becoming *righteous* in God's eyes and receiving His reward of eternal life.

Therefore, these unsaved, unjustified, and unrighteous children who have not yet reached the age of accountability and have no saved parent intercessor from whom to receive sanctification must be made holy and righteous before entering the spiritual or literal kingdom of God.

To receive the true fulfillment of God's intent and purpose on the earth, Man (little boys and girls included) must be regenerated. They must be 'born again spiritually' to receive redemption and the renewing of their natures from a sinful nature to God's holy nature. Once this is accomplished, the pre-requisite for life in heaven and the new earth is completed, and eternal life is then attained.

If a child dies before having the opportunity to receive that which God ordained from the foundation of the world, due to Satan's interference and meddling, that child has had its rights violated. Therefore, if an unsanctified child has had life prematurely and unjustly stolen, they could justifiably be transformed at the beginning of the millennial reign of Christ to fulfill their God-ordained purpose.

God does not breathe life into a conceived human life without regard for the development of his or her life. He personally cares for and brings life into the world for a purpose, for an allotted time on earth (generally today, about 70 or 80 years). Although one may die before his or her time, in God's plan, He does not want "anyone to perish, but everyone to come to repentance" (2 Peter 3:9). God intends for all children to grow physically and spiritually, fulfill His will in their lives and bring Glory to Him.

> *For YOU created my inmost being, You knit me together in my mother's womb. I praise You because I am fearfully and wonderfully made; all the days ordained for me were written in Your book before one of them came to be.*
>
> *Psalm 139:13, 14, 16 (NIV)*

> *Before she goes into labor, she gives birth; before the pains come upon her, she delivers a son, who has ever heard of such a thing? Who has ever seen such things? Can a country be born in a day or a nation be brought forth in a moment? Yet no sooner is Zion in labor than she gives birth to her children.*
>
> *Isaiah 66:7, 8 (NIV)*

Here we see the rebirth of Israel as God's people during the Messianic (millennial) kingdom; this birth is remarkably quick and will bring much joy.

> *The city streets will be filled with boys and girls playing there. This is what the Lord Almighty says: 'It may seem marvelous to the remnant of this people at that time, but will it seem marvelous to Me?' declares the Lord Almighty.*
>
> *Zechariah 8:5, 6 (NIV)*

Children among the Jews were considered a blessing from God and were raised as members of God's chosen people. (Deuteronomy 6:6-8). What more logical, more opportune, and more desirable time and place could be planned for the children whose lives were cut short than to be reintroduced into the world with the natural human life that was prematurely taken from them.

The remnant of God's chosen people that return to the promised land with King Jesus is mostly an adult people, a people who have suffered horrible atrocities, persecution, and agony. It is highly improbable that very many of the world's young children will survive the exceedingly immense atrocity of the great tribulation.

As a little side note to history buffs: It is noteworthy that during the Greek/Roman periods of history, including the time Jesus ministered on the earth, paganism and spiritism were in their zenith, and children were looked upon with great scorn. Childhood was considered a very insignificant period of life in pagan cultures, and infants, especially girls, were routinely discarded and abandoned to die along the roadsides and in garbage dumps. Children were held in such low esteem that many times they would be mutilated and used by beggars just to gain the sympathy of people, and of course, their money.

Child abuse reached epidemic proportions then and is likewise reaching these same proportions today in our own neighborhoods. Just this past decade, a very young mother murdered her two young children. She buckled them up in the back seat of her car with the motor running, transmission in drive, got out of the vehicle, and let the car drive into a lake, killing her babies. Why? Because her boyfriend didn't like kids and she was afraid she might lose him.

Is this the end of the story for those two precious little souls, these babies that didn't know the saving grace of Jesus? Did God plan to only let them live a short period of time? No, on both accounts. Sin destroyed the lives of these two little bodies, but their spirit and soul live on for all eternity.

Will these two little ones receive a glorified body? Are they justified and righteous in the sight of God? I pray they are, but of the spiritual circumstances and their standing in the body of Christ, only our Triune God knows.

If in a similar situation, a child was to die before reaching the age of accountability without receiving sanctification through a believing parent, they are not justified. However, that little spirit and soul sleep and await the glorious return of our Lord and Savior Jesus, at which time this little child is transformed and restored to fellowship with God. Without sanctification and justification through faith, there is no one who is made righteous in God's eyes.

> *Therefore, thus say's the Lord: 'I am returning to Jerusalem with mercy; My house shall be built in it', say's the Lord of hosts, and a surveyor's line shall be stretched out over Jerusalem.*
>
> *Zechariah 1:16 (NKJV)*

> *Many nations shall be joined to the Lord in that day, and they shall become My people. And I will dwell in your midst and the Lord will take possession of Judah as His inheritance in the holy land and will again choose Jerusalem.*
>
> *Zechariah 2:11, 12 (NKJV)*

> *"The city streets will be 'filled' with boys and girls playing there" (Zechariah 8:5, NIV).*

According to Strong's definition, the word translated as built is "banah" and means to build, construct, found, set up, or to obtain children ("build" a family)—the root of ben (son) and banim (children).

"BURSTING WITH STAR FORMATION AND ENERGETIC STELLAR NEWBORNS."

Looming some 135 million light-years from Earth in the constellation of Centaurus is the bright emission line galaxy NGC 3749, seen here in an image from the Hubble Space Telescope. Astronomers can learn a lot about a galaxy by studying its spectrum of light, particularly the wavelengths of light that are emitted or absorbed by elements it contains. Galaxy NGC 3749 displays strong emission lines, which means, Expansion!

Hubble Eyes an Emission Galaxy

(Image Credit: ESA/NASA/Hubble NASAID Rosario et al)

The European Space Agency said in a statement—Hanneke Weitering

NeXT

CHAPTER 13

We too shall "Bloom like a Rose."

"And the Lord shall be King over all the earth. In that day it shall be—the Lord is one, and His name one" (Zechariah 14:9, NKJV).

"And they shall look upon Me Whom They Have Pierced" Zechariah 12:10, (KJV).

"They will gather together His elect from the four winds, from one end of Heaven to the other"

Matthew 24:31, (NKJV)

The Jews brought through the test of fire (the tribulation) as well as the Jews from Petra (those hidden and protected by God), go alive into the 1,000-year Millennial Kingdom with Jesus as their King. Both groups help to repopulate the earth during the Millennium along with the gentile survivors of the judgment of the nations (the sheep nations).

I will bring back my exiled people Israel; they will rebuild the ruined cities and live in them.

They will plant vineyards and drink their wine; they will make gardens and eat their fruit.

I will plant Israel in their own land, (the promised land); never again to be uprooted from the land I have given them, says the Lord, your God.

Amos 9:14, 15 (NIV)

I am very jealous for Zion; I am burning with jealousy for her. This is what the Lord says: I will return to Zion, and dwell in Jerusalem.

Zechariah 8:2, 3 (NIV)

The seed will grow well, the vine will yield its fruit, the ground will produce its crops, and the heavens will drop their dew. I will give all these things as an inheritance to the remnant of this people.

Zechariah 8:12 (NIV)

I will bring them back to live in Jerusalem; they will be My people, and I will be faithful and righteous to them as their God.

Zechariah 8:7 (NIV)

God will truly become the God of His people, and they will partake of His righteousness through Christ.

Behold, the days are coming, says the Lord, that I will raise to David a Branch of righteousness; a King shall reign and prosper, and execute judgment and righteousness in the earth.

Jeremiah 23:5 (NKJV)

The time period applicable to these scriptures is immediately after the great tribulation and upon Christ's second coming to set up His literal kingdom on earth.

The Jewish Talmud (ancient Rabbinical writings) identify the Millennium as a time characterized by the deliverance of the Jews from all their enemies, the recovery of Palestine, and the literal reign of their Messiah in glorious splendor.

Except for the belief that Jesus is the Christ (Messiah), most Christians and Jews have a very similar belief. Both groups believe the Messiah is going to rule and reign on the earth, and overthrow their enemy Satan, all ungodly governments and lawlessness, and establish a kingdom of righteousness.

In addition, the Christian believes the church, under Jesus as the Sovereign Lord, will reign over the earth with Jerusalem as the capital city. After the Great Tribulation, the Jews from all nations will be restored to the land of Israel, finally recognizing Jesus Christ as Lord.

The Jewish nation will then, at long last, be the center of one-world government, Christ's government. In addition to Israel, all the other nations and people of the Earth will be included in Christ's world-wide Millennial Kingdom. Notably, it will be a wonderful kingdom of holiness with a pure and blessed government.

There are many old testament passages in the scriptures that refer to Christ's coming return to rule and reign with His saints over the earth. The following are a few that support the new testament passages confirming these promises: (Isaiah 11:4; Jeremiah 3:17; Zechariah 14:9; Revelation 19:11-16; and 20:1-9).

These and many other passages in the old testament refer to the thousand-year millennial reign of Christ, but it is sometimes difficult to perceive the difference between the Millennial age and the

Perfect age. The Perfect age has its beginning at the culmination of the re-made "new heavens and a new earth." Moreover, it will occur at the termination of the thousand-year Millennial reign of Jesus after Satan and all His followers are cast into the eternal lake of fire.

There are many promises to Israel that will have partial fulfillment in the thousand-year Millennial period, but the ultimate fullness of fulfillment will only occur during the perfect age. There will never be a more glorious state in all of creation, including Eden, than this heavenly perfect age.

At the beginning of this eternal state, the new heavens and the new earth will be gloriously revealed, as the heavenly city of New Jerusalem, whose architect and builder is God, descends to the new earth.

Probably the most significant occurrence of the entire Millennial period is the actualized literal reign of Christ, with all the glorified saints from the earth reigning as priests of God and of Christ.

> *"And have made us kings and priests to our God; and we shall reign on the earth" (Revelation 5:10, NKJV).*

It is important for us as Christians to recognize that not only will Christ literally rule during this thousand-year period, but even beyond into the Perfect age of the ages to come. Jesus, who is our Lord and Savior, now rules and reigns over our hearts from the right hand of God and will continue to rule from there until His enemies are made His footstool (all of God's enemies are brought underfoot.

> *"The Lord said to my Lord, sit at My right hand, till I make YOUR enemies YOUR footstool" (Acts 2:34, 35, NKJV).*

The Millennial reign of Christ has been interpreted by theologians in several different ways, and due to these interpretations, the church has established differing doctrines. One position is that the Millennium is represented in the scriptures and only refers to Christ's spiritual rule today from the right hand of God in heaven. This is considered a Millennial interpretation.

A second position that has developed is the belief that Christ's spiritual reign is working through the church, spreading the gospel by its preaching and teaching. A position in which it is believed will bring eventual world peace leading to Christ's return. This is, by many, considered a post-Millennial interpretation. The interpretation that this book presents is the literal pre-Millennial belief that God, through His prophets, meant exactly what He said in actual real words that should be taken literally—not symbolically or spiritually.

The early church included Christ's chosen apostles and disciples, who, like you and me, were mostly ordinary men and women. The early church was probably not even capable of intellectualizing or spiritualizing the message and belief that was taught and preached.

From the simple message of the gospels, the early church all looked for the literal coming return of Jesus. They all expected Jesus to return and begin the actual 'thousand year' scriptural fulfillment of God's promises to Israel, with His literal reign on the earth.

The scriptures describe this thousand-year (Millennial) period as an almost perfect utopian society of peace, love, joy, and brotherhood, where all of humanity and nature live in total harmony and unity with Christ. We are given a description of a wonderful, glorious life as it could have been, and God probably intended it to be, in the Garden of Eden. But, no matter how grand Christ's Millennial kingdom will be, it will not be exactly as life was intended in the Garden of Eden.

Christ will "rule with a rod of iron," sin will not yet be eradicated from mankind's nature, and mortal death will still occur during this period. It is, however, a glorious period of peace and righteousness. A period when mankind uninhibited by Satan's influence will excel and prosper to a wonderful state of natural and spiritual excellence.

It becomes a transition period in which natural mortal mankind may be perfected and sanctified through the righteousness of Christ's supernatural reign. This will most likely occur when Mans' sin nature is repressed by his free will living under Christ's righteousness, and through God's grace, mans sin nature is substituted by God's holy nature. If a person rejects Christ during this final period, he or she will be rejected, and their sinful nature prevails to their utter destruction.

All of us as God's children receive sanctification (are made holy and separated from the world and sin) by faith through the blood of Christ and the regenerating and sanctifying work of the Holy Spirit in our lives.

God's desire for His chosen people in the old testament was that they would live holy lives, separated from the lifestyles of the nations around them—to achieve sanctification.

> *Now if you obey Me fully and keep My covenant, then out of all nations you will be My treasured possession. Although the whole earth is Mine, you will be for Me a kingdom of priests and a holy nation.*
>
> *Exodus 19:5, 6 (NKJV)*

To receive a true sanctification, the people of the earth (Gentiles included) will be required to maintain an intimate communion with their King and Lord Jesus Christ. They will be obliged to obey and submit to His rule and reign physically and spiritually through the sanctifying work of the Holy Spirit in their hearts.

This sanctification process will be a lifelong purification that will progressively transform mankind into 'Christ-likeness,' growing in grace and making a clear break with their sinful natures in order to live holy lives for God, according to His will.

Or, on the other hand, Man's evil nature will rise through disobedience for one last time. When Satan is released at the end of the 1,000 years, all evil mankind who have willfully rejected the righteousness and sanctification of God will be destroyed, and they will be cast into the lake of fire for eternity.

The actual future physical conditions on the earth will be like the Garden of Eden. In the book of Isaiah, it is described as a time when all animals, wild and domestic, live in peace with Man and each other. It is described as a time when nothing in God's creation will ever harm humankind, and little children will even be able to play with the cobra or lion and not be harmed. The human-race will then live in absolute harmony with one another and with Christ and with the glorified saints.

There will be universal peace and joy throughout all the nations, and the knowledge of the Lord will cover the earth as the waters cover the sea. Jerusalem will be Christ's center of government, and all the nations of the earth will come to Jerusalem each year to honor their King.

> *And it shall come to pass that everyone who is left of all the nations which came against Jerusalem shall go up from year to year to worship the King, the Lord of Hosts, and to keep the feast of tabernacles.*
>
> *Zechariah 14:16 (NKJV)*

God's present reign through Christ in today's world has many implications for the poor—both the spiritually poor and materially poor. This extends also to Christ's concern for the children of the world, and by direct example and expression, we see that God is concerned about the deprived and despised people of the world.

> *"...to proclaim liberty to the captives and recovery of sight to the blind, to set at liberty those who are oppressed; to proclaim the acceptable year of the Lord."*
>
> *Luke 4:18 (NKJV)*

In the previous chapter concerning the unjustified child's fate, we briefly discussed all those unsaved little children who died without knowing Christ. All those who are yet to be saved but shall be brought into the blessings of the Millennial Kingdom.

When the actual literal return of Christ is manifested through the glory of His reign over all human society, especially Israel, "God's holy people" (Romans 11:16), His love will abound.

His absolute eternal love will be manifested through the little children who have died but are yet to be saved and brought into the fullness of redemption. They will be victorious, experience Christ's justice, and brought 'back to life,' marvelously affirming to all the nations, His absolute supreme sovereignty, and righteousness with mighty miracles and signs.

There are several examples of God's grace and mercy to children who have died before their ordained time described in both the old and new testaments. Jesus himself has given us wonderful examples of His power and love by bringing life back to those who had died.

As a type and shadow of Christ, Elisha was a mighty prophet of enormous stature and gifts, whose ministry was affirmed by God with mighty miracles and signs. His ministry included the manifestations of God's power and love in bringing dead children back to life.

I believe the scriptures have proven by example and are telling us today that our God intends to extend His mercy and grace to again bless these children with life. The Jewish remnant and the nations entering the Millennium will be witnesses as God once again affirms Christ's Sovereignty.

When Christ returns to reign as King of kings and Lord of lords as promised, He will completely fulfill all the remaining Messianic prophecies and will rebuild 'the temple' as described in Ezekiel 40 thru 48—but with certain modifications. i.e., God will dwell among His people, sanctifying them with His Holy presence, so there would not be any need for a traditional Holy of Holies.

Since God physically resides with His "elect" people, the Jews, in the resurrected person of Jesus Christ, God the Holy Spirit will also now reside within them (Ezekiel 36:27).

Also, from the personage of God's holy children, 'the saints,' He emanates His presence through and from them in the manifested reflection 'of His glory'—His divine presence, the *Shekinah* glory.

When Jesus the Messiah descends from heaven upon the mount of olives, the veil of spiritual blindness will lift from the eyes of the elect, the 'chosen ones.'

> *I will set My glory among the nations; all the nations shall see My judgment which I have executed.*
>
> *And I will not hide my face from them anymore; for I shall have poured out my spirit on the house of Israel; says the Lord God.*
>
> *Ezekiel 39:21 & 29 (NKJV)*

"And I will give you shepherds according to My heart, who will feed you with knowledge and understanding" (Jeremiah 3:15, NKJV).

Do you get it yet, dear pilgrim? Yes, you are destined for glorious triumph!

You were slain and have redeemed us to God by Your blood out of every tribe and tongue and people and nation, and have made us kings and priests to our God; and we shall reign on the earth.

Revelation 5:9, 10 (NKJV)

As a royal priesthood, the saints' rule and reign with Christ right now by their worship, their prayers, and their works for the kingdom. This prophetic vision is literally fulfilled when Christ returns and sets up the actualized Millennial Kingdom of Heaven on Earth.

The Millennial Kingdom will then be a literal reign of Christ on the Earth and not simply a "spiritual exaltation" of the church.

"A King will reign in righteousness, and princes will rule with justice" (Isaiah 32:1, NKJV).

These princes are very probably the royal sons of the Most-High Sovereign King, "I AM"—we the saints, the 'sons of God', the heirs and joint-heirs with Christ,' the King who reigns in righteousness.

To more clearly understand God's long-range plan for mankind, especially the plan for Christ's Millennial reign on the existing earth; (although geographically, the seven years of tribulation will significantly alter its physical appearance)—You are encouraged to prayerfully read, study and contemplate the biblical prophecies in the scriptures as revealed by the prophets of both the old and new testaments.

Most of the prophecies concerning the Kingdom of Christ or the Millennial Kingdom identify its time of duration as one thousand years. The Bible clearly teaches that Christ's kingdom will be an eternal, everlasting kingdom of which there will be no end. However, the millennial kingdom is just one phase and can be considered the transitional phase before the perfect future "Age of Ages" that will begin upon the New Earth after all things are made new.

Notice that it is called the "Age of Ages," for just as the earth's past history is ordered into distinct and separate ages (sometimes referred to as dispensations, i.e., an ordering of distinct events under divine authority), the future eternal Age shall likewise be distinguished by many ages.

Both the old and new testament prophecies identify the beginning of the kingdom of God at the coming of the Messiah. Furthermore, we are told that the kingdom "is come" with Christ through His redemptive work for mankind. Therefore, God's reign only begins in the lives of those who accept Jesus Christ as Lord, at which time the kingdom of God also becomes a present spiritual reality.

The future literal (actualized) "Kingdom of God" has its beginning upon Christ's coming in glory (the 2nd coming) when He sets up His millennial kingdom. The spiritual kingdom of God also comes into the hearts of the Jewish people, and God's Holy presence is experienced in His chosen people (His elect).

God's presence is also seen in the manifestation of His glory through Jesus Christ the King and 'the saints.' We, the 'saints,' His elite—you and me, will rule and reign with Him in the actual physical earthly kingdom of Christ. In addition, we will rule and reign with Him in the future eternal kingdom of God that is also a literal kingdom but on the new earth.

The Millennial Kingdom is the final resting place for mankind to choose between good and evil. There will no longer be any deception or influence upon Man from Satan or any evil spirits. Any temptations to do evil things in the world will only come from Man's own inherited sin-nature. Christ will be ruling with a "rod of iron "and will swiftly and deliberately deal with all disobedience.

Just before the conclusion of this 1,000-year reign of Christ, the evil one, Satan, will be allowed to go free for "a little season" to deceive any who would choose him over Christ. This will be the occasion when Man's good and evil nature are unconditionally separated, and the sinful nature will be destroyed along with evil Man and cast into the lake of fire with Satan forever.

God has promised in the clearest language possible that He will establish His kingdom of righteousness on the earth in the future, and at this same time, the Holy Spirit will be poured out on Israel and the gentile nations. This uninhibited indwelling of God's spirit will transform the spirits of all-natural mankind, who are followers of Jesus Christ, and their nature will be renewed by the Holy Spirit.

When the children of Israel return to their own land, it will be to possess and occupy all that was promised to Abraham. The boundary of the land that was promised was vast, and it extended from the Mediterranean Sea to the Euphrates river. Starting at the River of Egypt and Kadesh on the south, the land extends across the desert to the Euphrates River on the east; then from Hamath on the north (about 60 miles from Damascus) to the Euphrates River.

The extent of the land includes all the land east of Israel that is today only a barren desert, but the scriptures tell us that it "will bloom like a rose." This area includes much of the lands now occupied by Jordan, Saudi Arabia, Iraq, Syria, Lebanon, and of course, Israel.

When God made His covenant with Abraham, He committed Himself to a plan for a future Kingdom on the earth to be ruled and reigned over by His Messiah. His plan included the establishment of a kingdom in which His elect "chosen ones" and the gentile nations alike would enjoy and live—a kingdom of glorious splendor much like the Garden of Eden.

> *Never again will there be in it an infant that lives but a few days, or an old man who does not live out his years; he who dies at a hundred will be thought a mere youth; he who fails to reach 100 will be considered accursed.*
>
> *Isaiah 65:20 (NIV)*

Even though some of the subjects of the kingdom (not the reigning saints) may sin and die during the millennial age, others who remain righteous may possibly, according to scripture, die in a good old age. Those who die who are less than a hundred years old will still be considered a child, and their death shall be disgraceful.

> *"And I bestow upon you a kingdom, just as My Father bestowed one upon Me, that you may eat and drink at My table in My kingdom."*
>
> *Luke 22:29, 30 (NKJV)*

This is no doubt one of the strongest proofs that the kingdom will be literal and material.

> *"The Millennial Kingdom is the manifestation of the glory of Christ when He shall sit on the throne Of His Glory"*
>
> *Matthew 19:28, (NKJV)*

The early church not only believed in the pre-Millennial coming of Jesus Christ in all His glory but even made this belief a proclamation of the church. The early Church not only taught and preached the good news of Jesus Christ but also believed that He would reign with His saints on the earth for a 1,000-year period of righteousness and peace.

Our future life with our triune God includes the marvelous glory of sharing in the sovereignty of Christ's kingdom as joint heirs. It is beyond our natural human understanding but is promised to be of immense magnitude with fabulous overflowing blessings and honor.

> *Worthy is the Lamb who was slain to receive power and riches and wisdom and strength and honor, and glory and blessing!*
>
> *Revelation 5:11, 12 (NKJV)*

This proves that the saints, God's children, and His heirs partake of these exceedingly wonderful divine gifts during their eternal lives as they share Christ's inheritance throughout His millennial reign and forever.

It says in Revelation 11:15, *"the kingdoms of this world have become the kingdoms of our Lord and of His Christ and He shall reign forever and ever!"* Then as another conclusive proof of our inheritance, we are told in Daniel 7:18, *"But the saints of the Most High shall receive the kingdom and possess the kingdom forever, even forever and ever."*

> *They will build houses and dwell in them; they will plant vineyards and eat their fruit.*

> *For as the days of a tree, so will be the days of My people; My chosen ones will long enjoy the works of their hands.*
>
> *They will not toil in vain or bear children doomed to misfortune; for they will be a people blessed by the Lord, they and their descendants with them.*
>
> *Isaiah 65:21-23 (NIV)*

The Gentile nations will also receive overflowing blessings and will share in the glory of Christ's kingdom, but the Jews (God's elect) and the city of Jerusalem are the central figures in the absolute glory of the Millennial kingdom. And in those days, the Jews will be highly revered by the gentile nations.

> *Thus says the Lord of hosts: in those days ten men from every language of the nations shall grasp the sleeve of a Jewish man, saying, 'let us go with you, for we have heard that God is with you.'*
>
> *Zechariah 8:23 (NKJV)*

When Jesus returns to the present earth, He will destroy the army that has come up against Jerusalem and then imprison Satan, removing all his evil deceptions and influences from the earth.

Jesus will then proclaim His government the only government on the earth, and the Millennial reign of Christ will commence. Thus, "the day of the Lord" is revealed to the whole earth.

The saints of both the old and new testaments have waited throughout history for the world to get to this point in the fulfillment of the Bible's prophecy. But more significantly, those who participate in the first resurrection will have now received their rewards and inheritance from God.

The wedding of the Lamb to the bride of Christ, the church, will have occurred between Jesus and all the 'saints,' including the tribulation martyrs who have their names written in the Lamb's Book of Life. All the faithful of the old testament will have attended the wedding as distinguished guests, and all the heavenly hosts of angels were present as spectators.

Therefore, the Lamb's Book of Life appears to be for those who have accepted Jesus before His revelation at Armageddon, and the Book of Life appears to be for the other faithful of all ages, including those who died under the age of accountability throughout history.

> *Who are these arrayed in white robes and where did they come from? these are the ones who come out of the great tribulation and washed their robes and made them white in the Blood of the Lamb…they shall neither hunger anymore nor thirst anymore; the sun shall not strike them, nor any heat.*
>
> *Revelation 7:13, 14, 16 (NKJV)*

These martyrs who were killed during the last three and a half years of the tribulation (the Great Tribulation) must be those who will serve the throne of God forever because no sun, light, or heat will ever again fall on them.

This is also an indication that these (the last martyrs) do not return to the earth during Christ's millennial reign but remain in heaven. They may even dwell in the City of New Jerusalem that God has prepared for the 'saints' prior to its descent to the "new earth" after the millennial reign is completed. These saints will therefore remain with God and serve Him during this time and forever.

The other saints who return with Christ will have their special appointments from God and will have direct access to the throne of God in heaven and the kingdom of Christ on the earth. Some of these will no doubt have specific duties and responsibilities in Christ's government, others to the Jewish nation, and still others to the nations of the world.

> *Thus, say's the Lord: I will return to Zion, and dwell in the midst of Jerusalem. Jerusalem shall be called the City of Truth, the Mountain of the Lord of Hosts, the Holy Mountain.*
>
> *Zechariah 8:3 (NKJV)*

> *Jerusalem shall be inhabited as towns without walls, because of the multitude of men and livestock in it. For I, says the Lord, will be a wall of fire all around her, and I will be the glory in her midst.*
>
> *Zechariah 2:4, 5 (NKJV)*

> *And I will make them one nation in the land, on the mountains of Israel, and one King shall be King over them all; (Israel and Judah)*
>
> *Ezekiel 37:22 (NKJV)*

It is clear from the scriptures that it is God's purpose to set up a kingdom on this earth over which a Son of King David is to reign forever. This promise was given to David through Nathan the Prophet.

> "*And your house and your kingdom shall be established forever before you; Your throne shall be established forever*"
>
> *2 Samuel 7:16, (NKJV)*

> *God, who at various times and in various ways spoke in times past to the fathers by the prophets, has in these last days spoken to us by His Son, whom He has appointed heir of all things, through whom also He made the Worlds:*
>
> *Who being the brightness "Of His Glory" and the express image of His person and upholding all things by the word of His power?*
>
> *Hebrews 1:1-3 (NKJV)*

We will have everlasting life of joy, love, peace, and purposeful activity of every conceivable kind. Eternal life will be the most exciting and challenging experience throughout all of God's creation.

All the assigned responsibilities and activities we receive and accomplish will progressively reveal God's long-range plan, His purpose for mankind, and the ultimate eternal quality of His future heavenly kingdom of God.

In the scriptures, there are numerous examples of "mentoring," and its importance is described by Paul in *2 Timothy 2:2:*

> *And the things that you have heard from me among many witnesses, commit these to faithful men who will be able to teach others also.*

Like the saints who rule and reign with Christ, we will also have this responsibility towards natural mankind. We will convey knowledge, wisdom, and the talent necessary to utilize the vast resources of God's kingdom that will further Man's development and increase his opportunities.

Once the kingdom has been established on the earth, the ten tribes of Israel (including those of the remnant) are all brought back from the nations of the earth into the land. Then together with the two tribes of Judah, they become "one nation under God."

The Lord then makes a new covenant with His people, Israel and Judah, forgiving their iniquity and remembering their sin no more. The re-born nation of God's elect (Jewish) people now come into actual possession of the full extent of the land according to the promise. And the land now includes the great desert, which "blossoms as the rose."

The land, as previously described, stretches from the river of Egypt and the Mediterranean Sea to the Euphrates River. And now, the temple and the city of Jerusalem are rebuilt after the divine plan.

The Levitical sacrifices and the ancient form of worship with Christ's modifications are reestablished as a remembrance of Jesus' sacrifice for the salvation of the world. Jerusalem is made the center of praise and the joy of the whole earth, with the Lord Jesus Christ in its midst as her glory and everlasting light.

The above is substantiated by the following scriptures. You are encouraged to study these for yourselves:

Genesis 15:18; Deuteronomy 11:24; Isaiah 11:11, 13; 13:9; 32:15; 33:14; 35:1, 2; 49:12-23; 49:12-23; 51:3; 60:10; Ezekiel 20:33-38; 20:40-42; 36:33-36; 37:16-24; 37:26; 38:18; 39:21; 39:25, 28; 40:1; 43:17; 47:13; 48:29; 48:1517, 30-35; Joel 3:2, 12; Hosea 1:11; Amos 9:9, 10, 14, 15; Josh 1:4; Jeremiah 31:31-33, 38; 32:40; 40; 50:4-5; Zechariah 14:10-11; Matthew 13:30, 41; 25:14-30; Luke 19:12-27; Acts 17:31; Romans 11:26-27; Hebrews 8:8-11

> *Therefore, the Lord will wait, that He may be gracious to you; and therefore, He will be exalted, that*

He may have mercy on you. For the Lord is a God of justice; blessed are all those who wait for Him.

Isaiah 30:18 (NKJV)

"And they shall rebuild the old ruins, they shall raise up the former desolations, and they shall repair the ruined cities" (Isaiah 61:4, NKJV).

20 There shall no longer be an infant who lives only a few days nor an old man who has not filled out his days. For the child shall die a hundred years old, but the sinner being a hundred years old shall be accursed.

21 They shall build houses and inhabit them and they shall plant vineyards and eat the fruit of them.

22 They shall not build and another inhabit; they shall not plant and another eat; for as the days of a tree are the days of My people, and My chosen ones shall long enjoy the work of their hands.

Isaiah 65:20-22 (MEV) Modern English Version

Younger generations are sometimes reluctant to trade what they now perceive as the "real life" on earth for the "imagined" life they may or may not ever have in heaven. However, the real tragedy is their lack of knowledge about the eternal life God has promised will come and their misunderstanding of the "kingdom of heaven" that is available to the believer today through Jesus Christ.

Compared to the "Kingdom Of Heaven" that will literally be realized on all the future everlasting habitations throughout God's incredible creation, this should totally electrify them. Religion has left them totally unmotivated to either desire heaven or to fear hell.

This confusion has also left them totally vulnerable to Satan's deceptions and the consequence of his easily understood worldly enticements. Hell!

I hope you catch the vision from this message, and you write it down as the Bible encourages in Habakkuk 2:2: *"Write the vision, and make it plain on tablets, that he may run who reads it."*

Pray that you will get this understanding and begin to dream and desire that this revelation remain locked within your heart. I pray that your testimony will be so strong that the world will say, "this is not possible"—but that you will have the faith to believe that with God…

ALL THINGS ARE POSSIBLE!

CHAPTER 14

A Place of Meaningful, Purposeful work

One of the purposes for which I was ordained to write this book is to help clear up the confusion over the spiritual and literal Kingdoms of heaven. I believe mankind has become so over religious that he has placed a tremendous burden of confusion on a very simple concept.

Some of this confusion might possibly be eliminated by just examining the various biblical facts of life (natural, spiritual, and supernatural) concerning the promises of God. We will begin this inquiry by simply reviewing a few of the teachings regarding our eternal life, the Millennial Reign of Christ, and the future perfect age. We will, by necessity, keep it to a simple topical study.

By eliminating, what I call, the 'religious overburden' of confusion, the concluding chapters of this book should provide you with a better understanding and appreciation of God's literal Kingdom of Heaven and His long-range plan for mankind. In addition, you should joyfully embrace the extraordinary vision, "Of His Glory."

I have read that we are not speculating when we prayerfully study prophecy, but I'm not sure this is really 100% true, at least not always. Sometimes a truth might also be reached without concrete evidence, whereas the conclusion is solely based on logical reasoning that infers the premise is correct—but is it?

The subjects presented in this book have been prayerfully studied, and each conclusion has been reached by reasoning,

Biblical evidence, theory, and divine inspiration. I cannot, however, honestly, say that 100% of every word of this text is divinely inspired by God or state "thus saith the Lord!" I do know the Lord initiated the subject and the purpose for the book. And it has been His inspiration, guidance and instruction that clearly guided it to final completion.

I am only advising you of this to encourage you to develop the habit of studying the issues for yourself, especially those that are controversial. If you don't receive the peace of confirmation in your spirit concerning the validity of an issue, search out the truth for yourself through study and prayer.

Believing that this has encouraged your spirit, I now prayerfully present the remaining chapters of this work for your study and discernment. The information presented is supported with Biblical evidence when and where appropriate. Some of the information and visions are based upon the results of reasoning, theory, and logical conclusions. However, I am convinced the primary influence comes through divine inspiration from the Holy Spirit.

The intent is for you to catch the vision of God's long-range plan for your own eternal life, and for that of all mankind. It is important that you grasp the truth of the vision and pass it on to others for their acceptance and redemption, so they too, will grasp the truth of the vision and pass it on.

"REPENT, for the Kingdom of Heaven is at hand"

Matthew 4:17, (NKJV)

This statement not only professes that it has come and is present in the church, "The Body of Christ," but, that it is also very close to actual consummation with the Lords soon appearing, our Blessed

Hope. Immediately after Christ's decent with His righteous army, His 'elite' glorified Saints,

> *"The armies in heaven, clothed in fine linen, white and clean, followed Him on white horses" (Revelation 19:14, NKJV).*

> *His feet will stand on the mount of olives which faces Jerusalem on the east, and the mount of olives shall be split in two, from east to west.*
>
> *Zechariah 14:4 (NKJV)*

Then the ghastly effects of God's wrath *"will strike down all the people who fought against Jerusalem."*

> *Their flesh shall dissolve while they stand on their feet, their eyes shall dissolve in their sockets, and their tongues shall dissolve in their mouths.*
>
> *Zechariah 14:12 (NKJV)*

> *The beast and the false prophet were cast alive into the lake of fire burning with brimstone. And the rest were killed with the sword which proceeded from the mouth of Him who sat on the horse. And all the birds were filled with their flesh.*
>
> *Revelation 19:20, 21 (NKJV)*

A quick foretaste of life after the Great Tribulation:

After Christ's victory, that old dragon Satan, is bound with chains and cast into the bottomless pit for 1,000 years. Throughout all of Christ's Millennial reign Satan will remain imprisoned and will not be allowed to interfere with Man's life again until the 1,000 years are finished. Then, *"Satan will be released from his prison."*

Immediately after concluding the final event of the *"Day of the Lord"* and Satan is removed from the earth, the angels will go out across the world and gather the Jews (God's elect) back to Jerusalem and to Christ.

Most of mankind that remain on the earth after the rapture of the 'Saints' who don't die during the two three-and-a-half-year periods of the tribulation are scattered throughout the earth. One exception will be the 144,000 Jews who are redeemed (raptured) from earth just prior to the second three and a half period called the 'Great Tribulation.' This great tribulation will bring the greatest time of trouble ever to come upon mankind.

A great number of the people who become righteous believers during the tribulation will die, with most of these being martyred for their faith. The total population of the earth will be significantly reduced, except for perhaps a billion people who will manage to come through the terror of this awful period alive.

Have you ever seen photographs of the Jews after they were set free from the World War II death camps? Or the photographs of Berlin that were taken after Germany's surrender, or the horrifying photographs of Hiroshima and Nagasaki Japan after the devastation of the atomic bomb?

Even closer to our own present time, have you seen any of the scenes in the science fiction movies that depict the cities of the earth destroyed? Have you ever seen any of the movies by Arnold "The Terminator" Schwarzenegger that shows the world's future cities as piles of rubble and heaps of concrete and steel?

Well, dear pilgrim, these fictional pictures are not far off from the actual, future magnitude of the total unparalleled devastation and ruin that will be worldwide. The cities we now know and inhabit will have been almost totally obliterated from the face of the earth.

Many of these will also very probably be completely contaminated by chemical, nuclear and biological fallout. Famine, pestilence, and disease will likewise have taken their toll. Most of the cities of the world will very probably become giant waste dumps. A literal wasteland! The whole earth will have been shaken by unprecedented monumental volcanic eruptions, earthquakes, the sun's scorching heat, war, plagues, fire, huge wrecking-ball sized hail stones, oxygen depletion and catastrophic worldwide drought.

The earth will have truly been 'beaten with an ugly stick' and billions of people will die horrible deaths. The whole ecosystem of the world will become completely devastated with its plant life, animal kingdom and natural resources almost completely obliterated.

Mankind will be in danger of almost turning the whole planet earth into a barren, totally polluted wasteland. Man's destructive technology and preference for sin will be increased far beyond their actual physical human wisdom. The geography of the entire earth as we know it today will almost become unrecognizable and practically beat to a pulp.

I can assure you that when you and I return with Christ and see the awful destruction, we won't recognize much of what remains on the earth. We certainly won't be going to the islands for a little vacation because they will no longer exist.

We won't be climbing a high mountain to assess the damage, because they will have all become a plane; and we won't be climbing to the top of any high-rise building to view a city's skyline, because they will all be mounds of rubble and charred piles of concrete, steel and glass. Remember the photographs of the World Trade Center after the terrorist attacks of 9/11?

But praise God, before mankind annihilates himself, Christ will return to save mankind from himself. He will then set up the forerunner of the literal Kingdom of Heaven, "Christ's Kingdom" on the earth. Our hero, Jesus, saves the day!

I'll just bet you thought in the future you would be in heaven floating on clouds and playing a harp like I mentioned at the beginning of this book. Right? No way! Grab a broom, you've got some serious cleaning up to do. But first, maybe we should ask the King how we can best serve Him and the Kingdom—He is our Lord, you know!

Whatever specific appointment God has assigned to us in life, He desires that we bring Him the glory produced through our faithful stewardship. He expects us to share with others the resources and capabilities He has placed under our control, as we are led by the Holy Spirit.

During our future millennial reign with Jesus, we will likewise, through our assignments, provide godly leadership, encouragement, and support to the remaining people of the earth. And mankind will again be given the responsibility to properly manage and "subdue" the earth—to restore and develop it to its fullest potential just as God always intended from creation.

As the restoration of the earth begins, the nation of Israel will be restored and placed in its appointed place of honor.

> *I will multiply men upon you, all the house of Israel, all of it; and the cities shall be inhabited, and the*

> *ruins rebuilt. I will multiply upon you man and beast; and they shall increase and bear young; I will make you inhabited as in former times and do better for you than at your beginnings. Then you shall know that I am the LORD.*
>
> *Ezekiel 36:10-11 (NKJV)*

Work! Work! Work! It will never be as glorious and fulfilling on our present earth as it will be in the future literal 'Kingdom of Heaven.' It will begin on the first day of the Millennium and continue throughout all of eternity. Please note I did not say labor, but 'work,' for there is a significant difference between the two.

> For a quick comparison: 'work' is wonderful, rewarding and exciting, like holding, hugging and loving a child, giving yourself completely to the nurture of the child. 'Labor,' on the other hand, is strenuous and burdensome, like the labor of giving birth to a child—even painful!

Many people believe work is a curse from God because of Adam and Eve's sin, as stated in the following passages of scripture: *"in the sweat of your face you shall eat bread till you return to the ground" (Genesis 3:19, NKJV).*

> *"Cursed is the ground for your sake; in toil you shall eat of it all the days of your life"*
>
> *(Genesis 3:17, NKJV).*

"Toil" is a word that means "to labor," work very hard and long, accomplish only with great laborious effort and sacrifice.

The Bible never calls work a curse, but a gift from God—He gave Adam and Eve work to do and projects to accomplish for His purposes long before they were commanded to leave the Garden of Eden.

> *"Then the Lord God took the man and put him in the Garden of Eden to tend and keep it"*
>
> *(Genesis 2:15, NKJV).*

> *"So, Adam gave names to all cattle, to the birds of the air, and to every beast of the field…"*
>
> *(Genesis 2:20, NKJV).*

God created Man in His image, an image that shows us that God is a worker! So, our God, who can only do what is good, shows us that work is good. He shows us that it is gratifying and has dignity, value, and purpose.

The work that God assigns to people today is meant to be a blessing, not a curse. The work that He will assign to the natural people on the earth during the Millennium will be provided as a blessing. Likewise, the work that God will assign to His children, "the Saints," during the Millennium will be provided as an amazing glorified blessing.

As God's sinless holy race of people, and we 'the saints' advance beyond the Millennial Reign of Christ into the perfect Kingdom of Heaven, God will extend and enhance all our assignments, perfecting the blessing of work to its supreme ultimate potential.

God provides mankind an assignment of work to meet all his personal, material, physical and spiritual needs. God's intent is to bless His people and to accomplish His purpose (His long-range plan) throughout all of creation, and to bring Him the Glory He intended when He created Man.

This makes us all co-workers with Him now and throughout all of eternity as we continue to fulfill our assignments to the fullest. As we accomplish the innumerable tasks associated with our specific assignment's we bring honor to ourselves and incredible blessing and Glory to Him. We not only enhance our eternal lives, but more importantly bring the greatest magnificent glory to God our Father as we employ of the knowledge, wisdom, talent and love He has placed within each of us, His co-workers.

The work that mankind does in advancing the actual physical and spiritual Kingdom brings fulfillment to God's will for all of creation, reflects the work of God and brings all the Glory to Him.

> *Then God saw everything that He had made, and indeed it was very good. So, the evening and the morning were the sixth day.*
>
> *Genesis 1:31 (NKJV)*

The work of God's creation was finished! However, this does not preclude any of the future enhancements outlined in His long-range plan. His creation is forever and always expanding, for He will re-make the quality and grandeur of many of its attributes beyond our ability to comprehend.

> *And on the seventh day God ended His work which He had done, and He rested on the seventh day from all His work which He had done.*
>
> *Genesis 2:2 (NKJV)*

Mankind was appointed to have dominion over all the earth, to manage all things of the earth, and to glorify God with their work in fulfilling His divine purpose. God expects immortal mankind to people all His creation, bringing Him unparalleled eternal glory as they faithfully manage all the earth's resources.

He desires infinite enrichment, development, and utilization of all its substance to fulfill mankind's eternal needs, and He wants Man to explore and "subdue" all its glorious wonders. He created the entire cosmos for mankind's eventual habitation. Therefore, Man's dominion over the earth is to become all-inclusive of the universe.

> *Also, your people shall all be righteous; they shall inherit the land forever, the branch of My planting, the work of My hands, that I may be glorified.*
>
> *Isaiah 60-21 (NKJV)*

God originally created Man to work, and He fully expects it in the future Kingdom of Heaven. Mankind is to have God's full authority over creation as managers and will have all the ability necessary to carry out His work, with Christ as the Chief Overseer, the Director of Operations.

It now takes, and in the future will likewise take, all manner and sorts of talents, skills, abilities, and people to do what God has planned for all of creation. Although the Bible doesn't describe the physical characteristics of eternity with very much detail, it does explain that meaningful, purposeful work will be a part of God's future peopled society.

> *"They shall build houses... They shall plant vineyards... My elect shall long enjoy the work of their hands" (Isaiah 65:21, 22, NKJV)*

Jesus Christ will rule and reign over the earth with His ambassador's "the Saints," and we, "the Saints," will be the highest-ranking diplomatic officials of His entire government. In receiving this appointment, we will be acknowledged as His holy representatives and the authorized messengers of Christ's righteousness and justice, forever.

He will Sovereignly position every person within the Kingdom—the natural Jewish and Gentile people and the glorified righteous Saints. All of these including the special Saints, His "elite Body"—the glorified church, will be appointed to a hierarchy of occupational, vocational responsibilities to serve in His Kingdom and do His work throughout all habitable earth's.

Mankind will be assigned to manage all the habitable earth, care for it and obtain benefit from its vast resources. In fulfilling their assignment, Man will bring unprecedented glory to God for His abundant blessings and richness. And we, "the Saints," as His co-workers, will delightfully share in *"His Glory"* as the people of the earth bring fulfillment to His will.

As you will recall from our previous discussions, all the Saints, including you and me, will have already received our glorified bodies like Christ's. In addition, we will have already received all our many wonderful crowns and rewards as God's holy children and joint heirs with Christ.

Having returned to earth with Christ, this great multitude of Saints will have also received their divine appointments, the imparted knowledge of God Almighty and His divine wisdom to carry out the work assigned. And it will all be carried out precisely, according to His will.

> *"When He comes, in that day, to be glorified in His Saints and to be admired among all those who believe"*
>
> *(2 Thessalonians 1:10, NKJV).*

As glorified Saints, having the countenance of God's love and a recognizable reflection *"Of His Glory,"* we are gloriously accepted by mankind as Christ's holy ambassadors. After Jesus' resurrection, His body still resembled that of a man and was recognizable as Himself when He met with His followers, but He also had an unmistakably divine countenance.

When we (the Saints) receive our glorified Bodie's we will also have the appearance of our natural mortal bodies, male and female, but we will be like Him. However, we will not have any need for a distinct sexual gender because our bodies will be supernatural, and we will have no desire or need for human sexuality.

Besides, the eternal joy and pleasure we will experience as a reflection *"Of His Glory"* is infinitely greater than any human experience. However, the ability for procreation will still exist within God's holy race of natural immortal people and they, not the Saints, will continue to populate the universe forever.

> *Those who are wise shall shine like the brightness of the firmament, and those who turn many to righteousness like the stars forever and ever.*
>
> *Daniel 12:3 (NKJV)*

The 'wise' are the godly Saints who show their wisdom by the way they live and the affect their lives have in bringing others to a righteous way of life. Their shining means they will be transformed, and God's glory will be reflected in and through them.

> *"And just as we have borne the likeness of the earthly man, so shall we bear the likeness of the Man from heaven" (1 Corinthians 15:49, NIV).*
>
> *"...and star differs from star in spender"*
>
> *1 Corinthians 15:41, (NIV)*

"Then the righteous will shine like the sun in the Kingdom of their Father"

Matthew 13:43, (NIV)

"The path of the righteous is like the first gleam of dawn, shining ever brighter till the full light of day"

Proverbs 4:18, (NIV).

Once the government of the Millennial Kingdom is set up by Christ and all His systems are go, the actual 1000-year reign of Jesus Christ begins. There is, however, a time of 75 days after the second three and a half years (1260 days) of the Great Tribulation in which the transition and preparation for Christ's Reign will most likely take place *(Daniel 12:11, 12).*

The first 30 days of this additional 75 days referred to in *Daniel 12:11 (1290 days - 1260 days = 30 days)* is probably the period in which the judgment of the sheep and goat nations will be conducted.

In addition to this time, *Daniel 12:12 refers to a period of 1335 days that is an extra 45 days (1335 days - 1290 days = 45 days) and* is probably the time that will be necessary to completely set up the government of Christ's Kingdom. It is also the time in which He will establish His hierarchy of management and assign various leadership roles to many of the remaining natural people of the earth.

11 And from the time that the daily sacrifice is taken away, and the abomination of desolation is set up, there shall be one thousand two hundred and ninety days.

12 Blessed is he who waits and comes to the one thousand three hundred and thirty-five days.

Daniel 12:11, 12 (NKJV)

At no other time in mankind's history will the devastation that comes upon the whole earth be more pronounced materially and physically, as well as psychologically terrifying than the three and a half years of the Great Tribulation. The natural created environment, the man-made built environment and the social/cultural environment of all the peoples of the earth will be totally devastated.

The restoration process that will be necessary to restore order and replenish the earth's resources will be announced to the whole world by the new Commander in Chief, the Lord of lords, King of kings, Jesus Christ the Son of the living God Almighty, "I AM!"

All people who remain on the earth will bow down before His Name, the only Name. Some of the remaining people will be so terrified at the time of Christ's return that many will probably die of fright, be killed by followers of Antichrist or even commit suicide before any degree of social order can be brought back to the earth.

The hearts of many of the people who accept Antichrist will no doubt fail them due to His total complete victory over the enormous army that is assembled to destroy Jerusalem. All of those who rejected Antichrist and suffered for Christ to the end will conversely be utterly overjoyed.

"Blessed is he who waits," and comes through the judgment of the sheep nations, for it is all these who will triumphantly enter the Millennial Kingdom of Christ.

The restoration plan will be announced to the whole world, and all peoples (nations) of the earth will unite under His banner of love, righteousness, and justice. Then, along with the leadership teams composed of God's holy 's Saints,' the greatest urban (world) renewal project in history will be commenced.

The organizational skill that Jesus displayed when He fed the 5000 plus women and children will again be witnessed by the world in His marvelous plan of reconstruction.

The holy city of Jerusalem and the new temple that Jesus will have built is going to have center stage in the restoration process, and much attention and work will be devoted to its completion. We are told in Ezekiel 48:35 that the name of Jerusalem in that day is "Jehovah-Shammah," the Lord is there.

He also tells us that the new city will be approximately 9 miles square but with the suburbs, ten miles square, and it will sit within an area called the "Holy Oblation" or "Holy District." The new temple or sanctuary will be built (probably at the site of ancient Shiloh where Joshua set up the tabernacle) and it will be located about 12 to 15 miles north of the new city. [illustration on page 119 and 120]

He further describes the entire tract of land that is designated the Prince's portion that the fifty-mile square "Holy District" is located within. This tract is bounded on the north by the border of land given to the tribe of Judah and is also aligned with the northern boundary of the "Holy District."

Then fifty miles to the south the tract is bounded by the border of land given to the tribe of Benjamin and is also aligned with the southern boundary of the "Holy District." The tract is further bounded by the Mediterranean Sea on the west and the Euphrates River about 540 miles to the east for a total land area of approximately 27,000 square miles; about the size of South Carolina or Maine.

The total tract of land is designated for the Prince, "our King," the Lord of lords Jesus Christ and His holy Saints. Therefore, since it is Christ's personal track, we can be assured that it will be blessed more abundantly than any place on the face of the earth. It is also noteworthy for us to know that Jesus is sometimes referred to as the Prince, because He is David's descendant and He fulfilled the Davidic covenant—thus, He is the Prince of God's people, the Jews.

We will discuss the city and the temple in more detail later, but first, let's get a perspective on the overall restoration of the world that will be the first order of business for all of mankind who remain and enter the Millennium alive.

The earth's ecosystems will need to be restored to a level that will support the basic food requirements of the people. Existing farmlands will need to be re-claimed and new farmlands developed in new fertile land areas. Crops of all types all over the world will need to be planted, cultivated and harvested to feed the nations. Therefore, a very high priority will be given to developing the total food delivery system.

> *The wilderness and the wasteland shall be glad for them. And the desert shall rejoice and blossom as the rose; It shall blossom abundantly and rejoice.*
>
> *Isaiah 35:1-2 (NKJV)*

Eventually, over the course of many years, all of nature will flourish and be restored to God's original natural order, perfection and beauty. Man will, as it has always been since Adam, have the responsibility for maintaining and managing all the earth's natural resources.

There will also be a tremendous undertaking to clean up the mess left behind due to the Tribulation. Some cities and towns will very probably be annihilated from the face of the earth, while others will be so horribly demolished that rebuilding on the same site will be totally out of the question.

Others will be enormous piles of debris that will be impossible to build over. However, there will be some cities such as Jerusalem that will be able to be rebuilt on the same site. Ezekiel describes the rebuilding of Jerusalem on the site of the old, and in addition mentions that the landscape has significantly been changed.

Many of the sites of the old cities will probably become enormous building material resource areas. These areas will very likely provide an immediate source from which a great variety of materials can be secured for recycling and re-use in the re-building process. In addition, these new cities will very probably be near these great resource mines.

The entire infrastructure of the man-made built environment will need to be rebuilt to ideally support all the earth's new systems. Some of the existing systems will be rebuilt, but many will have to be newly developed to ultimately provide for all the natural, physical and material needs of the nations.

You should be aware that most of the international, national, and local public utility, communication, transportation, sanitation, health care, and socio-economic support systems across the world will have been severely damaged or destroyed. The whole earth will be war-torn and ravaged.

In many cases, previously inhabited areas of the earth will be spoiled beyond restoration. We're talking about "Little House on the Prairie" type of new beginning—outhouse included!

The leadership and direction to the nations will come from Christ's Saints (you and me)! His Holy Ambassadors. With God's imparted knowledge and wisdom, we will go out into all the earth to help establish His Rule and Reign over all the people and nations under Christ.

We, the 'Saints,' will also very likely show the way and direct the Lord's reconstruction plans over the whole earth, with the remaining natural men and women managing and performing the work of restoration and rebuilding.

All the physical and spiritual needs of the people will be met. The Saints' will teach and instruct the people of God's unending love, righteousness and justice that is administered to them through His Son Jesus. They will be taught that Jesus' rule over the whole earth will be swift but just. Disobedience will be dealt with very quickly and punishment administered with a "rod of iron," meaning physical punishment, including death, to the offender.

> *You shall not live, because you have spoken lies in the Name of the Lord. And his father and mother who begot him shall thrust him through when He prophesies.*
>
> *Zechariah 13:3 (NKJV)*

The above passage relates to anyone who prophesies during the reign of Christ. Prophecy is expressly forbidden during this time because Christ will now be physically present and will have fulfilled *all* prophecy. So, if any word of prophecy is spoken, it will be a lie that is meant to deceive the hearer. Thus, the false prophet will be swiftly dealt with, even by his own family.

I have read commentaries by several men of God who have stated that there will be no death, no sickness, and not even a weed on the earth during the Millennium. However, in addition to the above scriptural passage, there are many others that prove physical death is still present and not just for the wicked.

If sin and death are still on the earth, then it seems obvious sickness and weeds will still be around. But it is reasonable to believe, without Satan around, they certainly won't be as prevalent as today.

> *"He shall strike the earth with the rod of His mouth, and with the breath of His lips He shall slay the wicked" (Isaiah 11:4, NKJV).*

> *"He who dies at a hundred will be thought a mere youth; he who fails to reach a hundred will be considered accursed" (Isaiah 65:20, NIV).*

Even though Satan is bound during this Millennial period, sin is still present because mankind's sinful nature remains unchanged. However, this in-born nature may be repressed to extinction during the Millennium allowing Christ's nature to reign supreme in the heart of Man. We must remember that Man is still mortal during this period, not immortal. Sickness and death will still be prevalent in the world, although significantly diminished. Man will have an extended long life, for even a person of 100 years will be considered a child.

Man's life span could reach 500, 600 or maybe even 900 years, meaning that many people might live their lives to the very end of Christ's Millennial Reign. After the millennium, the living righteous men, women and children who enter the perfect age, will live throughout eternity with God.

Mankind, as God's holy race of people, will then be rewarded with transformed immortal bodies and receive their inheritance of the renewed earth.

Unfortunately, the old sin nature will prevail in many of the millennial people, and they will reject Christ. They will also follow Satan to the bitter end, suffering total defeat, and then cast into the lake of fire for eternity.

> *They went up on the breadth of the earth and surrounded the camp of the Saints and the beloved city. And fire came down from God out of heaven and devoured them.*
>
> *Revelation 20:9 (NKJV)*

The nations under Christ's Reign are obliged to honor and be obedient to His rule. They are always to persevere in love and obedience, to have faith in Him, and through Him receive God's righteousness. However, as we have seen, some will choose the way of rebellion and disobedience and will be punished.

> *And it shall come to pass that everyone who is left of all the nations which came against Jerusalem shall go up from year to year to worship the King, the Lord of Hosts, and to keep the Feast of Tabernacles.*
>
> *Zechariah 14:16 (NKJV)*

The Feast of Tabernacles was the last of the sacred festivals under the old covenant and marked the completion of the harvest and historically commemorated the wanderings in the wilderness. This Feast was traditionally held in the middle of the month of Tishri (October), lasted seven days, and was very popular and extremely joyous in nature. It was a lot like the present 21st Century's* Christmas holidays.

* The 21st (twenty-first) century is the current century of the Anno Domini era or Common Era, in accordance with the Gregorian calendar. It began on January 1, 2001 and will end on December 31, 2100. The first century of the 3rd millennium. Anno Domine, Latin for "Year of Our Lord," AD.

As you can probably see by now, there will be much to do during the first several years just to get things back into some degree of order. Everyone will have a job to do, and they will do it with more vigor and joy than anything mankind has ever done before.

They will no doubt sing and praise the Lord the whole day long in all they do. The people of the earth will understand and truly know that there is peace, safety, prosperity, and righteousness throughout the earth. They will see and grasp the vision of the future literal Kingdom of Heaven on earth, and all the nations will bow before the King and receive His blessing.

Most occupations and vocations the people of earth have today will also be needed during Christ's Millennial Reign, however, as previously discussed we know with certainty the role of the prophet is no more. We should also know there will not be any sinful occupations allowed in Christ's Kingdom. However, a majority of all the meaningful occupations and vocations we have today will be with us during Christ's Reign.

The emphasis and prominence of the various occupations will very definitely be of either greater or lesser importance in Christ's Kingdom than today. Even the work performed in a specific occupation may be different than it is today. For example, consider the professional wild animal trainer and any associated occupations or vocations related to the animal kingdom.

*The term-built environment is referring to all those surroundings created for humans, by humans, and to be used for human activity.

Since there will not be any "wild" animals on the earth, we will not need any "wild" animal trainers. However, we will certainly need people in occupations that will be responsible to oversee the nurturing and care of all the animals of the earth. Can you think of a prominent occupation today that will perhaps be less important or more important during the Millennium? Such as the military, doctors, lawyers, politicians, police and firemen, morticians, guns and gun stores just to name a few.

With Satan's influence eliminated from the world, the effects of his evil will no longer plague or deceive mankind. Therefore, the world will either not need or will have a much lesser need for occupations related to those areas that were previously under his influence.

Occupations, vocations and special skills the Lord has led each of us to pursue and develop during our natural lives on the earth may possibly be related to the assignments we, 'the saints,' receive during His reign. Our acquired expertise may become one of the main prerequisites for receiving God's advanced knowledge and wisdom in each of our special areas of work. Then, we will each receive a special assignment that will be needed to lead, mentor and advance mankind's future growth and achievements—bringing inexpressible glory to God.

The greatest adventure we could ever imagine awaits the Saints and all of mankind in the actualized literal Kingdom of Christ and the future eternal Kingdom of God. Everything in the universe has purposeful activity, and the Lord declares that Man will have joyous and purposeful employment of their gifts and skills in bringing tremendous glory to God.

> *For you shall go out with joy and be led out with peace; the mountains and the hills shall break forth into singing before you, and all the trees of the field shall clap their hands. Instead of the thorn shall come up the cypress tree, and instead of the brier shall come up the myrtle tree; and it shall be to the Lord for a name, for an everlasting sign that shall not be cut off.*
>
> *Isaiah 55:12,13 (NKJV)*

> *"For the earth shall be full of the knowledge of the Lord as the waters cover the sea" (Isaiah 11:9, NKJV).*

The greatest truth that any person can possess with the heart and mind is to experience and know the truth about God. At the beginning of Christ's Reign, every person who believes in Christ will personally know the Lord and have intimate fellowship with Him, have direct access to Him, and will receive the imparted fullness of the Holy Spirit in their lives.

Not every person who will enter the Millennial kingdom from the tribulation will personally know Christ as Savior and Lord. However, the knowledge of the Lord will fill every man, woman, and child who come into the Millennial Kingdom, and there will not be one person on earth who will not know God the Father, Son, and Holy Spirit.

> *No more shall every man teach his neighbor, and every man his brother, saying, 'know the Lord,' for they all shall know Me, from the least of them to the greatest of them, says the Lord.*
>
> *Jeremiah 31:43 (NKJV)*

> *"It shall come to pass that before they call, I will answer; and while they are still speaking, I will hear" (Isaiah 65:24, NKJV).*

Having the knowledge of the Lord and seeing His Glory manifested in the person of Jesus Christ and all the Saints, every Jewish and gentile person who accepts Christ as Savior and Lord will receive the fullness of the Holy Spirit. And upon their acceptance, they will receive a greater outpouring than *"when the day of Pentecost had fully come" (Acts 2:1-4).*

The nation of Israel will be born again and rise as the most glorious nation in all the world, revered by mankind all over the world. With the knowledge of the Lord and the fullness of His Spirit in their lives, the natural abilities of Man will increase to a much higher plane than mankind has ever experienced. With God living in and through him, Man's creative spirit will be continuously propelled to reach higher and higher in his search for ways to bring unending Glory to God as he serves the throne of Christ.

Imagine how magnificent the earth will become during the 1,000-year millennial reign of Jesus compared to today's *built environment and the amazing new architectural designs of all the new cities to be developed throughout the world. Comparing the 21st century buildings designed by today's architects and those by the millennial architects during this 1,000-year period is beyond one's imagination.

Please copy the following link onto your browser to see what is currently regarded as 'Amazing!' (Ctrl + Click if you are reading an 'e-book.')

https://www.pinterest.com/harrowp/architecture-is-amazing

By truly knowing God, mankind will possess the wisdom to exercise his knowledge, his purpose, his position, and his power of authority and dominion over all of God's creation on this earth. Man will finally have dominion over the earth just as God originally intended for Adam, and as exercised by Jesus during His ministry on the earth. The spiritual, intellectual, and personal growth of mankind during Christ's Reign of righteousness will progress to a height of accomplishment greater than mankind today could ever imagine. Under Christ's Reign, the whole earth will flourish in a state of absolute, total magnificence and become an actual realized paradise of life that will be a holy reflection…

OF HIS GLORY!

CHAPTER 15

Truly, "It's a Wonderful Life"!

In Christ's Kingdom, there is only one hero, and that is Him! What more could anyone want in a hero that the King, our Lord, Jesus Christ doesn't have? He is the very hero generation after generation has been searching for, Generation 'X, Y and Z' included. He is all we will ever need!

If you've heard His story or read 'The Book,' you know He's the *One* who will be charging mankind's enemy with His mounted posse. He's the one who will terminate all the evil gang members. He's the hero who will capture that old desperado Satan. And He's the only one who can take that old enemy, the earth Baron, and put him in leg irons and keep him behind bars during the millennial reign of Jesus for the thousand years.

Sorry, Roy and Gene, but you've just never come up against anyone quite like the old evil Baron. Father God had to call in the big Gun on this one cause that old Baron is one mean, the ornery devil.

Some of you may remember Roy and Gene and the wonderful place occupied by the people of Happy Valley and how they all lived happily ever after. Well, that's the truth, almost. But there is a matter about a jailbreak in about a thousand years that will spoil their peace for a little while, but not really for very long because Jesus is surely going to 'smoke-em.'

All our favorite heroes have had sidekicks to support and help them in addition to just being their good old buddies and true friends. Well, our hero, Jesus, also has His friends, His sidekicks, so to speak. His sidekicks will be participating with Him in bringing peace, prosperity, security, and joy to His glorious city and the whole earth during His millennial reign.

These participants, the Saints, will share in His glory and have the same character of Holiness and Righteousness as His own. And above all, they will each one become a living glorious reflection "Of His glory."

These are the same glorified 'Saints' (you and me) who famously return with Christ from heaven to defeat Satan and his army. We are the ones who will help set up the government of the Millennial Kingdom and assist with the restoration of the earth while all this is taking place. We're not just casual observers looking on from some distant hill watching our Hero win the day for mankind. No way! We're the participants with Him. We're the ones sharing His glory—we, too, are heroes!

> *The Spirit Himself bears witness with our spirit that we are children of God, and if children, then heirs—heirs of God and joint heirs with Christ, if indeed we suffer with Him, that we may also be <u>glorified together</u>.*
>
> *For I consider that the sufferings of this present time are not worthy to be compared with the glory for which shall be revealed in us. For the earnest expectation of the creation eagerly waits for the revealing of the sons of God.*
>
> *For the creation was subjected to futility, not willingly, but because of Him who subjected it in hope, because the creation itself also will be delivered from the bondage of corruption into the glorious liberty of the children of God.*
>
> *Romans 8:16-21 (NKJV)*

We're the heroes natural mankind will be looking for during the Millennial Reign of Christ. We will be there to help them reach the attainable heights God intends for them to reach in holiness, righteousness, and victory over sin.

As Christ's ambassadors, we will be His representatives to the people. We'll share in His reign by fulfilling many roles, not the least of which will be as a teacher, mentor, and overseer of the Kingdom. But always under Christ's Kingship—so, don't ever be deceived to believe otherwise.

We discussed a few chapters back how many in previous generations did not have any heroes. They were a generation who had their purpose and destiny clouded with so much 'new age' garbage the truth couldn't be found. Well, I've got news for them, and for you as well, Jesus is the answer! He's the real Hero, and He is offering to share everything He has with you or anyone who will accept His call.

He's willing to start sharing right now, through the rapture, the marriage of the lamb, His second coming, His Millennial Reign, the perfect age, and even into eternity forever and ever. There's no higher position in all eternity for mankind than that of a Saint, a child of God, adopted into the Father's family through His only begotten Son, Jesus Christ.

If you haven't yet accepted Jesus' call, or if you've just pushed him out of your life, pray this prayer right now and accept His call:

> *Heavenly Father, I come to you in the name of Jesus. Your word says, "everyone who calls on the name of the Lord will be saved."*
>
> *Acts 2:21 (NIV)*
>
> *I am calling on you and ask Jesus to come into my heart and be Lord over my life. I confess with my*

> *mouth Jesus is Lord, and I believe in my heart that God raised Him from the dead.*
>
> *Romans 10:9 (NIV)*

I am now born again and a child of God! I am saved! I will live my life for you! Thank you, Jesus.

Now I know I can say without reservation that we will all meet very soon in the air, translated to be like Him. And dear Saint, we will all 'shine' with the beautiful radiance Of His glory. As His holy ambassadors to natural mankind, we will have the incredible reflections Of His glory and will minister to their needs as directed by our Lord and King, Jesus.

This new world with Jesus as King is going to be as good as it gets until sin is finally put down for good at the end of the Millennial Kingdom. Then, after God remakes the heavens and the earth, it will become eternally glorious.

> *The heavens will pass away with a great noise, and the elements will melt with fervent heat; both the earth and the works that are in it will be burned up.*
>
> *2 Peter 3:10 (NKJV)*

> *"For behold, I create new heavens and a new earth and the former shall not be remembered or come to mind" (Isaiah 65:17, NIV).*

Until sin is totally eradicated from mankind's nature, no kingdom that includes natural Man will ever have the opportunity to become a perfect Kingdom. Therefore, even the Millennial Kingdom will never make the grade. However, this news is not as tragic as you might think.

The Millennial Kingdom or Christ's Kingdom—whatever your favorite phrase might be for this 1000-year Reign of Christ on earth; it is to become the most glorious, incredible, joyous, stupendous, and totally awesome Kingdom to ever develop upon the earth of mortal Man.

Mankind will reach such vast new heights of achievement over this 1,000-year period that no one today could begin to imagine or even comprehend the actualized fullness of knowledge.

The peace, prosperity, and joy of this Kingdom will be incredibly glorious. If mankind today could get just a glimpse of Christ's mature Kingdom, they would very probably claim to have seen heaven. If they were to see one of His glorified Saints, they would most surely believe they had seen Jesus Himself. And the brightness of the glory throughout Christ's Kingdom will be so radiant. They would have to cover their faces.

Do you get the picture, dear brother and sister? This Kingdom is just so magnificent it cannot even be described. Even with life becoming incredibly glorious under Christ's rule, sin will still exist, and Man will continue to say no! As unbelievable as it seems, some will still reject Christ and unfortunately pay the awful price. Please keep in mind that this future glorious 'Kingdom of Christ' is just a foretaste of what is to come in the 'Perfect age' and even beyond into the 'Eternal age' of the 'Kingdom of Heaven.'

It is going to become so good; one couldn't believe it would ever get any better! Let me explain: Immediately after the millennial reign of Christ, the Perfect age begins, and according to scripture, this is only one of the ages that we will experience in the glorious "Age of the Ages." (An age {aeon} is defined as an immeasurably long period of time: a unit of time possibly equal to one billion years as used in geology)

"HALLELUJAH! For our Lord God Almighty reigns. Let us rejoice and be glad and give Him GLORY!" (Revelation 19:6, 7, NIV).

I have to say, I hope you are getting as excited reading this as I am in writing it—God is so good! The more we learn of His Kingdom and His plan, the more we all grow in love with Him. Just to know that we are His children, His saints, His heirs, and as such, we will have inherited all this and more. We have not only become spiritual reflections of His glory in this mortal life, but in the future resurrection life to come, we, the 'Saints" will become a true manifestation of the reflection, of His glory.

Just stop a moment and mull that thought over a bit—we will get back to this later in the following chapters.

From God's creation and from His word, we can see that God is very ordered and systematic about everything He does. There is no disorder, confusion, or haphazard occurrences in all the universe. The tadpole did not just sprout legs one day, and then the next day, Man walked the earth.

There was a very definitive plan from the foundation of the earth, and as God worked that plan, it all became that which was planned. Not only did He know the plan, but He also foreknew the results of His plan. Knowing the future, He then made special provisions in the plan to nullify certain undesirable occurrences from becoming permanent.

He knew that Satan would rise up during the execution of the plan to sabotage His ultimate desired objective, so He provided solutions to every adverse situation ahead of time. Therefore, God's plan has never changed, nor has He changed the desired objectives and the ultimate goal for mankind that was established at the foundation of the world.

"I the Lord do not change. So you, O descendants of Jacob, are not destroyed" (Malachi 3:5, NIV).

Being the master organizer that He is, it is doubtful He would assign every Saint in heaven a position on this earth during the Millennial Reign of Christ, at least not initially. Since the remaining population of natural mortal mankind that will enter His Kingdom is so small compared to the total number of the Saints, we can presume that some of the saints will be occupied elsewhere for a season.

Remember, too, the saints have all been transformed into supernatural creatures with the inherited traits and capabilities of Christ. Thus, we, the saints, in serving and glorifying our God, will have the distinct privilege of supernaturally traveling throughout God's whole universe.

We will not only be able to traverse at will throughout the planet earth, but even throughout the heavens and into the third level of heaven. We will be capable of traversing beyond the universe to the "sides of the north" where God Almighty resides.

We also know from scripture that the martyrs from the "Great Tribulation," who are the last ones to become righteous believers and die for their faith, will serve God's throne forever.

> *And I said to him, 'Sir, you know.' So, he said to me, 'These are the ones who come out of the Great Tribulation and washed their robes and made them white in the blood of the Lamb."*
>
> *"Therefore, they are before the throne of God, and serve Him day and night in His temple. And He who sits on the throne will dwell among them. They shall neither hunger anymore nor thirst anymore; the sun shall not strike them, nor any heat...*
>
> *Revelation 7:14-16 (NKJV)*

The heavenly city, "New Jerusalem," that God has prepared for all the righteous saints throughout history is now in the Heaven of Heavens. God is awaiting that glorious day when the new heavens and new earth are made, so the City of New Jerusalem can begin its descent to the new earth where it will remain for all of eternity.

During the Millennial Reign of Christ, this city will no doubt be occupied by a certain number of the saints who remain in heaven with God. Perhaps they are assigned to put the final finishing touches on all those many mansions in the Father's house as proclaimed by Jesus 2,000 years ago.

They no doubt will also be discovering the mysteries of God's creation and preparing for the advent of the 'perfect kingdom' on the new earth and throughout all of God's creation in the universe.

As God's children, we will have already received our full inheritance and have access to all the levels of heaven, and especially before the throne of God the Father. All the saints in heaven will have the fullness of God's glory abiding within them and will become fully manifested as a perfect reflection of His glory while in His presence.

As the saints enter and leave God's 'Kingdom of Heaven,' or the third level of heaven where our God resides and reigns supreme, the actual radiance of the reflection of God's Glory as it is manifested in the saints will be inexpressible.

If mortal men were exposed to the fullness of this reflection, they too would need to have their eyes screened, as Moses did. Remember, he even had to screen his shining face from the Israelites after just seeing the reflection of God's back on Mount Sinai.

Natural mortal Man will never see the fullness of God's radiant glory, nor the full reflection of God's glory through the saints. Only a very limited degree or level of His glory will be reflected through the saints, His angels, and through the Lord Jesus Christ during the Millennial Reign of Christ.

The measure of His glory that will be witnessed by natural mankind will only be as determined by the Father. However, it will bring wonderful joy, praise, and thanksgiving, to the Lord, and possibly at certain times, it may even become a more intensified radiance than at other times.

As the Spirit of God works through His anointed saints, His holy children, in ministering to Man's needs, we would expect the anointing of His glory will flow in varying degrees. The scriptures are very clear that no Man may see the fullness of His glory and live, but we, the saints, His children, are able.

> *And He said, 'Please, show me Your glory.' Then He said, 'I will make all My goodness pass before you, and I will proclaim the name of the LORD before you.*
>
> *I will be gracious to whom I will be gracious, and I will have compassion on whom I will have compassion.' But He said, 'You cannot see My face; for no man shall see Me, and live.'*
>
> *Exodus 33:18-20 (NKJV)*

Revelation 20:9 tells us that at the end of the Millennial Reign of Christ, Satan and his army will be instantly devoured by fire from our Father, God. Could this possibly be the actual awesome radiance of God's Glory. A radiance that will only be exposed to Satan's army of followers as they surround the camp of God's saints and the city of His 'Elect' people, the Jews?

Let me recap and highlight the reality of the heavenly fullness to which you, my dear brother and sister, will be ascending. You will be transformed from this mortal human existence (an eternal spirit living in a mortal body) only because you have accepted Jesus Christ as your Lord and Savior. Nothing else works!

Your blood-bought redemption through Jesus has provided you with an opportunity far beyond human comprehension. As a natural mortal creature with God's Holy Spirit living within and through you, the absolute highest level of spiritual maturity is readily available to you today. Since you are the righteousness of God in Christ Jesus and are precious in His sight—He will do anything for you, if you'll just simply ask.

> *"If you then, being evil, know how to give good gifts to your children, how much more will your heavenly Father give the Holy Spirit to those who ask Him!"*
>
> *Luke 11:13 (NKJV)*

> *"For He made Him who knew no sin to be sin for us, that we might become the righteousness of God in Him" (Corinthians 5:21, NKJV).*

When Christ returns, we will have already taken part in the first resurrection (probably during the rapture of the church) and received our transformed, glorified, supernatural bodies like Christ's. We will have also previously ascended into heaven and stood before the judgment seat of Christ.

During this our judgment, we receive our crowns and rewards. Then, as members of the church, we are joined with Jesus in the marriage of the lamb and celebrate the honor of His glory with Jesus at the marriage supper.

We then subsequently return to the earth in our transformed bodies with Jesus at His second coming and begin our reign with Jesus over the Millennial Kingdom of Christ.

Quite a lot will be occurring in your life from today up to the beginning point of the Millennium, wouldn't you agree? Well, as a little added excitement to your life, do you have any notion about the total length of time under discussion here?

Every indication from Bible prophecy is pointing to His soon return, but, of course, no one knows exactly when this will happen except our Father God. However, we do know that the time is very near, and we should all be looking up for *"our Blessed Hope."*

> *"...looking for the blessed hope and glorious appearing of our great God and Savior Jesus Christ" (Titus 2:13, NKJV).*

As I have mentioned previously, there are many good books available about the end-times, the rapture of the church, and the seven-year Tribulation. So, if you haven't yet acquired a good working knowledge of these events, you are encouraged to study these upon completion of this book.

In the conclusion of our recap, let me again emphasize to you the awesome splendor and magnificence of your future new eternal body. You have seen Jesus face to face and beheld all His glory, and instantly your mortal body became like His, Glorified and Eternal. You have seen God the Father in all Of His Glory and have seen God the Holy Spirit. In other words, you have been in the very presence of the Triune God, "I AM."

You have seen His host of Angels and the Glory of Heaven. You have seen, now know, and have stood side by side with all the righteous saints of all history since Adam.

Your new glorified body radiates with the brightness of God's Glory, and you, dear Saint, are holy, holy as the Lord and a perfect reflection of His glory, hallelujah! Glory to God! For all of eternity, you will be with God, your Father, forever, and ever, forevermore.

Higher than the Angels, His heir and a joint heir with Jesus, of all God's glory.

Can you now begin to see the vision God has for you? Do you realize who you are and in Whom you are? Today, even today, you reflect God's glory, and everything you do should and is to bring glory to Him. Today, your outward reflection and radiance are only like the flicker of a small candle. But tomorrow, the radiance of your reflection of God's Glory and Essence will transcend even beyond human understanding. And your countenance will become just like His! A true, fully perfected reflection of His glory. Awesome, wouldn't you say?

With the very presence of Almighty God being reflected through you and all the other holy saints, natural Man will be living in the physically realized presence of Almighty God throughout the whole earth. In addition, Man will be living in the actualized presence of Almighty God in the person of Jesus Christ, the King of the whole earth.

Have you grasped the full meaning of all that will occur over God's planet earth? Prior to the return of Jesus to establish His Millennial Kingdom, there will have existed only one state of mankind—natural mortal mankind.

Now for the very first time in all of creation, two will exist, natural mortal mankind and supernatural immortal mankind (the saints). Natural mortal mankind, however, will only continue to exist in God's creation for the duration of the 1000-year Millennial Reign of Christ.

At the end of the Millennium, another first will occur in creation; Goodness will be eternally separated from evil. Natural 'Mortal' Mankind who remains loyal to Christ as God's holy (righteous) people miraculously become Natural 'Immortal' Mankind. At the time of this transformation, the righteous are also divinely protected like Noah, while the heavens and the earth are made new as God has promised.

All the righteous Natural 'Immortal' Mankind who are miraculously removed from the present earth returns to the New Earth as God's holy, sinless race of people. Upon their return to the new earth, they not only remain fruitful and multiply upon the new earth, but they will continue to populate the whole of God's creation, the 'new Heavens,' throughout the entire cosmos for all of eternity.

Following this glorious new beginning after the Millennium, there will continue to be two very distinctively different states of mankind. The first state is 'Natural' Immortal Mankind, who will people the universe as God has always intended and as promised to Abraham. The second state is 'Supernatural' Immortal Mankind, who are the glorified saints of God—you and me.

Just as there are various distinctive states of God's Angelic creatures, there will likewise always be in the future age(s) to come at least two very distinct and very blessed unique states of mankind—the 'Glorified saints' and all of 'Supernatural Immortal Man,' translated into the Glorious Magnificence of "God's Grandeur." Such is and has been the legacy of mankind since the foundation of the earth. No mere Man can even begin to fathom the difference—but with the revelation of God's Holy Spirit, you, dear Saint, can and will *"catch the vision."*

Maybe you have not previously considered your godly inheritance, but you dear Saint, as a blood-bought Christian, you are God's heir. As His heir and a joint heir with Jesus, we are destined to receive the greatest of all blessings in God's Kingdom.

We will receive the actual fully realized characteristic manifestation of God's righteousness, and then as His 'Glorified saints' will become the loving reflection "Of His Glory" throughout the whole created universe, and very probably even beyond.

You are to become one of the elites, along with all the other righteous saints who will be Eternally glorified by God the Father and receive a Supernatural/Spirit body that will be transformed from earthly mortality to heavenly immortality. A body with the very essence of heavenly life that transcends higher than all of God's creatures. A body with a certain quality and a state of godliness beyond all human comprehension.

Remember that "lower than Elohim" in Psalm 8:5 is really saying 'Higher than the angels and is a state of eternal heavenly quality that is now built-in, but not yet fully manifested. Even Lucifer, who was the most magnificent of all God's creatures before his rebellion, would have been no match for the magnificence of God's elite heirs, we the children of the Most High, God Almighty.

Why do you think Satan has been so adamant in all his dastardly endeavors? He desires to destroy mankind by any means necessary and to keep mankind in bondage with all his lies, tricks, and deceit. He knows that God's long-range plan includes this very special elite group of saints.

He understands that God's children (you and me) will be exalted to the absolute highest state of existence next to our Triune God Himself. And he knows and is embittered, that we will gloriously rule and reign throughout all of God's heavenly realm for eternity.

A state of existence Lucifer could never have reached even if he had never rebelled. A state of perfected glorious existence he has no doubt coveted since the very foundation of God's creation. He not only coveted the state to which we will ascend, but he desired an even higher state. He coveted a state of perfection even higher than Almighty God.

Satan is jealous of you and me and will do anything and everything within his power to steal Man's rightful inheritance. He especially wants to steal the Godly inheritance of the righteous saints who will, for all eternity, be a magnificent reflection of God's Triune Glory throughout all of God's Holy Realm. He does not want us Transcending to the height and breadth of heavenly life available now only to God the Father, Son, and Holy Spirit.

It can't and won't ever get any better than this! This is the absolute ultimate—the Highest Honor God will ever bestow upon any of His creatures. This honor is reserved just for the saints and has been since the very foundation of the world. It is an honor bestowed only upon the "sons of God," God's children, the saints, His heirs, and the joint heirs with Jesus Christ, you and me!

All of this is yours, all of this is for anyone, anyone at all who will just do one thing, one little thing—freely accept the gift God has provided to the world. Accept Jesus as Lord! If you haven't yet accepted, please turn back to the beginning pages of this chapter and pray the prayer of salvation from your heart.

Accept God's gift and prepare to receive all that God has stored up just for you. No matter who you think you are, where you've been, whatever you might have done, or even if you have been deceived into believing you are unworthy, whether you're 8 or 108, God's free gift is yours if you'll just reach out and accept Jesus Christ as your Lord and Savior.

One thing to always remember is that God, at the very moment He breathed life into you at conception, placed a very special gift, a special ability, a special talent within you that only you will be able to fulfill in God's Kingdom.

You may not yet know what that gift is, or perhaps your life has been such a disaster (or you think it has) you have nothing left to believe in. Perhaps you're one of those caught in 'Generation X or Y and can't relate to Gen 'Z' thinking.' The Christian Gen-Z millennials have confirmed on a recent Barna release (mentioned earlier) that (96%) of these said witnessing for Jesus is part of being a Christian. Additionally, Christian millennials are identified as having the strongest beliefs in the Bible and *read it more* than any other previous generation: 87 percent say they do so multiple times a week. If this is, you please *"Catch the Vision,"* pass it on!

Well, I've got news for you! God has strategically placed within your spirit a gift (a special seed) that will bring a harvest that only you can make happen, only you can fulfill, and if you don't make it happen, it won't be fulfilled. To make it happen, you must accept Jesus as Lord and let Him be the center of life in your heart. You may, during your natural mortal life, never see the fulfillment of that special gift placed in you by God.

However, the full manifestation of its growth and harvest will be gloriously fulfilled through you as a child of God during Christ's Millennial Reign. It will even continue into the future age of ages as you fulfill your very special position in God's elite family. A position so special that only you can fill it, and if for some reason you decline God's offer, then the position will just not be filled.

This reminds me of that old movie classic 'It's a Wonderful Life' with Jimmy Stewart. His life was such a wonderful blessing to so many, but he never realized it until he saw himself from the outside looking in. You may be in that same frame of mind right now and can't see your own value or the effect your life has on others.

Go on, go outside and look in, look at the good affects and the bad. You'll see the good outweighs the bad. Besides, all the bad has already been forgiven and forgotten! It truly is 'A Wonderful Life.'

It's been all uphill until now, but you've just reached the top, the place where Jesus has been waiting just for you. You've just touched the "Capstone," and from Him, it's all downhill from now on, and from here, it really gets better. Jesus Christ lived a perfect human life in order to be the perfect sacrifice for you and for me. *Hebrews 1:3 NIV* and *Hebrews 2:14 NIV* reinforce Jesus' identity:

> *The Son is the radiance of God's glory and the exact representation of His being, sustaining all things by His powerful word. After He had provided purifi-*

> *cation for sins, He sat down at the right hand of the Majesty in heaven.*
>
> *Since the children have flesh and blood, He too shared in their humanity so that by His death He might break the power of him who holds the power of death—that is, the devil.*

The most wonderful life we will receive from God will occur after the 1,000-year Millennial reign of Christ, which will last throughout all the Age of Ages for an Eternity. When God spoke to Abraham and told him he would be the 'father of many' and then compared the stars, sand of the sea, and even the dust of the earth to confirm what He promised to Abraham, Isaac, and Jacob.

The Milky Way and Andromeda Galaxy

The Andromeda Galaxy is the closest spiral galaxy to the Milky Way. It's the most distant object you can easily see with the naked eye (under good observing conditions). Andromeda is 220,000 light-years in diameter and is one of the 35 objects that make up what is called the Local Group. Andromeda lies, of course, within this constellation.

The Andromeda galaxy could be considered the big brother of the Milky Way, as it contains over a trillion stars compared to our 200-400 billion and is approximately 220,000 light-years across to our 100,000. Our galaxy is thought to look much like Andromeda.

Both Andromeda and the Milky Way got to their current size by eating up other galaxies within which they collided. Expansion of the Universe causes most galaxies to move away from us, but Andromeda and the Milky Way are actually headed towards each other. Is this a hint of what this collision might mean?)

Andromeda and the Milky Way are good neighbors, but eventually, our neighbor is going to move in with us—the Milky Way and Andromeda are approaching each other at 320 miles per second, and they will eventually collide. There's no need to panic, though, as Andromeda is over 2 million light-years away, and the collision won't happen for another 2 or 3 billion years, unless God has planned a sooner merger. Astronomer John Dubinski of the University of Toronto has an excellent animated simulation from multiple perspectives of what this galactic dance could look like. See 2 Peter 3:8 (any version).

The importance of understanding the magnificence of the continuing expansion of the "Universe of Universes" is to have the faith, knowledge, and wisdom to understand God's plan. We should thoroughly seek the path God has intended us to follow under the guidance of His Holy Spirit. We serve an incredibly "Great and Powerful" Father God, who created all that there is and all that there ever will be for Eternity. He says what He means and means what He says.

We will not know everything that God has planned for His children until we see Him, as He is, and we become transformed into and become the full manifestation…

Of His Glory!

Note:

If you desire more information regarding God's expanding Universe, please copy the following links to your browser or click on the link if you are reading an e-Book and see God's creation as we know it today. You may be totally astonished by your future!

https://www.youtube.com/watch?v=DKPRDCAOnXM

https://www.youtube.com/watch?v=HWxBTHVhc3I

https://www.youtube.com/watch?v=pM-aRrlCjGs

ANDROMEDA GALAXY

The Immense Andromeda galaxy, also known as Messier 31 (M31), is captured in this new image from NASA's Wide-field Infrared Survey Explorer (WISE). Blue highlights mature stars, while yellow and red show dust heated by massive newborn stars. Also seen in the photo are two satellite galaxies: M32, located just a bit above Andromeda to the left of the center, and the fuzzy blue M110, located below the center of the great spiral arms. (See illustration credits)

CHAPTER 16

Our share of Christ's Glory

This life is but a foretaste of the life to come, a mere shadow of the life to be lived in the very presence of God, and in the coming 1,000-year millennial reign of Christ that is the final chapter of mortal life as we know.

At the conclusion of Christ's reign, the sinful nature that Man has struggled with for seven thousand years will, at last, be forever overcome by the righteousness of Christ. Then, perfected righteous mankind will be promoted by God to the eternal position of sinless human-beings just as He has planned from the very foundation of the earth.

This sinless, holy race of people who have spiritually partaken of the tree of life through Christ will receive eternal life and the very nature of Christ. Then, once the new heavens and new earth are re-made, God will then cause His people to be brought into the land.

It is at this new beginning when God's 'elect,' sinless Holy race of people fulfill God's will as they continue to populate the New Creation of the habitable universe for all of eternity. Moreover, in addition to the complete fulfillment of His purpose, all that they accomplish brings great glory to our God.

Prior to the commencement of this "Perfect Age," the renewed New Heaven and New Earth that is prepared exclusively for mankind will be purged of all evidence of the previous Creation. Everything that was tainted by Satan and his evil influence, including all records of previous human life, will be burned up. God tells us that even our memory of this past life will be forgotten.

Nothing of the old creation that would point to human life in antiquity will remain, for it will all be burned up and vaporized out of existence. Even as glorious and magnificent as the Millennial Kingdom of Christ will be, it too will all be burned up and not remembered.

> *But the day of the Lord (God) will come as a thief in the night, in which the heavens will pass away with a great noise, and the elements will melt with fervent heat; both the earth and the works that are in it will be burned up."*
>
> *"Looking for and hastening the coming of the day of God, because of which the heavens will be dissolved, being on fire, and the elements will melt with fervent heat.*
>
> *2 Peter 3:10, 12 (NKJV)*

Besides, the New Creation of God's Perfect Age will be so incredibly wonderful that the old will simply be forgotten. Compared to humankinds ties to a new eternal life, nothing in this present life, or the world, will even be worth remembering!

The actual one-thousand-year reign of Christ that precedes the 'Perfect Age' will be much like a dress rehearsal compared to the actual Eternal performance that mankind will live out as God's natural immortal, holy people. It is His plan and purpose that this Holy race of people populates the New Creation to bring glory to God throughout all the ages to come.

Even the stage and all the scenery will be freshly made for this Heavenly event. In addition, all the sinful desires in Man's heart that developed during the seven thousand years will, at the end of this millennial period, be cast into the Lake of Fire with Satan forever.

What this one-thousand-year reign of Christ will bring into realized physical fruition can only be imagined by inference, but from history, we see the greatest examples of physical accomplishment in those cultures that are developed spiritually.

Thus, as mankind matures spiritually under the reign of Jesus Christ Himself, without the negative influences of Satan to hinder the growth and development of mankind's spirit, the whole earth will experience its greatest increase since time began.

Mankind under the reign of Jesus, guided by the 'saints' of God and led by God's 'elect,' the revived Hebrew nation will develop into the most awesome physical and spiritual world conceivable. It will be so majestic that even the most creative movie studio in Hollywood couldn't begin to depict its glorious incredible magnificence.

As an architect ordained of God at the age of nine to enter this profession, I am eagerly awaiting this age of unparalleled splendor as a saint of God. I know that when I see Him, I will not only become glorified like my Lord and Savior Jesus, but God has also promised me and you as joint heir's with Jesus that we will rule and reign with Him over the peopled habitations (earths), beginning with the millennial earth, and on throughout God's eternal creation.

During Christ's millennial reign, I can't imagine anything to be more gratifying than mentoring natural mortal mankind in their unparalleled development and dominion over the whole earth. Nothing could be more rewarding than to serve in the literal presence of Jesus as mankind rightly subdues the earth and brings it into its golden age of unparalleled splendor.

God has placed certain special abilities within each of our spirits at conception that will only become fully enhanced and realized during our glorified eternal lives. Therefore, all that we become in this life and the next will bring great glory to our God.

We are truly blessed as God's children, and as each of our special abilities come into fruition, they become the means through which we will experience a significant part of our purposeful activity during the millennial reign of Christ and even into the ages beyond.

What special abilities has the Lord ordained in your life? Perhaps you don't even realize that you possess a special calling, or maybe you haven't yet experienced the revelation knowledge regarding your own special area of ordination. If you haven't, please don't be overly concerned because God has already placed that very special ability within your spirit. And it will become wonderfully manifested in your life, in God's due time and season.

Your own special calling could quite possibly be related to a very special assignment in Christ's new Kingdom and one that only you can fulfill. You must understand that in His government, there are many key appointments and positions, a good many of which have no comparable likeness on the present earth. Sounds intriguing, don't you think?

Follow in Father Abraham's footsteps, go where God is directing you even if you don't know where he is leading you. You are blessed! Believe!

There will be a multitude of positions, professions, vocations, etc., that do not even exist today, and there are many that exist today that will significantly change or perhaps even disappear from society. Since there are many activities in society today that exist solely because of Satan's evil influences over mankind and the environment, they will either be eliminated or modified to serve the Kingdom's new society in a totally different way.

Can you think of some that might become of less importance or possibly just vanish during the millennial reign of Christ? Well, certainly anyone connected with the vast complexity of the world's war machine will be out of a job! What about lawyers, judges, and the law enforcement professions? Jesus will rule with a "Rod of Iron," and His actions will be swift! He doesn't need a court to prove anyone's innocence or guilt. He knows because He is God!

Mankind will most certainly have some basis of enforcement due to being under Christ's rule, but the nature of the professions in this area will very definitely be different than today. What change would you anticipate in the health care professions and its vast array of related support services? With Satan's influence over sickness and death being totally eradicated from the earth, wouldn't you expect big changes in this area?

The world societies as we know them today will almost totally disappear as the new world government, Christ's government, expands and grows totally fulfilling all the requirements for an almost ideal utopian order within the changing world society.

However, as the scriptures have advised, Christ will rule during His Millennial age with a rod of iron, and all transgression will be dealt with swiftly and surely. Unfortunately, death will still exist, and any grievous sin or rebellion against Christ and His government will be quickly and very sternly dealt with in a most decisive manner.

Just as in the example of "Ananias and Sapphira" (Acts 5:5), certain types of transgressions will most assuredly bring almost immediate death to the transgressor. The scriptures also very clearly tell us that the good don't die young during the millennium, but surely the sinner will die before he has fulfilled his days.

> *No more shall an infant from there live but a few days, nor an old man who has not fulfilled his days; for the child shall die one hundred years old, but the sinner being one hundred years old shall be accursed.*
>
> *Isaiah 65:20 (NKJV)*

The societal culture of mankind doesn't cease during Christ's reign. It blossoms like a beautiful flower bringing all manner of glory to God. It will be awesome compared to human society today that is likened to a seedling struggling to stand upright amid all the tangled and choking weeds.

However, the societal culture that will crawl out of the ashes and rubble of the great tribulation will have been all but obliterated from existence by the time Christ returns (the second coming of Christ), and He begins to set up His millennial Kingdom.

Upon the commencement of Christ's millennial Kingdom, the societal culture of remaining mankind that enters the Kingdom could be likened to a bud having just formed on a twig. Then, throughout Christ's reign of a thousand years, as this bud continues to grow, it will completely blossom into a fully mature, majestic tree with a multitude of beautiful flowers, unlike any the world has ever seen.

Stop and imagine just for a moment; If it was possible to transport the following people from their own time and place into today's world with all our technological advancements, what would be their reaction? Would they have been able in their own time and place to even begin to imagine in their wildest dreams and ever been able to describe what they had seen that we take for granted today in our societal culture?

Looking back about a thousand years, what do you suppose would be the reaction of Macbeth (1040—1057); Thomas Becket (1118—1170); Omar Khayyam (+/-1123); or what about Marco Polo (1254—1324) sitting in a Stealth bomber traveling from continent to continent; or Kublai Khan (1216-1294) watching China's armed forces on parade; or even better yet, imagine just 529 years ago transporting Christopher Columbus (1492) in a manned space shuttle, landing him on the moon and then returning him to New York City for a ticker-tape parade.

Just what do you think these renowned men of the earth would think? What would be their reaction to this experience? Would they even be able to explain what they saw upon returning to their own time? Imagine Columbus describing the earth and its many continents to the Queen. Remember, the earth is flat according to the greatest minds of the age. Flat indeed!

Would any of these men of renown still be conscious after an experience of this magnitude? I think not! They would very likely have the mother of all culture shocks, and as some might say, "it would blow their minds!"

Well, dear saint, what would you think if you could see all the future advancements that will become a reality in Christ's kingdom? If today, you were to witness the advancements made by the new society in which we and natural Man will all be participants, with Jesus as the Lord of lords and King of kings, I would venture to say, "it would blow your mind!"

Just think, as a joint heir with Jesus, you will not only have a very special place in His Kingdom but an even more special assignment. Your assignment will be to help natural mankind achieve their very best, to be all they can be, in the Kingdom. As Christ's ambassador, you will either directly or indirectly affect their lives and help them attain the absolute highest order of mortal human excellence and spiritual perfection available in His Kingdom.

I, for one, now know that I have been ordained by God as an architect for a very special purpose. Throughout my life and career, I have been developing certain creative abilities that might become heavenly enhanced and used by God to bless natural Man during the rebuilding and continual advancement of Man's built environment. The millennial age will be the greatest, most glorious, and magnificent worldwide renaissance of humankind's culture of all time, the vast splendor and opulence of which I can't even begin to imagine.

But I do know that it shall, in all its splendor, bring unparalleled glory to our Father.

The absolute majesty of His Kingdom will be an ever-present sign of His glory to all of mankind, and it will likewise be an awesome example of the abundant love He has always had for His people.

One of the most glorious projects to ever be accomplished on the face of this earth will be the development of Christ's seat of government at Jerusalem and the new city that will be built over the site of the existing city. The prophet Ezekiel not only gives us a very detailed description of the new city, but he likewise describes the vast land area designated for the twelve restored Tribes that surround the "Princes (Jesus) Portion," in which the "Holy Oblation" (Holy Place) is situated.

This Area called the "Holy Oblation" is a fifty-mile square area (50mi. x 50mi.) the north and south boundaries of which align with the same boundaries of the Prince's Portion and similarly, extend from the southern boundary of the existing city of Jerusalem to the town of Yamun Jordan. (About 15 miles south of Nazareth)

This fifty-mile square area (2500 sq. miles) is further divided into an area on the north, twenty miles (N-S) by fifty miles (E-W) designated as the "Levites Portion," and immediately below it another area of the same dimensions designated as the "Priest's Portion." The last section is specifically designated as the area for the new city of Jerusalem and is ten miles (N-S) by fifty miles (E-W), with the additional twenty miles of land on the east and west sides of the city for food.

The new city of Jerusalem is ten miles square, including a 1/2-mile-wide strip on each side designated as the suburbs. The city is further described as having a wall around its perimeter, with each side having three gates, each of which are named after the Tribes of Israel, giving us a picture of the future *"New Jerusalem."*

Ezekiel 48 very aptly defines this division of the land and its extension from the Mediterranean Sea to the Euphrates river on the east. It encompasses an area that is today a desolate, barren desert land that the scriptures tell us will blossom as a rose and become a land of great fertility. It is very probably the land that we, the saints, the joint heirs with Christ, will have as our earthly abode along with Jesus. (The "camp of the saints," mentioned at the end of the Millennium in Revelation 20:9). [See illustrations on pages 118, 119, 120, and 121].

Just imagine the glorious splendor of God's own sub-division filled with this elite group of saints promoted to rule and reign with Christ over the earth. The whole area will be filled with the awesome reflection of His glory, as the radiance of our Lord's glorious presence is seen in addition to our own glorious reflection of His glory because we have seen Him as He is.

In addition to the new city, Ezekiel describes the new Temple or Sanctuary that will be built, not in the city, but in the middle of the Holy Oblation located near or at the ancient location of Shiloh, where the Tabernacle was kept from the time the children of Israel seized the promised land, up until it was moved into Solomon's Temple. (This location is close to the present town of Qabalan Jordan).

> *A highway shall be there, and a road, and it shall be called the Highway of Holiness. The unclean shall not pass over it, but it shall be for others. Whoever walks the road, although a fool, shall not go astray.*
>
> *Isaiah 35:8 (NKJV)*

This highway leading from the northern boundary of the New City to the Sanctuary in the center of the Holy Oblation is about twelve to fifteen miles long and no doubt will be the most beautiful parkway—boulevard in all the whole world. The Sanctuary itself is to be located within what will become the most gloriously beautiful area in all of God's earthly creation.

We are also told that living waters from a life-giving spring will be located under the sanctuary that will flow to the city of Jerusalem. One-half of the waters will then each go out from the city to the Dead Sea to heal its waters and to the Great Sea (Mediterranean), producing an exceeding abundance of many fish.

> *And in that day, it shall be that living waters shall flow from Jerusalem, half of them toward the eastern sea and half of them toward the western sea; in both summer and winter it shall occur.*
>
> *Zechariah 14:8 (NKJV)*

> *And it shall be that every living thing that moves, wherever the rivers go, will live. There will be a very great multitude of fish, because these waters go there; for they will be healed, and everything will live wherever the river goes.*
>
> *Ezekiel 47:9 (NKJV)*

> *Along the bank of the river, on this side and that, will grow all kinds of trees used for food; their leaves will not wither, and their fruit will not fail. They will bear fruit every month, because their water flows from the sanctuary. Their fruit will be for food, and their leaves for medicine.*
>
> *Ezekiel 47:12 (NKJV)*

Great physical changes will have taken place throughout all the areas prior to the beginning of the Millennial Reign of Christ due to the great earthquakes and volcanic eruptions.

These changes will level the land surface of Palestine and raise the Dead Sea, so its waters can flow both into the Mediterranean and the Red Sea.

> *And the LORD shall be King over all the earth. In that day it shall be—"The LORD is one," and His name one. All the land shall be turned into a plain from Geba to Rimmon south of Jerusalem.*
>
> *Jerusalem shall be raised up and inhabited in her place from Benjamin's Gate to the place of the First Gate and the Corner Gate, and from the Tower of Hananeel to the king's winepresses. The people shall dwell in it; and no longer shall there be utter destruction, but Jerusalem shall be safely inhabited.*
>
> *Zechariah 14:9-11 (NKJV)*

> *And it shall come to pass that everyone who is left of all the nations which came against Jerusalem shall go up from year to year to worship the King, the LORD of hosts, and to keep the Feast of Tabernacles.*
>
> *And it shall be that whichever of the families of the earth do not come up to Jerusalem to worship the King, the LORD of hosts, on them there will be no rain.*
>
> *Zechariah 14:16-17 (NKJV)*

> *The mountains will melt under him, and the valleys will split like wax before the fire, like waters poured down a steep place.*
>
> *Micah 1:4 (NKJV)*

Within this beautiful land, and even throughout the whole earth, the entire animal kingdom will be as it was in the original garden of Eden. No animal will harm mankind nor will any animal harm other animals, but they will all be like domesticated pets.

The whole earth will become a remarkable place without Satan's influence and his many malignant activities that have for 6,000 years twisted and deceived mankind. No longer will he control and dominate the earth's climatic environment producing all the adverse weather conditions that have always caused widespread problems for mankind.

> *The wolf also shall dwell with the lamb, the leopard shall lie down with the young goat, the calf and the young lion and the fatling together; and a little child shall lead them.*
>
> *The cow and the bear shall graze; their young ones shall lie down together; and the lion shall eat straw like the ox. The nursing child shall play by the cobra's hole, and the weaned child shall put his hand in the viper's den.*
>
> *They shall not hurt nor destroy in all My holy mountain, for the earth shall be full of the knowledge of the LORD as the waters cover the sea.*
>
> *Isaiah 11:6-9 (NKJV)*

The earth won't be restored to complete Edenic conditions as it will be in the New Creation that God has promised after the conclusion of the Millennium, but it will be much closer to these conditions than mankind (since Adam) has ever known or even conceived. It will be a far more marvelously ordered and productive earth than even the imagination could conceive. The sum total of all advancements that will be forthcoming due to Man's increased brainpower, knowledge, wisdom, and the influence of the Holy Spirit, along with the very presence of Christ Himself, will be so far advanced it will be incomparable to Man's present level of accomplishment.

In addition, mankind will have the benefit of being wonderfully blessed by the mentoring saints that will be ruling and reigning with Christ. All the satanic influences that mankind has had to contend with throughout history will be eliminated, and in its place, mankind will have the loving influences of the glorified, righteous saints.

This 'elite' group of God's heirs and joint heirs with Christ we have been discussing throughout the last fifteen chapters includes you and me, dear saint. We are to become a blessing to all of mankind as we serve with Jesus imparting God's blessings upon His Elect, the physical and spiritual nations of Israel.

Just as it was before the flood, mankind's patriarchal years will be restored, and God's people will live long, productive lives. No longer will the earth endure any of the debilitating effects of disease or the many maladies of old age the people of earth have been plagued with since Adam.

This is probably due in part to the atmospheric and climatic changes that will occur during the millennium and the worldwide effect of the life-giving and healing waters of the "New River" that flows out from beneath the "New Sanctuary." In addition, the scriptures tell us the leaves of the trees that grow along the riverbank are for "medicine," so even if one should happen to get sick, the leaves that grow from the life-giving waters will provide healing.

> *They shall not build, and another inhabit; they shall not plant, and another eat; for as the days of a*

tree, so shall be the days of My people, and My elect shall long enjoy the work of their hands.

Isaiah 65:22 (NKJV)

Thus, says the LORD of hosts: 'Old men and old women shall again sit in the streets of Jerusalem, each one with his staff in his hand because of great age.

Zechariah 8:4 (NKJV)

Along the bank of the river, on this side and that, will grow all kinds of trees used for food; their leaves will not wither, and their fruit will not fail. They will bear fruit every month, because their water flows from the sanctuary. Their fruit will be for food, and their leaves for medicine.

Ezekiel 47:12 (NKJV)

The atmosphere and climate of the whole earth will be dramatically changed from what we now experience and in which mankind has lived since the flood, but still quite different than man even experienced before the flood. The atmosphere of the Millennial earth will be as beautiful and healthful as the earth itself. The moon will shine to make the most spectacular moonlit nights ever experienced by man, being like the light of day provided by the sun, but a very pleasant brightly glowing reflected light, not the harsh, direct light of the sun.

And the sun will shine seven-fold, bringing its light to the earth seven times more productive than the present sun. This sunshine will be brighter but not as destructive as the ultra-violet rays of our present sunshine that has been the cause of so much pain and suffering, bringing intense heat to portions of the earth, as well as skin cancer to mankind.

This light of the sun is filtered no doubt by the earth's new atmosphere, and only the productive rays that help make the earth a fertile garden penetrates its protection. This life-giving light will flood the earth with its seven-fold abundance, and its fruitful warmth will blanket the cold climatic areas most people would consider being uninhabitable on today's earth.

> *Moreover the light of the moon will be as the light of the sun, and the light of the sun will be seven-fold, as the light of seven days, in the day that the LORD binds up the bruise of His people and heals the stroke of their wound.*
>
> *Isaiah 30:26 (NKJV)*

> *The sun shall no longer be your light by day, nor for brightness shall the moon give light to you; but the LORD will be to you an everlasting light, and your God your glory.*
>
> *Your sun shall no longer go down, nor shall your moon withdraw itself; for the LORD will be your everlasting light, and the days of your mourning shall be ended.*
>
> *Isaiah 60:19-20 (NKJV)*

The "Shekinah Glory" that departed from the Temple during the Babylonian era will again manifest its Holy presence in the New Temple and will illuminate the land around the Temple. It is also highly probable that the whole area of the Holy Oblation will become radiant with the brightness of His glory, providing an everlasting light upon the revived nation of Israel and as a sign of His glory to all the nations of the earth.

This is again a representative picture of the future perfect age to come when the brightness of His glory is manifested in the magnificent *New Jerusalem* when the nations of the earth will walk in its light. When we read the scriptures and see the various examples and occasions when God's Glory is shone as a light to mankind (other than the figurative examples), it soon becomes obvious that there is an aura of brightness associated with God's presence.

There is not only an inherent quality of heavenly light manifested from the very presence of God, but this same heavenly light emanates from the very presence of all of God's Holy Angels, His Glorified Holy saints, His Holy Spirit, and of course His Only Begotten Son Jesus, the Christ.

Knowing this, it stands to reason that the radiance of His glory will shine forth from the new Temple, the abode of the Prince (Christ), and from the abode of the saints who together reside in the area called the "Princes Portion." The radiance of the entire area would be as a picture of the future New Jerusalem that will magnificently shine with an unparalleled brilliance of His glory.

In addition to the awesome physical and spiritual development of the new city of Jerusalem, the new Temple, and all the areas within the Prince's Portion, there are other noteworthy examples. There will also be additional physical and spiritual developments throughout all the lands of the revived twelve tribes of Israel, and of course, a great renaissance of revival both physical and spiritual throughout the whole earth that will be unparalleled in human history.

The new and the re-built cities, along with the development and improvement of all the infrastructure of the world's various systems of transportation, communication, information, and the very fabric of societal culture under the leadership of Christ's government, will be astonishing.

However, even with the most perfect conditions and the perfect King, many people and nations will only remain in submission to Christ's Reign by His Rule with the rod of iron. Thus, the obedience God receives from many of these people will not be given out of love but out of fear.

> *The glory of Lebanon shall come to you, the cypress, the pine, and the box tree together, to beautify the place of My sanctuary; and I will make the place of My feet glorious.*
>
> *Isaiah 60:13 (NKJV)*

> *"For the nation and kingdom which will not serve you shall perish, and those nations shall be utterly ruined"*
>
> *(Isaiah 60:12, NKJV).*

> *"You shall break them with a rod of iron; you shall dash them to pieces like a potter's vessel" (Psalms 2:9, NKJV).*

Throughout the whole earth, the Glory of God will be seen and witnessed firsthand as the ruins of the previous societies that have experienced widespread destruction and terror are removed, and glorious new cities and towns are built to replace them.

As mankind begins the struggle of re-building, they soon discover that the new world government and the Head of the government, Jesus, is very personally involved with the welfare of all the people of the earth. They will know that He is genuinely concerned with the simple basics of their food and shelter, as well as their physical and spiritual well-being.

The teams that will be sent out into the world to help the nations begin the enormous task of clean-up and re-building will include a great number of the saints. These saints, the "sons of God," will carry the message of Christ's Reign throughout the whole earth and proclaim the sovereign power and glory of His government of righteousness.

These same saints who returned with Jesus in Glory at the second coming and witnessed the final defeat of the armies who came up against Jerusalem will minister to the needs of the people with great compassion and Christ's righteous love.

Considering the dreadful consequences from the worldwide devastation, it is very probable that mighty miracles will be performed throughout the world in Jesus' name, and being witnessed by all the nations of the earth will bring unprecedented homage to the King of kings.

The saints will be accepted and welcomed as the Holy ambassadors of Jesus and His righteous government. Besides, with their supernatural, spiritual, and physical guidance, they will lead and mentor the people (nations) across the earth into Christ's kingdom and usher in His new world order.

The scriptures tell us that Israel is to become the "Chief Nation" of all the nations of the world. In addition, it states that mankind will revere God's 'elect' nation as the leader throughout the "Millennial Age," and Israel will be a major blessing to all the Gentile nations.

> *But you shall be named the priests of the LORD,*
> *they shall call you the servants of our God. You shall*

eat the riches of the Gentiles, and in their glory you shall boast.

Instead of your shame you shall have double honor, and instead of confusion they shall rejoice in their portion. Therefore, in their land they shall possess double; everlasting joy shall be theirs.

Isaiah 61:6-7 (NKJV)

Their descendants shall be known among the Gentiles, and their offspring among the people. All who see them shall acknowledge them, that they are the posterity whom the LORD has blessed.

Isaiah 61:9 (NKJV)

For as the earth brings forth its bud, as the garden causes the things that are sown in it to spring forth, so the Lord GOD will cause righteousness and praise to spring forth before all the nations.

Isaiah 61:11 (NKJV)

As the nation's continuing to become self-sufficient and blessed with abundance, some of the people continue with an outward appearance of serving God and honoring Christ. However, we know from scripture that they are 'fakes,' and at the end of the thousand years, many of those who are still alive will allow themselves to be deceived by Satan after he is released from prison, and they all end up in the lake of fire.

Those people who reject the righteousness of Christ during the Millennium, whether or not they fake their relationship and die without accepting Him or remain alive to the very end, all have their names blotted out of the book of life and are cast into the lake of fire with all the other unrighteous throughout history. The only explanation as to why anyone would be so stupid has to be what I call the 'deception of things.'

I have surmised from my own experience that mankind can get so caught up in personal material possessions and worldly accomplishments that his prideful use and selfish pleasure of those things can eventually overshadow and take the place of the spiritual things of God.

Man can thereby unwittingly deceive himself, even without any influence from Satan. If mankind would just recognize the scriptural fact that it is God alone who owns all things, then they would see that we just receive the use of these things from God as a blessing, not for possessing.

When all the basic worldwide systems are again functioning and producing, mankind will begin to experience the glorious blessings of God through the one-world government of "Christ's Kingdom." Then the obedient nations of the earth will begin to experience a wonderful progression of advancements and an overabundance of blessing, upon blessing, upon blessing.

As mankind continues to honor God, His King, and the Kingdom, Man's knowledge, wisdom, and capabilities for achieving new heights and dimensions of creativity to glorify God become enhanced exponentially. Every person on the earth will have purposeful activities and responsibilities. There will be no poverty, no hunger, no lack, for those nations (people) that obey and honor the Lord. But the Scriptures do point out that if the nations don't worship the LORD, they will receive punishment, and God's abundant blessings will not be showered upon them, nor their endeavors.

> *And it shall be that whichever of the families of the earth do not come up to Jerusalem to worship the*

> *King, the LORD of hosts, on them there will be no rain.*
>
> *Zechariah 14:17 (NKJV)*

One of the most blessed events that will take place at the commencement of Christ's Kingdom is the 'blessing of children' given to the newly revived nation of Israel upon their entrance into the Millennial Kingdom of Christ. Of all the nations of the earth, the Jews have always been the ones who most revered children and considered them a wonderful blessing from God.

We previously discussed how the pagan religions despised children and considered them a curse, so much so that they would throw a perfectly healthy infant on the garbage heap to rid themselves of the unwanted little curse. Well, the Jews were just the opposite, for all children were greatly loved and welcomed into their lives.

Children without parents were brought into the Jewish home and raised by a mother and father just the same as their own natural children. Both parents took on the responsibility for raising the children, and both natural children and adopted children were nurtured and raised to Glorify God and serve Him with all their heart and soul. Jesus Himself loved and welcomed little children with open arms. He many times confirmed His feelings to the disciples and all that were around Him, and with word and deed showed them the value and significance He placed on children.

> *"Let the little children come to me, and do not forbid them; for of such is the Kingdom of Heaven"*
>
> *Matthew 19:14, (NKJV)*

He also showed great compassion to the families of children, as well as the little children themselves who prematurely died before they had an opportunity to fulfill their appointed days. We see from scripture many examples of Christ raising people back to life, especially little children, giving them another opportunity to fulfill the days God has given them. (Matthew 9:18, 24-26; Mark 5:35-42; Luke 7:13-15; Luke 8:49).

These examples also provide us a picture of the future time when Christ presents all those unrighteous children, who have prematurely died before their time, to God's 'elect,' the revived Jewish Nation.

These are the ones we previously described that include all the countless millions of abortion babies, still-born babies, and all those millions and millions of children who died before the age of accountability who were not counted as sanctified by a saved parent.

This count includes all the unsaved children from the descendants of Adam to the beginning of the Millennial Kingdom, from their conception to the age of accountability. Any child who never reached an age of accountability due to some abnormality but may have lived way beyond the norm for the age of accountability is included in this group. And just as all the others, they are brought back to life in a natural, perfectly formed, and perfectly functioning body to live out their days as God has ordained.

> *Before she was in labor, she gave birth; before her pain came, she delivered a male child. Who has heard such a thing?*
>
> *Who has seen such things? Shall the earth be made to give birth in one day? Or shall a nation be born at once? For as soon as Zion was in labor, she gave birth to her children.*
>
> *Isaiah 66:7-8 (NKJV)*
>
> *Lift up your eyes and look around; all your sons gather and come to you. As surely as I live, "declares*

the LORD, "you will wear them all as ornaments; you will put them on like a bride.

Though you were ruined and made desolate and your land laid waste, now you will be too small for your people, and those who devoured you will be far away.

The children born during your bereavement will yet say in your hearing, 'This place is too small for us; give us more space to live in.' Then you will say in your heart, 'Who bore me these I was bereaved and barren; I was exiled and rejected.

Who brought these up? I was left all alone, but these—where have they come from?'

Isaiah 49:18-21 (NIV)

You are to distribute this land among yourselves according to the tribes of Israel. You are to allot it as an inheritance for yourselves and for the aliens who have settled among you and who have children. You are to consider them as native-born Israelites, along with you they are to be allotted an inheritance among the tribes of Israel. In whatever tribe the alien settles, there you are to give him his inheritance, declares the Sovereign LORD.

Ezekiel 47:21-23 (NIV)

'This is what the Sovereign LORD says: On the day I cleanse you from all your sins, I will resettle your towns, and the ruins will be rebuilt. The desolate

land will be cultivated instead of lying desolate in the sight of all who pass through it.

They will say, 'This land that was laid waste has become like the garden of Eden; the cities that were lying in ruins, desolate and destroyed, are now fortified and inhabited.'

Then the nations around you that remain will know that I the LORD have rebuilt what was destroyed and have replanted what was desolate. I the LORD have spoken, and I will do it.

Ezekiel 36:33-36 (NIV)

Sing, O barren woman, you who never bore a child; burst into song, shout for joy, you who were never in labor; because more are the children of the desolate woman than of her who has a husband, 'says the LORD.'

Enlarge the place of your tent, stretch your tent curtains wide, do not hold back, lengthen your cords, strengthen your stakes.

Isaiah 54: 1-2 (NIV)

The streets of the city shall be full of boys and girls playing in its streets. Thus, says the LORD of hosts: 'If it is marvelous in the eyes of the remnant of this people in these days, will it also be marvelous in My eyes?' Says the LORD of hosts.

Zechariah 8: 5-6 (NKJV)

There will no doubt be a tremendous resurgence of children, and a tremendous vitality instantly brought back into the revived Nation of Israel. As God's 'elect' undertake the rebuilding of the Jewish Nation for their natural and adopted heirs, they bring unprecedented blessings upon themselves. Furthermore, as they bless God for their Messiah and Redeemer, Jesus Christ, their spirits rejoice with worshipful praise of their Almighty Father God.

There will be literally millions and millions of children assigned to all the families of the twelve tribes throughout all the portions of land given to the revived Tribes of Israel. The land as described in Ezekiel 36:33-36 quoted above has become like the garden of Eden, and mankind now begins to enjoy the glorious Joy of the Lord as He has never, ever enjoyed since Adam and Eve were present in the Garden.

For all those saints who return with the Lord to rule and reign over the Millennial Kingdom with Jesus, and who have a special Ordained calling on their lives to minister to children, there will be no assignment on the earth more fulfilling and blessed than mentoring the families given the responsibility for raising and nurturing *all* of these wonderfully blessed children of the revived nation of Israel.

The whole world will likewise experience a tremendous resurgence of children, and a new youthful vitality will bless all the nations. Again, all those saints with that special gift for loving children, as Jesus Himself loves, will have a wonderfully blessed mentoring-ministry of working with the children and parents throughout the nations of the world.

The impact that all this will have on the people of the earth will be of major significance. Just as the extraordinary miracles Jesus performed during His ministry had a great impact on the lives of the people who witnessed them, causing many to believe in Him, this too will provide mankind undeniable proof that Jesus Christ is who

He says He is—the "Son of God!" "The King of kings and Lord of lords!"

You, dear saints, are the "children (sons) of God," the "heirs and joint-heirs" with Christ. If you haven't yet fully grasped the reality of this concept, it is absolutely the most Glorious of all rewards. There is absolutely nothing that will ever exceed the joy and pleasure of fellowshipping with our Triune God in His unapproachable Light and Glory as we see Him Face to face.

> *Who alone has immortality, dwelling in unapproachable light, whom no man has seen or can see, to whom be honor and everlasting power. Amen.*
>
> *1 Timothy 6:16 (NKJV)*

The actual experience of God's Glory is something that all born-again believers, whose names are written in the Lambs Book of Life, will receive at the consummation when we see Jesus Face to face and are brought into God's Glorious presence.

> *In bringing many sons to glory, it was fitting that God, for whom and through whom everything exists should make the author of their salvation perfect through suffering. Both the one who makes men holy and those who are made holy are of the same family. So, Jesus is not ashamed to call them brothers.*
>
> *Hebrews 2:10-11 (NIV)*

> *And the God of all grace, who called you to his eternal glory in Christ, after you have suffered a little*

while, will himself restore you and make you strong, firm and steadfast.

1 Peter 5-10 (NIV)

To him who is able to keep you from falling and to present you before his glorious presence without fault and with great joy.

Jude 1:24 (NIV)

Share in Christ's Glory.

Now if we are children, then we are heirs—heirs of God and co-heirs with Christ, if indeed we share in his sufferings in order that we may also share in his glory.

I consider that our present sufferings are not worth comparing with the glory that will be revealed in us. The creation waits in eager expectation for the sons of God to be revealed. ...and be given a Crown of Glory.

Romans 8:17-19 (NIV)

"And when the Chief Shepherd appears, you will receive the crown of glory that will never fade away"

1 Peter 5:4, (NIV)

So, will it be with the resurrection of the dead. The body that is sown is perishable, it is raised imperishable; it is sown in dishonor, it is raised in glory, it is sown in weakness, it is raised in power; it is sown a natural body, it is raised a spiritual body.

1 Corinthians 15:42-43 (NIV)

Who, by the power that enables him to bring everything under his control, will transform our lowly bodies so that they will be like his glorious body.

Philippians 3:21 (NIV)

For a thousand years, the Kingdom of Christ will continue to be advanced, and mankind's whole realm of the domain will have ascended to a higher place than even he can dream. But even with all the abundance and magnificent unparalleled glory of Christ's Kingdom, Man's sinful nature will still infect countless numbers of people who become subjected to the bondage of corruption.

For the earnest expectation of the creation eagerly waits for the revealing of the sons of God. For the creation was subjected to futility, not willingly, but because of Him who subjected it in hope; because the creation itself also will be delivered from the bondage of corruption into the glorious liberty of the children of God.

Romans 8:19-21 (NKJV)

After the thousand years of Christ's reign, His Millennial Kingdom will close, and the Eternal Kingdom of Heaven will be established in the Perfect Age. Beyond the Millennium, the whole universe will be cleansed and purified by the power of God, mankind's sinful nature will be totally purged from their hearts, and Christ's righteousness will abound forevermore.

When the thousand years are over, Satan will be released from his prison and will go out to deceive the nations in the four corners of the earth—Gog and Magog—to gather them for battle.

In number they are like the sand on the seashore. They marched across the breadth of the earth and surrounded the camp of God's people, the city He loves. But fire came down from heaven and devoured them.

And the devil, who deceived them, was thrown into the lake of burning sulfur, where the beast and the false prophet had been thrown. They will be tormented day and night forever.

Revelation 20:7-10 (NIV)

Then I saw a new heaven and a new earth, for the first heaven and the first earth had passed away, and there was no longer any sea. I saw the Holy City, the new Jerusalem, coming down out of heaven from God, prepared as a bride beautifully dressed for her husband.

And I heard a loud voice from the throne saying, 'Now the dwelling of God is with men, and He will live with them. They will be His people, and God Himself will be with them and be their God.'

Revelation 21:1-3 (NIV)

Just as the past age was an orderly unfolding of creation and a revelation of the Creator, so too will the future age(s) be ushered into an all-encompassing perfect age. Not an age (Aeon) that continues as a limitless eternity, but an ever-ongoing limitless succession of ages (aeon's) that continues for an infinite duration throughout eternity forever.

Beyond the Millennium we will experience an even more glorious eternal life throughout the new Heavens and the new Earth, an age of righteousness beginning another "Aeon" of the "Aeons." This new age (Aeon) is the future Kingdom that will bring the present age to an end and usher at the beginning of the perfect age promised in the scriptures and as proclaimed by the prophets.

The center of this perfect age is the Holy City, the New Jerusalem, known as the Heavenly Jerusalem, which is the dwelling place of God among His redeemed and glorified saints forever. A place illuminated by the "Glory of God" and the reflection "Of His glory" throughout the new Heavens and new Earth manifested by the glorious countenance of all His saints.

Unfortunately, mankind today as a group is all but ignorant of the Glory that is to come because throughout this present age, Satan has deceived (and continues to deceive) millions of people. But we as Christians can (and should!) do something about his lies because we have an ongoing responsibility to proclaim the Gospel of Salvation through Christ Jesus to all the nations.

In addition, and in conjunction, with the Gospel of Salvation, we should begin once again to proclaim the 'Good News of the Kingdom' that was preached by Jesus and His disciples before the Cross, *"Repent for the Kingdom of Heaven is coming!"*

Why, you may ask? Because mankind, and especially the young people of Earth, need to catch the vision of God's plan to negate the increasing onslaught of Satan's lies and deceptions concerning the earth and mankind's future.

<u>NOTE</u>:

I believe Generation 'X, Y and Z' has an opportunity to seize the moment and become that high-performance Omega Generation that can terminate the devil's offensive attack. Definitely, a cause to live or die for! Wouldn't you agree?

CHAPTER 17

Heaven is a Kingdom!

There has been a lot of talks lately about the many groups of people, other than Christians, whose 'end of the world' doctrines are capturing the hearts and minds of alarming numbers of people, especially young people. These unsuspecting innocent (and some not so innocent) people are foolishly subscribing to, and unfortunately getting trapped by, Satan's life-threatening treacherous lies.

Satan has successfully seduced many people with his own counterfeit plan for eternal life with the clever delusion of some mystical, supernatural realm in the hereafter. He has even tricked others with the assertion that mankind will attain the ultimate perfection of a joyous and blissful natural mortal life on earth.

Many people have perhaps heard of Jesus, but they have never been able to plug into Christianity. They usually cite any number of problems, but mostly personal doctrinal disagreements or misconceptions with some man-made church doctrine.

These people have absolutely no clue as to God's real plan for mankind. Therefore, instead of searching it out for themselves, many of them will take the path of least resistance, believing anyone who will feed them what their ears want to hear.

On the other hand, there are those who will diligently study, over long exhaustive periods, all the satanically inspired materials available from some off-the-wall group and then adopt their mystically alluring demonic doctrines. They become so totally, but unknowingly, open to satanic influences that they allow themselves to succumb to many unsound and malignant doctrines. Especially some middle eastern doctrines, sorry suicide bombers. There will be no sexual favors (virgins) for you—where you are going!

Sometimes they may even be allured into a state of total and complete submission to evil satanic forces that are disguised as something pure and mystically wonderful. The deceptions being perpetrated are many and varied, but they all have one single purpose, and that is to prevent any real understanding of God's truth from being heard.

> *For the time will come when men will not put up with sound doctrine. Instead, to suit their own desires, they will gather around them a great number of teachers to say what their itching ears want to hear. They will turn their ears away from the truth and turn aside to myths.*
>
> *2 Timothy 4:3-4 (NIV)*

Just 20 years ago, the year 2000 was marked as the end of time by numerous cults and ancient religious sects alike. Furthermore, many of the leaders of these cults were convincing and preparing their followers to commit mass suicide to escape the awful terror of the 'end' of the world they were proclaiming would occur. These followers were being brainwashed to believe that they would be assured of a special place with their leader (some of whom claimed to be god) in the glorious life he will lead them to in the hereafter.

Even some of the most brilliant, intelligent people on the earth are being deceived into believing the many lies espoused by the evil leaders of these groups. In many cases, these leaders themselves have become as highly revered by their unsuspecting followers as Jesus Christ is to the Christian.

To the unknowing person, the rationale and arguments these groups make are obviously very convincing. So much so that many

Christians are even being deceived by these scripture-quoting leaders. They completely manipulate God's word to give credence to their own self-serving interests in their arguments, thereby deceiving many people into following the infamous 'Piper.' It is sad to think that in the early spiritual training received by many of these people who are being deceived, they didn't at least learn that Satan himself can quote the scriptures. Besides, just because a person can quote the scriptures word for word doesn't make them a man or woman of God.

Each person should seek the knowledge of God for themselves to be able to rightly divide the word of truth. Unfortunately, many immature Christians have never received (or have received so little) of the Knowledge of God. They haven't gotten a clue as to what's true. Eve certainly thought the 'magnificently beautiful creature' in God's own garden was quoting God when she was deceived into eating from the tree of the Knowledge, of Good and Evil.

> *Be diligent to present yourself approved to God, a worker who does not need to be ashamed, rightly dividing the word of truth.*
>
> *2 Timothy 2:15 (NKJV)*
>
> *"My people are destroyed for lack of knowledge"*
>
> *Hosea 4:6, (NKJV).*
>
> *For this is good and acceptable in the sight of God our Savior, who desires all men to be saved and to come to the knowledge of the truth. For there is one God and one Mediator between God and men, the Man Christ Jesus.*
>
> *1 Timothy 2:3-5 (NKJV)*

To negate the plan of the evil one, we Christians need to stand up and once again proclaim to the world, "Repent, for the kingdom of Heaven is at hand." A fact that was true 2000 years ago and is still just as true today. But perhaps it's an even more significant and timely message today, considering the soon return of our Lord Jesus to set up His kingdom on the earth.

The disciples of Jesus thought that He would be physically returning within their lifetime when they preached the message of salvation through Jesus Christ. Instead, the spiritual 'Kingdom of God' was ushered in by the indwelling presence of the Holy Spirit in the Body of Christ, the Church.

The Millennial Kingdom is 'Christ's Kingdom,' and although a significant number of the citizens of Heaven (the saints) are now present with Jesus, the literal 'Kingdom of Heaven' will not actually become a fulfilled reality until the Perfect Age has begun. This Perfect Age, however, won't begin until Satan is finally defeated and cast into the lake of fire, mankind's soul is purged of all its sin nature, and natural Man is promoted to eternal holiness. By mankind having their sinful nature replaced with the very essence of God's nature, humans will receive the realized essence of His Image and Likeness, without flaw or blemish.

The actual height of spiritual and mortal accomplishment achieved by the people of the earth during the period of Christ's millennial kingdom, plus the role that We, the saints, play during this glorious period of peace and prosperity, will bring more Glory to God the Father than anything since time began. All things will be consciously done for the express purpose of bringing Glory to God. Therefore, the very nature of mortal achievement within the realm of the *'space-time continuum' will surpass even the world's most creative imagination. Click Link below or enter in your browser.

https://einstein.stanford.edu/content/relativity/q411.html

The populated cities of God's created universe throughout the 'Kingdom of Heaven' will be marvelous centers of activity of Heavenly immortal life. This new life will also exist without any of the social and physical maladies that currently plague our cities today. Peace and prosperity will greatly abound, and mankind will be totally uninhibited and gloriously blessed in all their endeavors.

The Bible contains numerous references to the Glorious lives' mankind will have in the future 'Kingdom of Heaven.' So, before we proceed any further, let's get a clear picture of just what we are talking about when we use the two most common phrases to describe this very real literal place.

As we have previously discussed, the two phrases, 'Kingdom of God' and 'Kingdom of Heaven' have been and continue to be used interchangeably in the same context. The word 'Heaven' is used to express several different concepts in the Bible. Therefore, due to its multi-use, 'Heaven' has even been used in reference to figurative, literal, spiritual, and divine experiences, in addition to being used as a substitute for the name of God.

> *"John answered and said, 'A man can receive nothing unless it has been given to him from heaven'*
>
> *John 3:27, (NKJV)*

> *"From that time Jesus began to preach and to say, "Repent, for the kingdom of heaven is at hand"*
>
> *Matthew 4:17, (NKJV)*

> *"The time is fulfilled, and the kingdom of God is at hand. Repent, and believe in the gospel"*
>
> *Mark 1:15, (NKJV)*

The 'Kingdom of Heaven' and the 'Kingdom of God', although used interchangeably in many instances, are, for the purposes of this book, two very distinctly different concepts. The 'Kingdom of Christ', on the other hand, is also, for the purposes of this book, a very distinctly unique concept. Unlike the other two, it relates only to the literal Reign of Christ during the 'one thousand year' Millennium. However, we do know from the scriptures that the phrase 'Kingdom of God' is generally describing a spiritual realm while the 'Kingdom of Heaven' is both a visual and literal place of varying levels.

Man has always had an innate curiosity about the things of God, especially Heaven. Perhaps you may have heard or even read about someone's experiences whereas they supernaturally visited the actual 'Realm of Heaven,' within which resided the actual presence of God.

All attempts at defining Heaven have been based upon a natural Man's limited human knowledge and his acquired earthly vocabulary from this temporal life on earth. Just as 'Paul' himself couldn't describe Heaven, I seriously doubt, based upon what he has told us, that the actual Sphere of our God's Realm is even capable of being described with a mortal vocabulary, especially English.

> *How he was caught up into Paradise (the third Heaven) and heard inexpressible words, which it is not lawful (possible) for a man to utter.*
>
> *2 Corinthians 12:4 (NKJV)*

We all know that God lives in Heaven, and the Bible describes the Heavens as several distinct levels, with God residing in the third level of Heaven, in contrast to the sky and the starry heavens visible from the Earth. Some Bible scholars even believe there is evidence of several more levels of Heaven in the Divine Sphere of God's Being, perhaps as many as twelve or maybe even twenty.

We know very little about the literal reality of Heaven and its physical characteristics, except for the information that God Himself has revealed in His eternal plan. Christ's promise to all those who believe in Him is that we shall join Him in Heaven and participate with Him in an everlasting life of joy, love, fellowship, and purpose.

He has planned for our lives in Heaven to be the most exciting and glorious experience in the whole Realm of Heavenly existence. He has prepared an eternal life for us that even transcends beyond the abilities of mankind's mortal understanding. It is a Life that can only be revealed after we receive our glorified eternal bodies and have transcended to our Heavenly status. An event that occurs as we come face to face with our redeemer and become glorified just like Jesus.

> *"And as we have borne the image of the man of dust,*
> *we shall also bear the image of the Heavenly Man"*
>
> *1 Corinthians 15:49, (NKJV)*

Heaven is a word used in the Bible to indicate many different things, conditions, and promises. The most common definition identifies Heaven as the permanent dwelling place of God and His heavenly host. In addition, we are told that it is the abode of those who are blessed to be with their God after death.

As young people growing up, we are reminded thousands of times that God lives in Heaven, and if we are good, we too will be able to live with God and the angels in Heaven. Sound familiar? So, Heaven becomes to the majority some mysterious ethereal and vaporous place up there, somewhere, "Where is Heaven," we ask time and again? "Up there, way up there above the sky," we are told. Then, down through the ages, this same explanation is passed on to generation after generation, identifying this celestial otherworld as the location where the Supreme Being lives.

Later in life, if we have had the opportunity to hear or read certain passages in the scriptures, we discover that this ethereal region is beyond the earth in the 'sides of the north.' We likewise discover that the scriptures reveal there are many different levels of heaven.

The image one gets of this unworldly spiritual region of space is intangible and immaterial in relation to our tangible earth, and it is often visualized as some vague, cloud-like, gaseous realm. We imagine it to be a wonderful place, but the most wonderful thing of all we are told is that we will be in the presence of God and will sing praises to him for all eternity. I, for one, have always thought this sounded boring for an existence that was to last an eternity. Besides, God could create some wonderful robots for this eternally repetitive event. Even when the concept was presented by a highly charismatic teacher using solemn emotional sighs and many wonderful adjectives to emphasize the description, it still had no appeal whatsoever.

The human mind, being a very complex machine, can be programmed to believe almost anything, but there are many who will question and synthesize all theoretical information for themselves, subsequently rejecting the ethereal concept of Heaven as infantile. Unfortunately, the picture painted most often is too vague and intangible for the unsaved, especially the unsaved younger generation who may not have any belief in an afterlife.

This is one reason why so many young people today are turning to numerous religious cults, subscribing to Satan's deceptive new age teachings, and have more of a belief in the Magic Kingdom and Star Wars than the future 'Kingdom of Heaven'. They have no benchmark upon which to base a comparison and have absolutely no idea of God's long-range plan, nor the marvelous vision He has for their eternal lives as His children and heirs of the Kingdom.

Man has only one frame of reference to use in any comparison or testing of any concept unless he has the benefit of counsel from the Holy Spirit. That frame of reference is his earthly experience and his specific level of knowledge in the world at the precise point in time of the comparison.

Without the guidance of the Holy Spirit, mankind is vulnerable to the outside influences of Satan and his many evil spirits who directly and indirectly influence the choices made by worldly men and women. Therefore, the choices mankind makes in the soulish realm alone may be unknowingly influenced by evil spirits even when following the counsel of respected friends and colleagues, who themselves are in the soulish realm without the benefit of the Holy Spirit's guidance.

Likewise, a Christian who may or may not be in the soulish realm at a particular point in time, who seeks the counsel of a trusted friend who is not a Christ-centered Christian, and then proceeds without the guidance of the Holy Spirit can, unknowingly, also have his choices influenced by evil spirits.

Therefore we, as Christ-centered Christians, are admonished to develop spiritually and be able to rightly divide the Word of truth for ourselves. We are likewise cautioned against becoming unequally yoked with unbelievers for the very same reason.

> *Do not be unequally yoked together with unbelievers. For what fellowship has righteousness with lawlessness? And what communion has light with darkness? And what accord has Christ with Belial? Or what part has a believer with an unbeliever?*
>
> *2 Corinthians 6: 14,15 (NKJV)*
>
> *"I will be a Father to you, and you shall be My sons and daughters, says the Lord Almighty" (2 Corinthians 6:18, NKJV).*

Being God's sons and daughters provides us a very special privilege that natural mankind will not enjoy when the literal 'Kingdom of Heaven' is fully realized. Just as the Saint's (God's sons and daughters) in the millennial 'Kingdom of Christ' have special privileges and status apart from natural mortal mankind, in the future perfect 'Kingdom of Heaven,' we too will have special privileges apart from all-natural immortal mankind.

Both groups will have everlasting life, but the saints, being supernatural, will have the distinct privilege of traversing across the physical limits of creation within the literal 'Kingdom of Heaven.' We, the saints, will also have direct access throughout God's Holy Realm of the limitless and literal Eternal Heaven and will be entitled to stand face to face with God in the *Heaven* of Heavens, the Holy abode of our Father.

Here we should stop to again distinguish between the future literal, visible 'Kingdom of Heaven' and the spiritual, invisible 'Kingdom of God.' In addition, we also need a clear working knowledge and understanding of the various uses of the word 'Heaven' in describing the many conditions and celestial places discussed in the Bible.

We are clearly told in the scriptures that the 'Kingdom of God' is spiritual and is available to all of mankind if they will receive Jesus Christ as their Lord and Savior. It is the 'Reign of God' in the universe over all His creatures, and being spiritual, it is not seen but is entered into by the New Birth.

This Kingdom is not physical but consists of righteousness, peace, and joy in the Holy Spirit. The 'Kingdom of God' is within all righteous believers. It is invisible and eternal, enabling us to become heirs of 'The Kingdom' God established through His shed blood on the cross.

> *Now when He was asked by the Pharisees when the kingdom of God would come, He answered them and said, "The kingdom of God does not come with observation; nor will they say, "See here!" or "See there!" for indeed, the kingdom of God is within you."*
>
> *Luke 17:20-21 (NKJV)*

> *Jesus answered, "Most assuredly, I say to you, unless one is born of water and the Spirit, he cannot enter the kingdom of God. That which is born of the flesh is flesh, and that which is born of the Spirit is spirit. Do not marvel that I said to you, 'You must be born again."*
>
> *John 3:5-7 (NKJV)*

> *"For the kingdom of God is not eating and drinking, but righteousness and peace and joy in the Holy Spirit" (Romans 14:17, NKJV).*

One's evidence that he has entered and is experiencing the actual 'Kingdom of God' is a life of righteousness, peace, and joy in the Holy Spirit.

> *"And I say to you that many will come from the east and west, and sit down with Abraham, Isaac, and Jacob in the kingdom of heaven."*
>
> *Matthew 8: 11 (NKJV)*

> *"Not everyone who says to Me 'Lord, Lord', shall enter the kingdom of Heaven, but he who does the will of My father in Heaven."*
>
> *Matthew 7:21 (NKJV)*

At the end of this present age that includes the Millennial Reign of Christ and is sometimes referred to as the 'end of time,' a new Heaven and a new Earth will be made. This new Heaven refers to the Heavens that encompass the new Earth and is the entire cosmos or universe within which the new Earth is contained. It is literally the place in which God's perfect presence exists within the sphere of perfected mankind's new habitation, the new Earth. When used together, the new Heaven and new Earth refer to the perfected state of the created universe and the final dwelling place of the righteous. Literally Heaven on Earth! The actual realized "Kingdom of Heaven."

Rooted deep in Jewish belief was the dream of a new Heaven and a new Earth, a literal re-creation of the universe that would occur following the 'Day of the Lord'. A time when the whole universe would be purified and cleansed by the power of God, as well as mankind's sinful nature being totally eradicated from the lives of God's new eternal righteous immortal people. The realized occupation of the land was then, and it remains today, an important part of God's plan for mankind. Abraham and his descendants were promised land, but Israel has only enjoyed a very minute part of that promise. However, God's desire has always been to extend His promised blessings to all the nations of the earth, which will be fulfilled when the new Earth appears.

The Hebrew word for earth 'erets' is frequently used in the phrase "heaven and earth" and may be correctly translated as the temporal scene of human activity, experience, and history. Its use in the scriptures suggests that our terrestrial planet is just a part of God's whole framework of the entire celestial cosmos, and therefore all habitable creation may be translated as 'earth.'

> *Now I saw a new heaven and a new earth, for the first heaven and the first earth had passed away. Also, there was no more sea. Then I, John, saw the holy city, New Jerusalem, coming down out of heaven from God, prepared as a bride adorned for*

her husband. And I heard a loud voice from heaven saying, 'Behold, the tabernacle of God is with men, and He will dwell with them, and they shall be His people. God Himself will be with them and be their God.'

Revelation 21:1-3 (NKJV)

"For as the new heavens and the new earth which I will make shall remain before Me," says the LORD, "so shall your descendants and your name remain."

Isaiah 66:22 (NKJV)

"But in keeping with his promise we are looking forward to a new heaven and a new earth, the home of righteousness"

2 Peter 3:13, (NIV)

Heaven is a place, an actual, real, literal, physical place. It is a place of indescribable beauty and glory. Heaven is the literal real Paradise of God somewhere out beyond the farthest star, out beyond the second level of heaven—the starry planetary heavens. This glorious third level of Heaven, the Heaven of Heavens, the home of our Triune God, is beyond the creation of the universe in the "sides of the North," according to Isaiah. It will always be, and it will never change.

When we speak about something being made new, it literally means 'renewed' or 'renovated.' It isn't destroyed and then re-created from scratch but is restored or brought back to its original state of newness, and often it is even brought to a state of superior condition exceeding the original. In the case of the earth and the heavens, God has sworn by Himself that He is going to purge His creation, the universe, and everything in it of sin. He will cleanse everything with fire that sin has touched and will not even leave a trace of remembrance of sin in existence.

If only the people of earth could grasp the truth of Billy Sunday's statement, they would be much more diligent in pursuing God's will in their own lives. They would be so much more devoted to teaching their children the importance of securing the eternal rewards of Heaven rather than spending their lives pursuing worldly goals. The heavens are part and parcel of God's creation, the universe, some of which is seen and some unseen. It will, however, become a most glorious visible paradise in the future age to come once all things are made new, and the universe is peopled with God's holy race of sinless mankind, as planned from the very foundation of the world.

It is important to note that we are only discussing the first and second levels of Heaven being made new, as defined in the scriptures. These first two levels have their existence within the created universe and are part of God's overall creation. The third level of Heaven is outside the realm of creation as understood by mortal mankind, is totally indescribable, and is God's private and holiest of domains. Therefore, God's actual realm is His glorious eternal, omnipresent Heaven of Heavens.

The Bible tells us that in the future perfect age, after all, things are made new, God will dwell with mankind, and His Heavenly city of 'New Jerusalem' will be the glorious capital city of Heaven on earth and the home of all His glorified saints throughout the whole earth.

> *'Then I, John, saw the holy city, New Jerusalem, coming down out of heaven from God, prepared as a bride adorned for her husband. And I heard a loud voice from heaven saying, 'Behold, the tabernacle of God is with men, and He will dwell with them, and*

> *they shall be His people. God Himself will be with them and be their God.'*
>
> Revelation 21:2-3 (NKJV)

I have read several accounts of mankinds future, their relationship with Heaven and have even heard the City of New Jerusalem called Heaven. I would agree that the Heavenly city of New Jerusalem will be more glorious than any mortal can imagine, but it is not Heaven. However, the new Heavens and the new Earth made by God for immortal mankind and the glorified saints is much more glorious than depicted in these accounts and is certainly much more all-encompassing than just the City alone. We are talking about the realized literal "Kingdom of Heaven" finally coming into its own realm of existence, ushering in the glorious, perfect age of ages and the beginning of eternal life as a reflection of His glory.

> *"In My Father's house, are many mansions; if it were not so, I would have told you. I go to prepare a place for you"*
>
> *John 14:2, (NKJV)*

> *"Don't let this throw you. You trust God, don't you? Trust me. There is plenty of room for you in my Father's home. If that weren't so, would I have told you that I'm on my way to get a room ready for you? And if I'm on my way to get your room ready, I'll come back and get you so you can live where I live. And you already know the road I'm taking".*
>
> *John 14:1-4 (MSG) The Message*

> *Thomas said, "Master, we have no idea where you're going. How do you expect us to know the road?" Jesus said, "I am the Road, also the Truth, also the*

Life. No one gets to the Father apart from me. If you really knew me, you would know my Father as well. From now on, you do know Him. You've even seen Him!"

Philip said, "Master, show us the Father; then we'll be content."

John 14:5-8 (MSG)

"You've been with me all this time, Philip, and you still don't understand? To see me is to see the Father. So how can you ask, 'Where is the Father?' Don't you believe that I am in the Father and the Father is in me? The words that I speak to you aren't mere words. I don't just make them on my own. The Father who resides in me crafts each word into a divine act."

John 14:9-10 (MSG)

"For behold, I create new heavens and a new earth; and the former shall not be remembered or come to mind"

Isaiah 65:17, (NKJV)

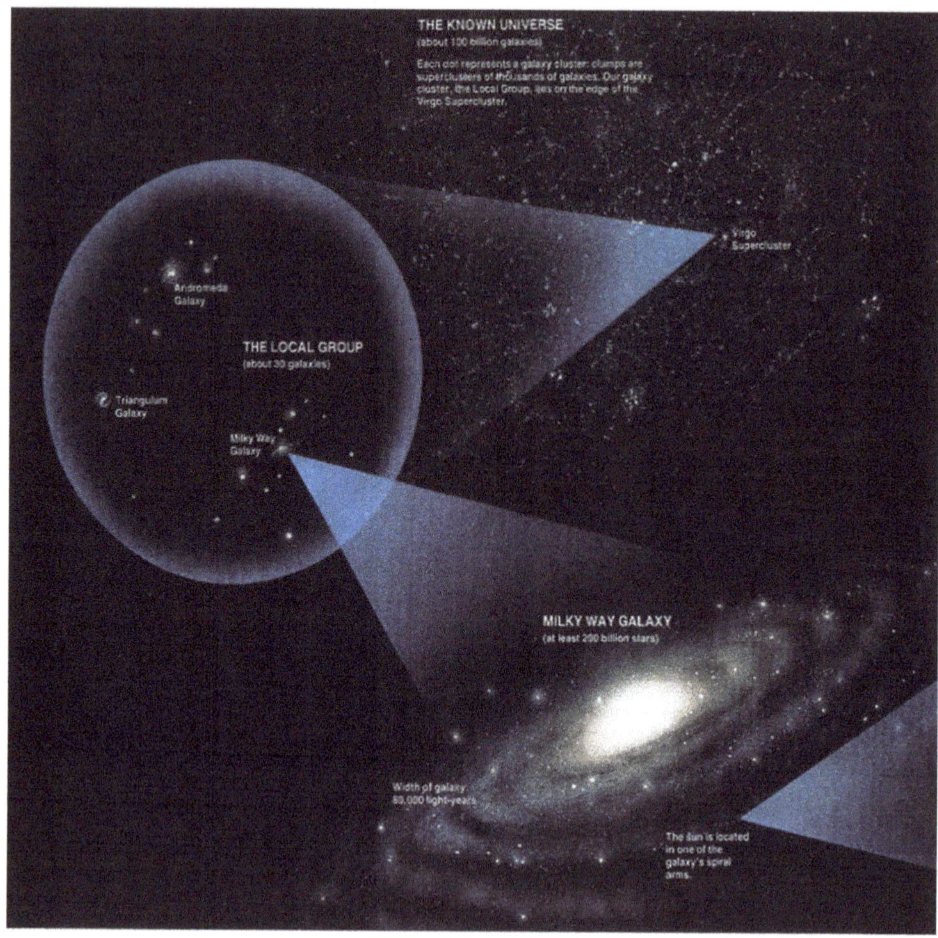

Illustration 1:
"THE KNOWN UNIVERSE"

God is omnipresent and, as such, must therefore dwell not only throughout all His creation but even beyond infinity. In God's "dwelling place$_{1}$" there are many "abiding places$_{2}$", and Jesus has gone to prepare "a place for you." Just how magnificent and inconceivable is this place He has been preparing?

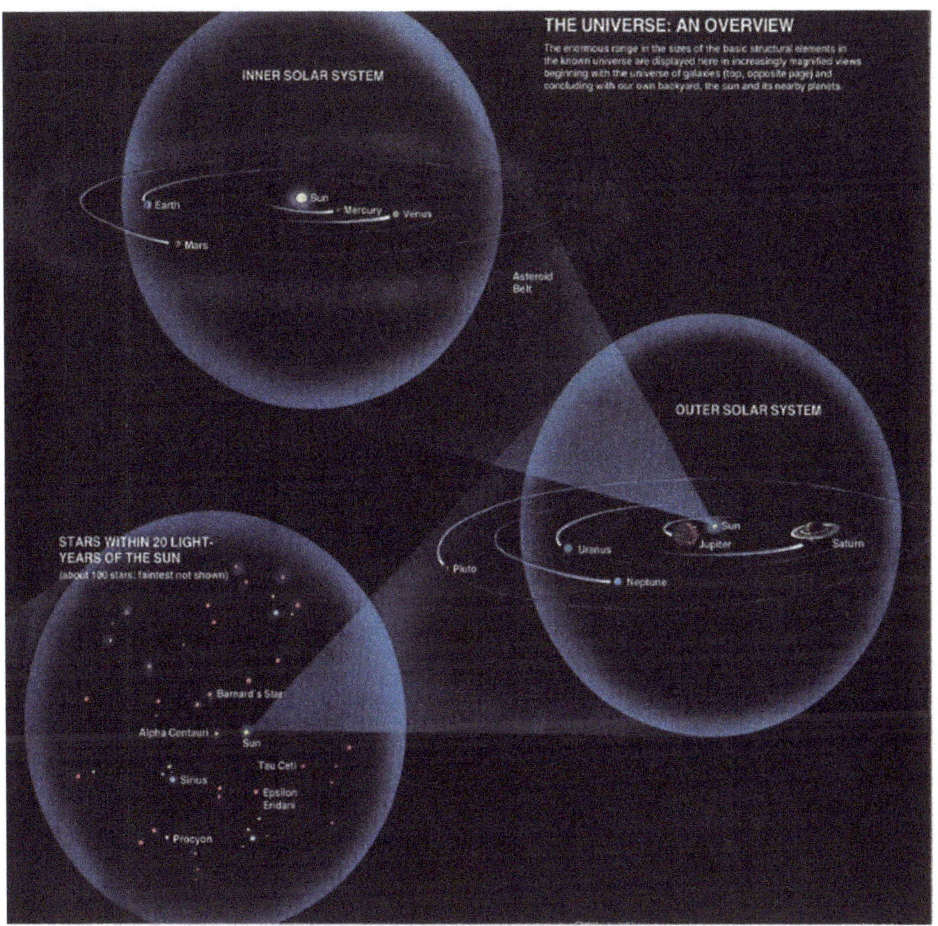

Illustration 2:
"THE UNIVERSE AND BEYOND"

Some current cosmological concepts indicate that many universes may exist in a common cosmos, a virtual sea of universes. Although our universe could not be observed from the outside as depicted above, it may very well be only one among a multitude of universes.

TERRENCE DICKINSON

CHAPTER 18

God's plan: Only the Universe?

At the close of the 1000-year Millennial Reign of Christ, Satan's army of followers is totally defeated and devoured by fire from Heaven. Satan himself is then finally and totally removed from the sphere of mankind's habitation and 'thrown' into the most awful place God ever created—Eternal Hell.

> *The devil, who deceived them, was cast into the lake of fire and brimstone where the beast and the false prophet are. And they will be tormented day and night forever and ever.*
>
> Then I saw a great white throne and Him (Jesus) who sat on it, from whose face the earth and the heaven fled away. And there was found no place for them.
>
> And I saw the dead, small and great, standing before God, and books were opened. And another book was opened, which is the Book of Life. And the dead were judged according to their works, by the things which were written in the books.
>
> The sea gave up the dead who were in it, and Death and Hades delivered up the dead who were in them. And they were judged, each one according to his works.

> Then Death and Hades were cast into the lake of fire. This is the second death. And 'anyone not found written in the Book of Life' was cast into the lake of fire.
>
> *Revelation 20:10-15 (NKJV)*

This Scripture identifies 'the great white throne judgment' that will take place somewhere in God's realm of Heaven. This event occurs outside of His creation during the renovation of the heavens and the earth by fire. It is the time of 'final' judgment that Peter called the "day of judgment and perdition" and is the judgment of the wicked dead.

> *But the heavens and the earth which are now preserved by the same word, are reserved for fire until the day of judgment and perdition of ungodly men.*
>
> *2 Peter 3:7 (NKJV)*

All the righteous dead and the 'end time' living church participate in the first resurrection prior to the Millennial Reign of Christ. Therefore, any righteous dead who die between the first resurrection and the second resurrection of the wicked dead must also rise at this second resurrection.

Verse 15 above implies that there will be some righteous and must therefore identify all the righteous who die during the 1000-year Millennial Reign of Christ. This group of the righteous dead will, of course, include all those who enter the Millennium alive from the Great Tribulation and are counted as righteous upon their death. Isaiah confirms the fact that death will occur during the millennium.

> *No more shall an infant from there live but a few days, nor an old man who has not fulfilled his days;*

> *for the child shall die one hundred years old, but the sinner being one hundred years old shall be accursed.*
>
> *Isaiah 65:20 (NKJV)*

The King James version uses the words *"whosoever was not found written in the book of life."* Therefore, since the righteous saints who are ruling and reigning with Jesus have stood before the Judgment Seat of Christ in Heaven, they have already received their crowns and rewards.

The only remaining righteous who are entitled to eternal life with God at the second resurrection will be those who come out of the Millennial Reign of Christ. All others will experience the second death and go to hell.

> *But the day of the Lord will come as a thief in the night, in which the heavens will pass away with a great noise, and the elements will melt with fervent heat; both the earth and the works that are in it will be burned up.*
>
> *Therefore, since all these things will be dissolved what manner of persons ought you to be in holy conduct and godliness looking for and hastening the coming of the day of God, because of which the heavens will be dissolved, being on fire and the elements will melt with fervent heat? Nevertheless we, according to His promise, look for new heavens and a new earth in which righteousness dwells.*
>
> *2 Peter 3:10-13 (NKJV)*

At the close of the Millennium, after Satan and his army are destroyed, there will be many unrighteous men and women still on the earth along with the living righteous. Just prior to the renovation of the heavens and the earth with fire, the living righteous will be miraculously transported out of harm's way, and the living wicked (ungodly) people of the Millennium will be destroyed in the fire that will completely consume the earth's atmosphere and exterior crust.

The "books" will be opened; the book of conscience (Romans 2:15); the book of words (Matthew 12:36, 37); the book of secret works (Romans 2:16, Ecclesiastes 12:14; the book of public works (2 Corinthians 11:15, Matthew 16:27); the book of Life (Exodus 32:32, 33; Psalms 69:28, Daniel 12:1; Philippians 4:3; Revelation 3:5; 13:8; 17:8; 20:12, 15; 21:27; 22:19) and all the wicked dead will be judged to determine the "degree" of their punishment.

> *"Some will receive a more severe punishment than others, but they will all receive a sentence to spend eternity with all the ungodly, the devil, the fallen angels, the devil's evil demons, the beast and the false prophet. "and they will be tormented day and night forever and ever."*
>
> *Revelation 20:10*

The other dead who are judged by the "Book of Life" at the great white throne judgment and receive eternal life with God appear to be the one-third of the faithful Jews who come through the Great Tribulation alive and enter the Millennial Reign of Christ; those faithful born during the Millennium and who remain faithful during their lifetime; the faithful Jews and gentiles who come out from the safety of Petra where they were protected during the Tribulation; plus those faithful gentiles who went into the Millennium with Christ for having protected the one-third of Tribulation Israel; and last, but not least, all the unjustified children who die before the age of accountability throughout history, including those unborn (miscarried) or still born children, and those killed by abortion throughout history, 'who lived again,' resided with the tribes of Israel, and remained faithful to their death during the Millennium.

Matthew 20:1-16 gives us a picture of God's grace and His gracious acceptance of all who turn to Him. A picture of redemption showing God's wonderful generosity that is even extended into the 1000-year Millennial Reign of Christ.

> *"For the Kingdom of Heaven is like a landowner who went out early in the morning to hire laborers for his vineyard...*
>
> *And when those came who were hired about the eleventh hour, they each received a denarius...*
>
> *So, the last will be first, and the first last. For many are called, but few chosen."*

When this judgment is over, the devil and all the wicked dead will be assigned to the "Lake of Fire" forever, and the entire universe will be purged of all sin and evil. Then righteousness will reign forever in the new heavens and the new earth, even throughout all of God's creation of the universe(s).

The exterior surface of this earth will be completely changed, and all that sin brought into existence will be forever destroyed. In addition, the entire cosmos will be purified and made free from the destructive forces of evil spirits and sin. The heavens and the earth will pass from its current 'state' of corrupt existence into a 'state' of perfect existence, just as the physical body of the Saint's will pass from corruption to incorruption and into a 'state' of perfected glory.

Though the Bible does not give us details of how God will transfer the people of the earth safely from the present earth to the new earth, they will no doubt be protected from God's wrath like Noah and his family were protected from the flood. All the living righteous, holy people of the earth who come through the millennium will be physically separated from the wrath of God that annihilates all the remaining sinful mankind from existence.

As the new heavens and the new earth that I make will endure before Me, declares the Lord, so will your name and descendants endure.

Isaiah 66:22 (NKJV)

"The heaven, even the heavens, are the LORD'S; but the earth He has given to the children of men" (Psalm 115:16, NKJV).

"For behold, I create new heavens and a new earth; and the former shall not be remembered or come to mind" (Isaiah 65:17, NKJV).

There will be no need for archaeologists on the new earth because everything of the past earth, including its crust, will be completely burned up without a trace. No future archaeologist, if there remains any such profession, will dig up any remnant of the previous creation, no lost city of Atlantis or its parallel—no lost city of Jerusalem to search out. It will all be gone forever. Not even the fossil of a bug will remain in existence.

Let's digress for a moment and discuss the geography of what is about to be burned up. The total area of the present earth is 196,938,796 square miles of the surface, with 71% of this total covered by water (oceans) or 139,826,545 square miles of our current earth's total surface area.

The highest elevation on the present earth is Mount Everest at 29,029 feet (approximately five and a half miles high); the lowest elevation is the Dead Sea at minus1286 feet below sea level. The hottest recorded temperature on a continent is the Libyan Desert, Africa, at +136 degrees F, and the coldest recorded temperature on a continent, Antarctica, at minus 128.6 degrees F.

This geography gives mankind a benchmark (frame of reference) upon which he measures and comprehends the physical sphere of his world. In addition, Man's understanding and comprehension of the cosmos usually begins and ends with his own solar system and the nine planets that rotate around the sun (the closest star). Even the sheer magnitude of our earth's solar system, which just happens to contain the largest known planet in our cosmos (Jupiter), is incomprehensible to most of mankind.

To get a real perspective of God's known creation, one must expand the mind to first visualize the 'one' star solar system of which we are a part, along with the estimated 300 billion other stars in our Milky Way Galaxy, and potentially 100 billion planets. A comparatively small galaxy that is only one galaxy out of billions and billions of galaxies in the known universe. A universe that, according to science, is continually expanding and increasing its volume at the rate of a trillion cubic light-years per minute.

('One' light-year equals 5.879 trillion miles). One of science's current cosmological concepts further suggest but cannot prove due to the geometry of space and other complex limitations, that many universes may be in existence.

During the 16th century, Copernicus suggested that the sun, not the earth, was the center of the cosmos. Since then, our sun has proved to be just one among hundreds of billions of stars in the Milky Way, and our galaxy only one among billions in the known universe.

Today, as we experience the 21st century, our universe is theoretically seen as merely one among an infinite multitude of cosmic bubbles in a far greater cosmos than we have ever before imagined, a universe within the 'Universe of Universes.' [See illustrations on page 296 & 297].

Based on the laws of astrophysics and the gravitational systems within God's created order of the cosmos, planets could exist and systematically function in the present order of the cosmos up to a size three times the mass of Jupiter (Jupiter's mass is 318 times greater than the earth's).

Scientists have determined that a planet more massive than this would be compacted by its own weight to Jupiter's maximum size (266,202 miles wide at its longest dimension) or even slightly smaller. By proportionally comparing earth's mass, density, and size to Jupiter's, this would equate to an allowable habitable planet having similar characteristics of today's earth, but increased to a diameter 139.33 times larger than our earth, or 1,104,315 miles across (The sun is 865,000 miles across at its widest dimension). However, God is not restricted by the above. He is its creator.

Taking into account the sun's present composition, mass, and stage of evolution, some scientists have mathematically forecasted that the sun will evolve into a huge ultra-hot giant that will increase in size between 300 to 400 times larger than the present sun (a potential diameter of 260 million to 346 million miles wide).

At this size, the sun would fill the center of our present solar system almost out to the earth's present orbit. The planets Mercury and Venus would be swallowed up, and the remaining planets would spiral outward to a new orbit farther from the sun.

The effect this would have on the earth itself is the surface temperature would reach 2,400 degrees Fahrenheit, at which temperature all its water would be blasted into space, and its surface converted into red-hot molten rock, burning up everything that ever existed on the surface. The oceans and polar ice caps would be almost instantly vaporized and would form an atmospheric blanket encircling the entire planet. It appears that the atmosphere of the earth could potentially return to God's created condition prior to the flood.

If the sun begins to be puffed up like an inflating balloon, then its brightness would continue to increase many times its current brightness. (This could account for the seven-fold increase in the sun's brightness during the Millennium.) But, even with the sun's increased brightness, the increase in temperature on the earth would only register a fraction of a degree unless the sun's thermonuclear reactions were accelerated to explosive proportions.

Science has determined that the galaxies, including the blackness of space in between, contain all the essential elements of dust and gasses for the formation of new stars and new planets. Within the cosmos today also exists the potential for the merging of two or more existing planets, stars, and galaxies into newly formed, much larger stars, planets, and galaxies.

The greatest of the galaxies are called the 'masters of the universe' or 'emperor galaxies' that are giant elliptical galaxies of dozens to hundreds of galaxies forming a group that can even exceed 50 trillion times the mass of the sun.

Man relies upon his benchmarks to help him comprehend the magnitude of an event or issue and can only base a comparison on his personal knowledge of a given situation or event. If he is taught to believe the earth is flat and the sky is a dome covering the earth, his ability to comprehend even the present earth's solar system is beyond his understanding.

This is exactly what the old testament fathers and the early church believed, and until the sixteenth century, the earth remained the single most important element in the whole of creation. Due to their lack of knowledge, natural mankind has always had limitations that have restricted their vision of the glorious future God has planned for His creation.

Well, Pilgrim, hopefully, the past several chapters have expanded your earthly benchmark into the vast and glorious future cosmos, the universe of perhaps universes.' Because God's planned creation is so immensely beautiful and enormously huge, even the world's most advanced supercomputers cannot begin to calculate or track its actual magnitude.

The Scriptures tell us that the earth is completely regenerated after its surface is burned up and that the new earth is made perfect and is wondrously magnificent. It is again made like the Garden of Eden and will remain forever—obviously requiring lots of sunshine for growth and continued maintenance.

However, it has been said by many current scholars and teachers of the Bible prophesy that the sun goes out forever, and the New Jerusalem provides the light for the new earth as it hovers over the earth. This is simply not what the Scriptures are telling us, but they do say that the wonderful City of New Jerusalem will have no need for the sun or the moon in the city, as you can see from the following Scriptures for yourself.

> *The city had no need of the sun or of the moon to shine in it, for the glory of God illuminated it. The Lamb is its light. And the nations (the righteous from Adam) of those who are saved (the* saints*) shall walk in its light, and the kings of the earth bring their glory and honor into it.*
>
> *Its gates shall not be shut at all by day (there shall be no night there). And they shall bring the glory and the honor of the nations into it. But there shall by no means enter it anything that defiles, or causes an abomination or a lie, but only those who are written in the Lamb's Book of Life.*
>
> *Revelation 21:23-27 (NKJV)*

And there shall be no more curse, but the throne of God and of the Lamb shall be in it, and His servants shall serve Him. They (the saints*) shall see His face, and His name shall be on their foreheads. There shall be no night there: They (the* saints*) need no lamp nor light of the sun, for the Lord God gives them light. And they shall reign forever and ever.*

Revelation 22:3-5 (NKJV)

The sun shall no longer be your (the Saint's) light by day, nor for brightness shall the moon give light to you; but the LORD will be to you an everlasting light, and your God 'your glory'.

Your sun shall no longer go down, nor shall your moon withdraw itself; for the LORD will be your everlasting light, and the days of your mourning shall be ended. Also, your people shall all be righteous; they shall inherit the land forever, the branch of My planting, the work of My hands, that I may be glorified.

Isaiah 60:19-21 (NKJV)

Praise Him, sun and moon; praise Him, all you stars of light! Praise Him, you heavens of heavens, and you waters above the heavens! Let them praise the name of the LORD for He commanded and they were created. He also established them forever and ever; he made a decree which shall not pass away.

Psalms 148:3-6 (NKJV)

My covenant I will not break, nor alter the word that has gone out of My lips. Once I have sworn by

My holiness; I will not lie to David: His seed shall endure forever, and his throne as the sun before Me; It shall be established forever like the moon, even like the faithful witness in the sky.

Psalms 89:34-37 (NKJV)

'For as the new heavens and the new earth which I will make shall remain before Me', says the LORD, 'So shall your descendants and your name remain. And it shall come to pass that from one New Moon to another, and from one Sabbath to another, all flesh shall come to worship before Me', says the LORD.

Isaiah 66:22-23 (NKJV)

Thus says the LORD: 'If you can break My covenant with the day and My covenant with the night, so that there will not be day and night in their season, then My covenant may also be broken with David My servant, so that he shall not have a son to reign on his throne, and with the Levites, the priests, My ministers. As the host of heaven cannot be numbered, nor the sand of the sea measured, so will I multiply the descendants of David My servant and the Levites who minister to Me.' …Thus says the LORD: 'If My covenant is not with day and night, and if I have not appointed the ordinances of heaven and earth, then I will cast away the descendants of Jacob and David My servant, so that I will not take any of his descendants to be rulers over the descendants of Abraham, Isaac, and Jacob.

Jeremiah 33:20-21; 25-26 (NKJV)

When Man thinks of the new heavens and the new earth, he uses his 'benchmark' of the present earth and only the sphere of existence he understands. He generally doesn't have the knowledge or wisdom to think beyond his current level of knowledge unless he is guided by the Holy Spirit, as is evidenced by the clearer understanding we have of the Scriptures today as compared to the Church's understanding of a thousand or even a hundred years ago.

The revelation of Jesus Christ and the end-time prophecies of the Old Testament make more sense today than at any other time in the history of their existence. After World War II and the atomic bomb, mankinds understanding of end-time events also exploded into reality.

Many of today's tragic worldwide events are rapidly fulfilling the remaining prophecies written in the Scriptures, an explosion of knowledge is filling the hearts and minds of Biblical scholars, and many students of prophecy are proclaiming "the bridegroom cometh."

> *"And at midnight there was a cry made, Behold, the bridegroom cometh; go ye out to meet him"*
>
> *Matthew 25:6, (KJV)*

God's long-range plan has always been the peopling of His entire habitable creation with a sinless, holy race of people—His very "elect," the natural and spiritual descendants of Abraham, just as we discussed in the beginning chapters of this book. This sinless, holy race of people will populate the entire universe in fulfillment of God's promise to Abraham, Isaac, and Jacob that Abraham's descendants would be as numerous as the dust of the earth, *"that if you could count the dust of the earth so could Abraham's descendants be counted."*

Therefore, the descendants of Abraham continue to populate the universe forever, the righteous saints of the Lord Jesus rule and reign forever along with Jesus as kings and lords and priests over God's entire wonderful creation, and the universe of universes' becomes the Kingdom of Heaven.

Although we have identified a number of 2 x 10^{28} for discussion purposes, the Scriptures infer the number of Abrahams descendants cannot be counted because God has indicated in His references to the dust, sand, and the stars as Abraham's descendants, Man cannot count these. Therefore, it appears that mankind continues to populate the universe throughout eternity and the actual number of Abraham's descendants spoken of in Genesis is 'infinity,' meaning there is no end to procreation in eternity.

If the Jews (God's Elect) inherit the promised land forever, then some form of the earth (habitable land) must exist forever, but does it exist at the same size? No! As the new heavens and new earth are made by God, it is more than logical that our present planet earth expands to a size much larger than it exists today.

The present planet earth itself very possibly becomes the molten core of new planet earth that is formed around it, much like the layering formation of a pearl around a speck of impure debris. In addition to our re-made existing planet earth, other habitable lands (planets), if not already in existence, will by necessity be made by God throughout the universe when he forms the new heavens and the new earth.

As stated earlier in this chapter, all the cosmic matter and essential material elements for star formation and planet formation now exist and are ever-present all around us in the cosmos. (See the front cover description of this book, page #7–8, of the Star-Forming Region NCC 2174 captured by the Hubble Telescope) The only requirement necessary for all of this to coalesce into planetary bodies is the action of a powerful force in the heavens that will bring about the required coalescing reaction. I'd have to say this is a no-brainer for our God, wouldn't you?

There are several reasons why the physical size of the new earth will, by necessity, be increased over its present size. One of the reasons, of course, is the vast number of Abraham's descendants' that God has identified in His promise, who, by the way, couldn't possibly all be contained upon a single planet that would fit into God's physical order and system of the universe.

For instance, if the new earth increased in size to the maximum physical diameter of 1,104,315 miles across as identified earlier, and if each human on the new earth was apportioned (given) an area of land the size of a football field, the entire new earth would only be capable of containing 3.8 trillion people—a far cry from the total population of Abraham's descendants God says will be greater than "the dust of the earth and the sand of the sea."

A mere difference of over 20,000 trillion, trillion, trillion people if just the calculated number we identified is the maximum. But, with the descendants of Abraham continuing to populate the universe forever, there must be somewhere, someplace, for this population to expand because there is no more death. Imagine the Glory our God will receive.

The other reason for an increase in the size of our planet earth is the physical size of God's new heavenly city, the 'New Jerusalem' that God has specially prepared for His saints. Many Bible scholars have stated that this new city will descend to the vicinity of the new earth as a stationary city floating above the earth—a city hovering in space with the new earth becoming a satellite planet-encircling the New Jerusalem, and from which the new earth will receive its light.

However, neither the law of physics nor the Scriptures support this notion, especially in consideration of our knowledge of its physical size and shape. Some believe the shape of the city is a cube, while others believe it's a pyramid, and there are convincing arguments for both. However, neither shape is in harmony with the law of physics nor fits the order, organization, or systems within the heavens of the cosmos for an orbiting space station, and that is exactly what it would be if it hovered above the new earth.

God has shown us through His order of creation and in the Scriptures that He is systematic, logical, and mathematical. Jesus very aptly confirmed this for us when He fed the 5,000 and had the disciples seat the people in groups of 50.

> *Now I saw a new heaven and a new earth, for the first heaven and the first earth had passed away. Also, there was no more sea. Then I, John, saw the holy city, New Jerusalem, coming down out of heaven from God, prepared as a bride adorned for her husband.*
>
> *And I heard a loud voice from heaven saying, 'Behold, the tabernacle of God is with men, and He will dwell with them, and they shall be His people. God Himself will be with them and be their God. And God will wipe away every tear from their eyes; there shall be no more death, nor sorrow, nor crying. There shall be no more pain, for the former things have passed away.'*
>
> *Revelation 21:1-4 (NKJV)*
>
> *Then one of the seven angels who had the seven bowls filled with the seven last plagues came to me and talked with me, saying, 'Come, I will show you the bride, the Lamb's wife.'*
>
> *And he carried me away in the Spirit to a great and high mountain, and showed me the great city, the holy Jerusalem, descending out of heaven from God, having the glory of God. Her light was like a most precious stone, like a jasper stone, clear as crys-*

> *tal. Also she had a great and high wall with twelve gates, and twelve angels at the gates, and names written on them, which are the names of the twelve tribes of the children of Israel: three gates on the east, three gates on the north, three gates on the south, and three gates on the west.*
>
> *Now the wall of the city had twelve foundations, and on them were the names of the twelve apostles of the Lamb. And he who talked with me had a gold reed to measure the city, its gates and its wall.*
>
> *The city is laid out as a square; its length is as great as its breadth. And he measured the city with the reed: Twelve thousand furlongs*. Its length, breadth, and height are equal.*
>
> *Revelation 21:9-16 (NKJV)*

*Note:

A furlong = One eighth Roman mile = one stadion = 606.954 feet, i.e.: 12,000 x 606.954 feet divided by 5,280 feet = 1,379.44 miles. The New Jerusalem is therefore laid out 'as a square' with each side approximately 1,380 miles long with the height of the city 1,380 miles high.

If the three gates are equally spaced on a side, then the center-line of each gate is 345 miles apart in a wall that is 300 feet** thick. ("Then he measured its wall: One hundred and forty-four cubits,"—*Revelation 21:17).*

**Note:

The Hebrew cubit of measurement is 25.025 inches. Therefore 144 cubits x 25.025 inches divided by 12 inches = 300.3 feet.

The New Jerusalem is the heavenly city of God, the city home of *all* the righteous children (the saints) of God, from Adam to every born again believer, who is 'the Church' and the 'bride of Christ', including all the righteous Jews and Gentile saints who accept and die for Christ during the first three and a half years of the Tribulation.

These glorious children of God (sons of God) will freely go in and out of the twelve gates into the new earth and the new heavens with access to the whole Sovereign reign of God's creation. They will have the 'elite' distinction of being ambassadors of God, ruling and reigning with Christ forever.

The many martyred Great Tribulation saints, and those that go into the Millennium alive and remain faithful till death, will have the glorious privilege and joy of serving the throne of God in the holy city of New Jerusalem for all of eternity.

> *Then one of the elders answered, saying to me, 'Who are these arrayed in white robes, and where did they come from?' And I said to him, 'Sir, you know.' So, he said to me, 'These are the ones who come out of the Great Tribulation and washed their robes and made them white in the blood of the Lamb.*
>
> *Therefore, they are before the throne of God, and serve Him day and night in His temple. And He who sits on the throne will dwell among them.*
>
> *They shall neither hunger anymore nor thirst anymore; the sun shall not strike them, nor any heat; for the Lamb who is in the midst of the throne will shepherd them and lead them to living fountains of waters. And God will wipe away every tear from their eyes.'*
>
> *Revelation 7:13-17 (NKJV)*

The city of New Jerusalem has the magnificent Glory of God filling the entire city with His Divine presence, and the whole city glows with an eternal brightness. *(Revelation 21:11).*

Previously, I mentioned that there are two physical geometric shapes that have been used to describe the physical characteristic of the city of New Jerusalem. One is the pyramid and the other a cube. The argument given for the City being in the shape of a cube is that it is the shape of the Old Testament temple, holy of holies, and because of this, scholars have surmised that it would follow that God's city would be of the same shape.

On the other hand, the pyramid shape is more in keeping with the shape of a mountain, and the city has been called the mountain of God in several Scriptures.

> *"Even them I will bring to My holy mountain"*
>
> *Isaiah 56:7, (NKJV)*
>
> *I will make them and the places all around My hill a blessing; and I will cause showers to come down in their season; there shall be showers of blessing.*
>
> *Ezekiel 34:26 (NKJV)*
>
> *And so terrifying was the sight that Moses said, 'I am exceedingly afraid and trembling.'*
>
> *But you have come to Mount Zion and to the city of the living God, the heavenly Jerusalem, to an innumerable company of angels, to the general assembly and church of the firstborn who are registered in heaven, to God the Judge of all, to the spirits of just men made perfect, to Jesus the Mediator of the new*

covenant, and to the blood of sprinkling that speaks better things than that of Abel.

Hebrews 12:21-24 (NKJV)

The Scriptures call the city a mountain, and a mountain is more like a pyramid than a cube. Therefore, it is more logical that the description infers that the pyramid shape is a more probable shape. Since the city wall with twelve gates is 300 feet thick, it is difficult to visualize a cube-shaped object of that size extending up almost 1400 miles due to the sheer size and potential weight of its exterior walls and the foundation necessary to carry its weight.

But a pyramid-shaped city could have a sloped, twelve-tiered foundation with a wall that high with twelve gates that could provide a structurally sound base to transfer the enormous loads to the foundations.

Note:

(Pyramid: A polyhedron with a polygonal [rectangular] base and triangular faces meeting in a single common vertex at the top called a 'capstone.' It is interesting to note that the Great Pyramid, the largest Egyptian pyramid, is called a square pyramid, due to its base being laid out 'as a square.')

It is also interesting to note that some scholars believe Job may have been the architect of the Great Pyramid and actually received its plan from God (Read the 38th chapter of Job—God is speaking to him of things no ordinary man would even begin to comprehend).

Comparing the relative size of the heavenly city of New Jerusalem, which is based on a typical floor to floor height in today's world be a 560,000-story building extending into our present earth's atmosphere. This gives us a very clear picture of the vast magnitude of the new city compared to buildings in today's planet earth.

Mount Everest, the earth's highest mountain, is five and a half miles high and is in the atmospheric area or zone called the troposphere that extends from the earth's surface up to about 6 miles. Starting at 6 miles and extending up to 28 or 30 miles is the zone called the stratosphere, within which the highest-flying commercial aircraft (the Concorde) could fly at the height of only 12 miles above the earth's surface. The earth's ozone layer is at the height of about fifteen and a half miles above the earth's surface and is the earth's filtering protector from all the very deadly radiation emanating from our sun and outer space, and without which all life would cease to exist on earth.

Above the stratosphere from 30 miles to 50 miles above the earth is the mesosphere where the temperature drops to -112 degrees F. The thermosphere is above the mesosphere, and it extends from 50 miles to about 310 miles above the earth's surface, where the temperature climbs steadily from -112 degrees F. to +1,895 degrees Fahrenheit.

It is within the thermosphere that the early manned space capsules orbited the earth at an elevation of about 110 miles, and later space shuttles orbited at an elevation of 170 miles above the earth's surface. Artificial satellites and space stations orbit at about 220 miles, and the Hubble space telescope orbits at about 375 miles above the earth's surface within the exosphere.

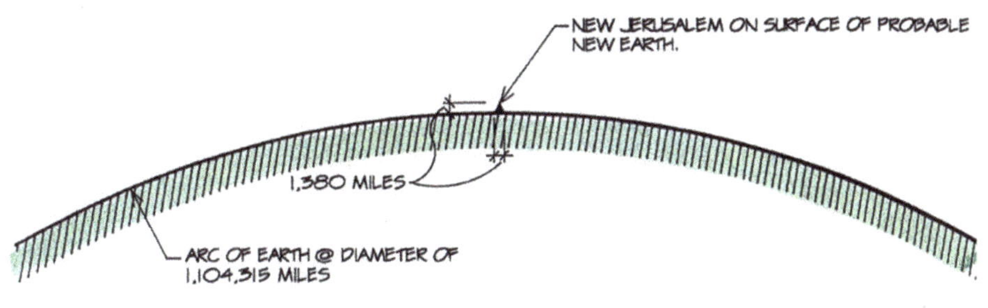

ILLUSTRATION:
View of the New Jerusalem if positioned on the surface of the New earth that is increased to the maximum allowable size according to the Law of Physics of the universe. (IF THE CITY IS A PYRAMID)

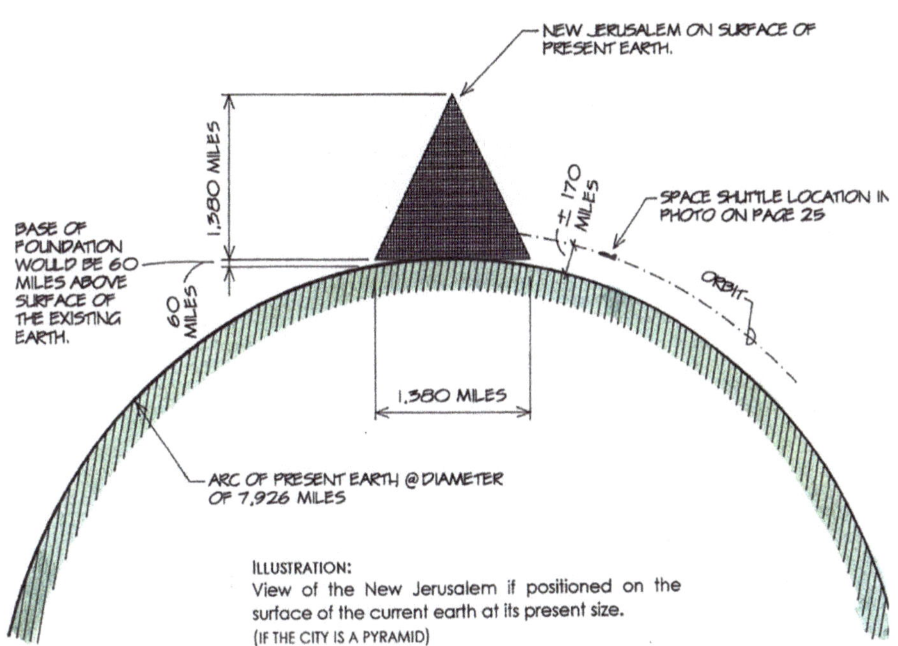

ILLUSTRATION:
View of the New Jerusalem if positioned on the surface of the current earth at its present size.
(IF THE CITY IS A PYRAMID)

PROBABLE COMPARITIVE SIZE OF THE NEXT NEW EARTH TO OUR HABITATAL EARTH TODAY

From about 310 miles above the surface of the earth begins the exosphere, which has no definite outer boundary but simply thins out until its density is no more than that of the interplanetary medium.

From an elevation of 400 miles space becomes an even greater hostile environment for Man, which contains cosmic radiation that can be fatal to an unshielded person, as well as the vacuum of space that can destroy an unprotected human body in just a few seconds by a major explosive decompression.

Based upon the inference that mankind will outgrow the new earth, the peopling of the universe will necessitate expanding human habitations throughout the billions and billions of galaxies in the universe. It is also a fact that the top of the city of New Jerusalem would extend 1380 miles out into a hostile space from the new earth if it is remade to a similar physical dimension as today's earth (a thousand miles further out than the Hubble space telescope.

It becomes obvious that God will increase the physical size of the new earth proportionally to a new atmosphere into its ideal and most perfect size, in the most perfect orbit, in a new solar system around the most efficient and perfect sun. All of this being made to accommodate the most perfect, heavenly city of New Jerusalem and the trillions of immortal natural humans occupying and possessing the land forever.

The relative size of the New Jerusalem extending above the surface of the new earth must be proportional to the earth upon which it sits to fit within God's order of the universe. The only way to accomplish this, unless God totally abandons the heavenly order of His creation, is by increasing the physical size of the new earth. Increasing the new earth's physical size even to the size indicated earlier still provides the harmony and equilibrium required by God's law of physics to maintain perfect order and balance in the galaxy.

It's not particularly important for us to know how large, but it is important to know the new earth and new heavens will, by necessity, be sufficiently changed to perfectly provide for God's and Man's habitation on the new earth and for the literal fulfillment of His long-range plan for peopling the entire universe. It is also quite obvious that a city with foundations, walls with gates and, *"a pure river of water of life, proceeding from the throne of God and of the Lamb"* is representative of a city that sits on the terrestrial ground, not a city that floats in space above the new earth.

Enter "Habitable planets in our Galaxy" in your browser to discover there are at least 300 million potentially *habitable planets in our galaxy,* NASA finds. See the artist's impression of a free-floating rogue planet being detected in *our* Milky Way *galaxy* using a technique called microlensing. Microlensing occurs when an object in space can warp space-time. Nov 5, 2020. It is an elongated and angled orbit that causes it to take 15,000 *Earth* years to complete one lap around its twin stars.

In the New City of Jerusalem, a river of Life, being both figurative as a picture of God's spirit flowing out to all mankind, and as a physical 'pure river,' will literally extend from the throne and flow out of 'the city' into the new earth, not into empty space. The Glory of God will so fill the entire city of New Jerusalem there will be no need for a special building such as a temple where His children (the saints) will communicate with Him.

> The glowing golden light of the city is:
> The Glory of God…and the Lamb. And the nations of those who are saved shall walk in its light, and the kings of the earth bring their glory and honor into it.
>
> *Revelation 21:24 (NKJV)*

> *But I saw no temple in it, for the Lord God Almighty and the Lamb are its temples. The city had no need of the sun or of the moon to shine in it, for the glory of God illuminated it. The Lamb is its light.*
>
> *Revelation 21:22, 23 (NKJV)*

This Scripture and other similar Scriptures at the beginning of this chapter do not refer to the outlying areas of the new earth outside the city but refer only to the actual physical city of New Jerusalem. There will be day and night outside the city, and the light that falls on this new earth will be the light from the new sun (the new sun must very definitely be a part of the new heavens.) God has told us in many different Scriptures that He plans to make a new heaven and a new earth. If He said it, He meant it!

> *Then He who sat on the throne said, 'Behold, I make all things new.' And He said to me, 'Write, for these words are true and faithful.'*
>
> *Revelation 21:5 (NKJV)*

We are told that the city itself is pure gold, like clear glass, and the foundations of the walls are adorned with precious stones. The city is perfect and has streets of gold lined with trees, as are the banks of the river of the 'water of life' that has its source from under the seat of the throne of God.

The trees along the bank are both beautiful and productive fruit trees that bear twelve kinds of fruit, a different one each month. These trees are the trees of life symbolizing the eternal life given to all who populate the new earth, and the fruit is for the inhabitants of the city, the saints who have their dwelling with God. These are the saints who are also called the 'overcomers' in the Bible.

> *He who has an ear, let him hear what the Spirit says to the churches. To him who overcomes I will give to eat from the tree of life, which is in the midst of the Paradise of God.*
>
> *Revelation 2:7 (NKJV)*

The leaves of these trees symbolize the absence of anything that brings physical or spiritual harm and are for the health of the nations who live outside the city and who occupy the new earth. These leaves serve as a remembrance to mankind that even in their new bodies (immortal) they are dependent on the Lord for life, strength, and health. They are preventive 'medicine,' not a cure for any sickness that will develop because all sickness has been removed from the earth.

This symbolic 'medicine' gives mankind a picture of the preserved health of the natural immortal people who live on the new earth, just as Adam's health and his descendant's health would have been preserved if he had eaten of the 'tree of life' in the Garden of Eden.

The nations (not the saints) who dwell on the earth outside of the walls of this beautiful city are the sinless, holy inhabitants with dwellings all across the new earth that will eventually include all habitable earth's throughout the galaxy, and then on to the other billions of galaxies throughout the universe as God's plan for peopling the universe unfolds throughout the age of ages.

It has been specifically promised that *"the meek shall inherit the earth"* (Matthew 5:5) and that the children of Israel shall dwell in it forever. So, if God's elect children will inhabit it forever, it will exist forever, in righteousness, for there will be no sin on the earth ever again.

> *And the nations (the body of righteous people) of those who are saved (the saints) shall walk in its light, and the kings (the saints) of the earth bring their glory and honor into it. Its gates shall not be shut at all by day (there shall be no night there).*
>
> *And they (the saints) shall bring the glory and the honor of the nations into it. But there shall by no*

means enter it anything that defiles or causes an abomination or a lie, but only those (the saints) who are written in the Lamb's Book of Life.

Revelation 21:24-27 (NKJV)

Also, your people (God's elect children of Israel) shall all be righteous; they shall inherit the land forever, the branch of My planting, the work of My hands, that I may be glorified.

Isaiah 66:21 (NKJV)

'For as the new heavens and the new earth which I will make shall remain before Me,' says the Lord, 'So shall your descendants (Israel's) and your name remain.'

Isaiah 66:22 (NKJV)

It is also obvious that God has always intended to populate the universe with a sinless, holy race of people, His elect people, the physical and spiritual (Gentile) Israel. We are assured of this due to the actual real presence of the 'tree of life' in the Garden of Eden, and also in the New Jerusalem, plus the presence of the 'river of life' that flows out from under the throne of God and His Christ.

The 'river of life' is both literal and figurative in the Scriptures because water has been used symbolically as an expression of the Spirit of God, and it also represents the real and literal eternal spiritual life that flows out from the presence of God to *all* the nations. Just as in the 'new birth' when Jesus comes into our heart, and we take on His Divine Nature and become a part of His Body, the Church, so will the eternal life-giving Spirit of God and His Holy Nature fill the lives of His 'elect' throughout the new earth.

Just as the temple of God was in the midst of Israel and within the Holy of Holies in the temple, God's spiritual presence was with Israel. However, as He was with Adam in the garden, God will physically return to the new earth at the beginning of the perfect age and reside with mankind.

The whole city of New Jerusalem will become like the new physical temple and the Throne of God 'the most holy place' or 'Holy of Holies,' while the earth and the entire habitable cosmos become the many courts around the temple that are contained within the entire Sanctuary of God's creation, the universe.

In discussing mankind during the perfect age, we should reflect on the life of Abraham, who has the sole distinction of being the Father of the Hebrews (Israel). He is our role model of a righteous man, a God-fearing man who was obedient to God's laws. Although faced with impossible odds, he had faith in God and trusted in God's promises for his life.

He also has the distinction of being second in importance of all-natural humans that have walked the earth, with Christ being number one. In many Biblical references, the God of Israel is even identified as the God of Abraham, and Israel herself is identified as the people 'of the God of Abraham'. He is today the prime example of a man of faith and the spiritual father of all Christian believers. It is because of his faith the Jew inherits the promised land on the new earth forever as God has promised, and we, the saints and His heirs, *"shall reign forever and ever."*

> *There will never be night again. People will not need the light of a lamp or the light of the sun. The Lord God will give them light. And they will rule like kings forever and ever.*
>
> *Revelation 22:5 (ERV)*

Israel (as a people) was the earthly bride of God just as the church is to become the bride of Christ. Israel was blessed and comforted with temporal (earthly) blessings, although now through unbelief, she is desolate and separated from God because of her rejection of Jesus, God's Son. Even so, the Bible tells us that *"she will be restored to righteousness and her children shall yet be as the sand of the sea."*

> *'For your Maker is your husband, the Lord of hosts is His name; and your Redeemer is the Holy One of Israel; He is called the God of the whole earth. For the Lord has called you like a woman forsaken and grieved in spirit, like a youthful wife when you were refused,' says your God.*
>
> *Isaiah 54:5-6 (NKJV)*

> *'Then it shall come to pass, when you are multiplied and increased in the land in those days,' says the Lord, 'that they will say no more, 'The ark of the covenant of the Lord.' It shall not come to mind, nor shall they remember it, nor shall they visit it, nor shall it be made anymore.' At that time Jerusalem shall be called The Throne of the Lord, and all the nations shall be gathered to it, to the name of the Lord, to Jerusalem.*
>
> *Jeremiah 3:16-17 (NKJV)*

These natural men, Jew and Gentile, will have offspring forever in the 'new earth' and God promises that He will always hear their prayer. With sin having been eradicated, there will be no impediment to perfect communication with God, forever and ever more.

In this future paradise, natural, immortal mankind will flourish in joyful and purposeful living under the rule and reign of Christ and the saints—the joint-heirs with Christ.

> *They shall build houses and inhabit them; they shall plant vineyards and eat their fruit. They shall not build, and another inhabit; they shall not plant, and another eat; for as the days of a tree, so shall be the days of My people, and My elect (Israel) shall long enjoy the work of their hands.*
>
> *They shall not labor in vain, nor bring forth children for trouble; for they shall be the descendants of the blessed of the Lord, and their offspring with them.*
>
> *Isaiah 65:21-23 (NKJV)*

From He who was almost dead, God brought forth seed unto himself and for His glory throughout eternity. Therefore, because of this faith, the descendants of righteous Abraham will populate the earth and expand out into the billions and billions of other new earths (planets) within the new heavens' as eternity progresses in a continuous infinite expansion without end.

All these, the holy race of people who will fulfill the long-range plan God has in motion today for mankind, are the actual and spiritual children of Abraham. They will be gloriously beautiful and perfect. Their assignment will be to continue to multiply and fill the earth just as Adam and Noah were assigned by God before them, only this time, sin will not be a factor with which mankind will have to contend.

> *The Lord your God will make you abound in all the work of your hand, in the fruit of your body, in the increase of your livestock, and in the produce of your land for good. For the Lord will again rejoice over you for good, as He rejoiced over your fathers.*
>
> *Deuteronomy 30:9 (NKJV)*

This prophecy confirms that in the 'new earth,' the descendants of the natural men and women who themselves are the descendants of Abraham who survived Armageddon, both Jews and Gentiles will enjoy children, crops, cattle, and fruit throughout eternity. In other words, prosperity beyond measure.

> *Beloved, now we (the believers) are children of God; and it has not yet been revealed what we shall be, but we know that when He is revealed, we shall be like Him, for we (the glorified saints) shall see Him as He is.*
>
> *1 John 3:2 (NKJV)*

John tells us that this knowledge (1 John 3:2) will purify our spiritual walk, and we will be glorified as Christ is glorified.

> *"And everyone who has this hope in Him purifies himself, just as He is pure"*
>
> *1 John 3:3, (NKJV)*

The two above scriptures are the most wonderfully awesome prophetic promises in the Christian church, a real life-giving doctrine when received into a heart of love that is powerful enough to separate one from the love of the world. As a part of God's long-range plan, this promise reveals the majesty of God's glorious legacy to be inherited by His children, a privilege shared with only the elite few believers (the saints) who choose Jesus as Lord and Savior. Those who wash in the Blood of the Lamb and have their names written in the Lamb's Book of Life will enter the gates to the Holy City, the heavenly city of New Jerusalem to live, rule, and reign forever and ever.

> *Love never fails. But whether there are prophecies, they will fail; whether there are tongues, they will cease; whether there is knowledge, it will vanish*

> *away. For we know in part and we prophesy in part. But when that which is perfect has come, then that which is in part will be done away.*
>
> *1 Corinthians 13:8-10 (NKJV)*

With all mortal limits removed, Man's capacity for knowledge and his God-given abilities will be gloriously unlimited. Mankind will significantly excel far beyond any previous mortal accomplishments, even including the astounding and marvelous wonders that are accomplished during the glorious Millennial reign of Jesus Christ.

Paul has told all Christian believers that in the ages to come, our Father God intends to shower us (His saints) abundantly with His exceeding riches. In addition to becoming like Jesus, when we see Him face to face and reign as joint heirs with Him, He will bless us far beyond the limits of human comprehension. Oh, the Glory of Heaven that we the glorified saints of God will receive and experience as reflections "Of His Glory."

> *But God, who is rich in mercy, because of His great love with which He loved us (the saints) even when we were dead in trespasses, made us alive together with Christ (by grace you have been saved), and raised us up together, and made us sit together in the heavenly places in Christ Jesus, that in the ages to come He might show the exceeding riches of His grace in His kindness toward us in Christ Jesus.*
>
> *For by grace you have been saved through faith, and that not of yourselves; it is the gift of God.*
>
> *Ephesians 2:4-8 (NKJV)*

> *Christians who are truly the "sons of God through faith in Christ Jesus" are promised an eternal life where "we shall always be with the Lord.*
>
> *Galatians 3:26 and 1 Thessalonians 4:17*

Then, even beyond the glorious existence prepared for the saints, God has promised eternal glorious life for all of mankind. An immortal but natural, human life that will be perfect, in absolute harmony with the will of God and through which man will bring God eternal joy and happiness. Mankind's blessings will be immeasurable as the peopling of God's universe unfolds, and sinless, holy mankind lives for God and is in the ever-presence of His glory.

> *"We will walk in the name of the Lord our God forever and ever"*
>
> *Micah 4:5, (NKJV)*

All of mankind will have the indwelling presence of God's Spirit within them and will forever be in the presence of God as manifested through the saints as heavenly reflections of His glory, and as seen in the actual presence of His Son Jesus Christ in all His glory. Mankind will also witness the 'Shekinah' Glory (visible presence of God) emanating from the holy city of new Jerusalem as well as the glory of God illuminating the entire holy city.

Do you truly trust Jesus?

Let us digress for a moment. In Matthew 14:29, Jesus invited Peter to join him and walk on water toward Him. He is also inviting you to join Him in the glorious supernatural life He has planned for you, following His example in faith, but what has been keeping you from getting out of the boat if you are still just sitting there contemplating what your *next* move might be?

> Jesus said to Peter, *"Come to Me,"* So Peter got down out of the boat. He walked on the water and he came towards Jesus. But then Peter saw that the wind was still blowing strongly. He became afraid and he began to go down into the water. He shouted to Jesus, *"Lord, save me!"* Immediately, Jesus put out His hand and took hold of Peter, *"You should trust Me more than you do. Why did you not believe that I could help you?*
>
> *Matthew 14:29-31 (Easy English Bible 2018)*

Our life should be focused on Jesus alone, not the storms that try to distract us from our faith. He may not come immediately upon our 'beck and call,' but He cares, and He will come to you if you trust in Him. If you read more of this scripture, you will discover, the storm did not stop until Jesus gets into the boat. Hallelujah!

> *When you go through deep waters, I will be with you. When you go through rivers of difficulty, you will not drown. When you walk through the fire of oppression, you will not be burned up; the flames will not consume you.*
>
> *Isaiah 43:2 (NLT)*

DEPICTION OF CHRIST REACHING THROUGH THE WATER

HAVENLIGHT FINE ART | PAINTINGS
BY YONGSUNG KIM
AD·WWW.HAVENLIGHT.COM/YONGSUNG-KIM

Encounter the Blessings of God's Grace. e-Book, click on or copy the following link onto your browser and believe that Jesus is always there to hold onto your hand.[6]

https://encounteringpeace.libsyn.com/blessing-of-gods-grace

CHAPTER 19

An unparalleled life of "Beauty and Glory."

I have heard it said that we the saints would have a city home in the New Jerusalem and a country home on the new earth; and what a country home the new habitable domain of Natural Immortal Mankind will provide for God's saints and His supernatural Elect descendants of Abraham during the "Aeon's of the Aeon's." Even most of the personal computers in the world today won't extend out to the numerical number of mankind that could inhabit the new habitable domain's, planned by God, if increased to the size mentioned in the last chapter.

If the new earth is increased to the maximum size that the law of physics will permit in the functional order of the universe, the new earth could have a surface area of over 3.8 trillion square miles. This is almost 20,000 times larger than the present earth, and its circumference would be 3.5 million miles as compared to 25 thousand miles for the present earth.

Based on a proportional comparison of the two using a classic movie as the basis upon which to make our comparison, the movie "Around the World in 80 Days" would have to be renamed "Around the World in 30 Years." This is representative of the comparable time it would take a comparable size balloon to circle the new earth.

The total number of Natural Immortal Mankind that could potentially occupy the new earth, if the total maximum population was based upon each person being apportioned an area the size of a football field, would be 2.4 quadrillion's (2.4×10^{15}) people. Presently the apportioned area of land for each person on the earth is the equivalent area of 24.5 football fields or approximately 25 times greater than the number we just used as a comparison.

What this all means is that even with this significantly high concentration of human population on the new earth of this enormous size, it would still require over 8.4 trillion new earth's (habitable planets) of this size just to contain the population of Abraham's descendants based upon the number, $2x10^{28}$ "dust of the earth." To Man, this is an incredibly large number, but is it for God? I doubt it very seriously, considering the immense size of just the current known universe.

Another interesting comparison is the relative height of the heavenly city of New Jerusalem on a planet the size of our present earth, compared with the example we just used as the maximum probable size of the new earth. Proportionally, the New Jerusalem with a height of 1,380 miles on the new earth is the equivalent of a 10-mile high building on the existing earth.

The proportional equivalent (footprint) size on the present earth is a square ten miles on each side. Coincidentally, the Millennial city of Jerusalem during Christ's 1,000-year reign is 10 miles square. A building 10 miles square and 10 miles high is physically impossible to construct today and would be almost twice as high as Mount Everest. But the Architect and Builder of the city of New Jerusalem is God Himself, so I am certain even a structure 1,380 miles high on the new earth is very possible with God.

Mankind has never built any building even one mile high, although visionary architect Frank Lloyd Wright designed one in 1956. The unstable conditions of today's earth is a limiting factor for building anything this size (the tallest building in today's world is Burj Khalifa in Dubai, the United Arab Emirates, which is 163 stories and 2,717 feet tall, just a little over half a mile.), but the new earth won't be under the curse nor have the instability of our present planet Earth, therefore what is impossible on Earth today will not be impossible on the new Earth.

The city of New Jerusalem will, no doubt, be the most incredibly beautiful and magnificent creation Almighty God will ever present to His elite children, the saints. It will be the most awesomely prepared city of mansions for the 'abiding place' of God and the *saints*. It will no doubt be identified as the 'first wonder of the universe' in comparison to all the immense glory of the new heavens and new Earth.

The entire city is prepared by God, built by God, and given to those who are faithful to God and obey His commands. The Scriptures describe the city, as well as any mortal, has the ability to understand, with the key to its indescribable beauty summed up in the simple phrase 'pure gold, like transparent glass,' and this is just a description of the street.

The city of New Jerusalem will be the most grandeur sight in all of God's entire creation, totally illuminated by the Glory of God, and will serve as the eternal dwelling place of God among His redeemed saints forever.

Frank Lloyd Wright's Design of a mile-high building called "The Illinois" compared to the 1,380-mile-high city of the eternal New Jerusalem is totally indescribable. On 16 October 1956, architect Frank Lloyd Wright, then 89 years old, unveiled his design for the tallest skyscraper in the world, a remarkable mile-high tripod spire named "*The Illinois*," proposed for a site in Chicago.

Also known as the Illinois Mile-High Tower, Wright's skyscraper would stand 528 floors and 5,280 feet (1,609 meters) tall plus antenna; more than four times the height of the Empire State Building in New York City, then the tallest skyscraper in the world at 102 floors and 1,250 feet (380 meters) tall plus antenna.

The single super-tall skyscraper was intended to free up the ground plane by eliminating the need for other large skyscrapers in its vicinity. This was consistent with Wright's distributed urban planning concept known as Broadacre City, which he introduced in the mid-1930s and continued to advocate until his death in 1959.

The above information was copied from an article published in the below link. Click on this link if you are reading an e-book, if not open this link in your browser to see the extraordinary genius of this architect.

https://lynceans.org/all-posts/
frank-lloyd-wrights-1956-mile-high-skyscraper-the-illinois/

My purpose for utilizing this illustration is to compare today's earth (Our current habitation) with God's long-range plan for immortal mankind. Wright's design for the "Illinois building" was based upon his belief in a vision of future urban planning. He could see in his minds-eye what our earth would become if we kept expanding in a horizontal direction. Well, he was right. Look at where we are today worldwide.

In the holy scriptures, God has given us a consistent vision of the future habitations that God promised to Abraham, Isaac and Jacob, stating that their descendants would be greater than the dust of the earth, the stars in the heavens and the sand of the sea. To visualize the manifestation of this promise, our universe is consistently expanding and appears to have been doing so since creation and will be continuing forever.

The description God gave for the New City of Jerusalem in the age of ages depicts a massive, colossal structure of such incredible size and beauty that it is difficult for the human mind to even comprehend. This City of the future has been calculated to be 1,380 miles high with a square base with each of the four sides 1,380 miles wide. To me, this is a revelation of mankind's future cities throughout the universe of universes, within God's amazing creation. Not just a single building but awesome mega-buildings within God's unlimited habitation surrounded by "Terrestrial Paradises" like the Garden of Eden.

Far-fetched to many but realistic in my minds-eye. Imagine urban sprawl to end all urban sprawl if going vertical isn't the order intended by our Father God.

> *But now they desire a better country, that is, heavenly: wherefore God is not ashamed to be called their God: for He hath prepared for them a city.*
>
> *Hebrews 11:16 (KJV)*

> *But ye are come unto mount Zion, and unto the city of the living God, the heavenly Jerusalem, and to an innumerable company of angels.*
>
> *Hebrews 12:22 (KJV)*

The two above verses are speaking of we the saints, dear friend, not the natural immortal people who will inhabit the new earth. You, dear child of God, not only live in the Kingdom, but you live with the King, forever. And you, dear Saint, are a wondrously glorified reflection "Of His Glory," and as such, you contribute to the glorious illumination of the New Jerusalem.

> *And the greatness of the kingdoms under the Whole Heaven shall be given to the people, the Saints of the Most High.*
>
> *Daniel 7:27 (NKJV)*

> *"Then the righteous will shine forth as the sun in the kingdom of their Father" Matthew 13:43, (NKJV).*

> *Those who are wise shall Shine Like the Brightness of the firmament, and those who turn many to righteousness LIKE THE STARS forever and ever.*
>
> *Daniel 12:3 (NKJV)*

Jesus is the personification of His Father's Glory, and we, the saints and righteous children of God through Jesus Christ are also glorified when we see Him face to face. We are made to be like Him, becoming God's heirs and joint heirs with Jesus, being transformed into the radiance of His Glory.

> *Who being the brightness OF HIS GLORY, and the express image of His person, and upholding all things by the Word of His power, when He had by Himself purged our sins, sat down at the right hand of the Majesty on high…*
>
> *Hebrews 1:3 (NKJV)*

Jesus is the radiance of His glory and the express image "of His Person" is the full and final revelation of God. We then, being like Him, reflect the pure radiance Of His Glory.

The entire city of New Jerusalem shines with the brilliance Of His Glory, the brightness of which manifests God's wonderful, perfect presence in the midst of His elect people (physical and spiritual Israel), as they continue to populate the universe(s) forever and ever in fulfillment of God's plan.

> *"Of the increase of His government (Jesus) and peace there will be no end" (Isaiah 9:7, NKJV).*

The 'saints,' as they carry out their respective God-given assignments to the nations, manifest God's wonderful luminous presence to the sinless, holy race of people throughout the entire glorious universe, with the perfect reflection of His glory that is eternally revealed through them.

> *"And they (the saints) shall bring the glory and the honor of the nations into it" (Revelation 21:26, NKJV).*

> *"No one shall enter 'but only those who are written in the Lambs book of life' (the saints) (Revelation 21:27, NKJV).*

A Re-visit to the glorious city, New Jerusalem:

The joy and abundant love of our Triune God will totally and completely permeate throughout the entire city of God, the New Jerusalem. The fellowship and glorious happiness shared by all the 'saints' of God will also be shared by the Angels of heaven.

Throughout all of eternity, we (the saints) will have the honor of loving fellowship with all of God's saints from Adam to the last righteous man, woman, and child who come into the heavenly city of God, as well as all the angels who have been with God for all the previous aeon's and aeon's.

But of all the glorious fellowship we will have, none will be more heavenly than the personal fellowship we will have with our Lord and our God. Imagine the absolute fullness of joy as Jesus puts His arms around you and hugs you in the purest, most holy agape love in all the realm of God's holy being. Oh! Wow! Come, Lord Jesus, Come!

> *You have come to God, the judge of all men, to the spirits of righteous men made perfect, to Jesus the*

> *mediator of a new covenant, and to the sprinkled blood that speaks a better word than the blood of Abel.*
>
> *Hebrews 12:22-24 (NIV)*

This glorious city that shines for all of eternity like a beacon of love to the nations of all the earth is the center of much discussion today, and rightly so, it is our future home with God. It has been said that a house is not a home without inhabitants, and this is likewise true of the New Jerusalem.

The New Jerusalem is not a city without inhabitants, so we, the glorified saints of God, 'His children,' along with the angels of heaven, our Lord Jesus Christ, and the presence of Almighty God Himself make this place the "City of New Jerusalem," the dwelling place *"Of His Glory."*

The base footprint of the city is 1,904,400 square miles of area and is approximately two-thirds of the land area of the United States mainland and three times larger than Alaska. The highest point in the US is Mount McKinley in Alaska, at an elevation of 20,320 feet, or 3.85 miles, high. Compared to the city of New Jerusalem, that is 360 times higher.

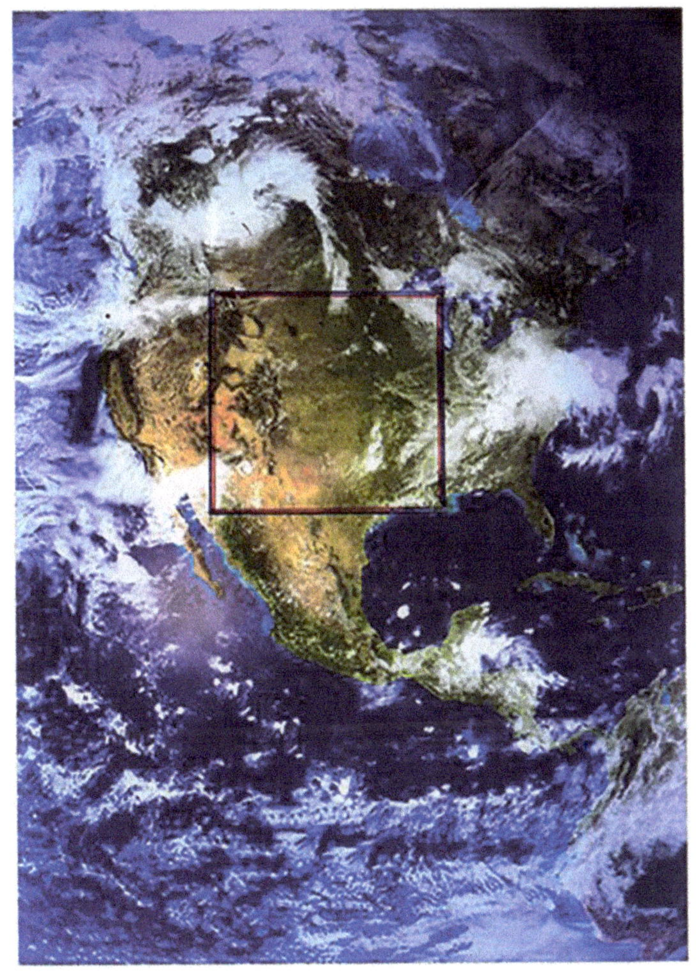

IMAGINE THE NEW CITY OF JERUSALEM
1,380 MILES WIDE AT EACH BASE ON THIS EARTH

The above square outline over the USA extends from Memphis to Phoenix 1,380 +/- mi E to W and from the US/ Canadian border to Austin 1,380+/- mi, N to S. & 1,380 high.

Credits: NASA Goddard Space Center Image:
Reto Stockli & Robert Simmon

It is interesting to note that a 'pyramid' is called triangular, square, or hexagonal according to whether its base is a triangle, a square, or a hexagon. In the case of the Great Pyramid in Egypt, it is called a 'square pyramid' because each side of its base is equal (756 feet). As stated earlier, it is also highly probable the holy mountain of God, the city of New Jerusalem, is likewise a three-dimensional pyramidal shape laid out as a 'square.'

> *The city is laid out as a square; its length is as great as its breadth. And he measured the city with the reed: twelve thousand furlongs. Its length, breadth, and height are equal. Then he measured its wall: one hundred and forty-four cubits*; according to the measure of a man, that is, of an angel. The construction of its wall was of jasper; and the city was pure gold, like clear glass.*
>
> *Revelation 21:16-18 (NKJV)*

*Note: If the Hebrew cubit of measurement is used (25.025 inches), the wall is over 300 feet thick, not 216 feet, as its wall is sometimes identified. This cubit of measurement is the same one used in the construction of the Great Pyramid that embodies much mathematical and astronomical knowledge. ie: the number 'Pi' (3.14159) denoting the ratio of the circumference of a circle to its diameter is determined from its dimensions.

> *And he carried me away in the Spirit to a great and high mountain, and showed me the great city, the holy Jerusalem, descending out of heaven from God, having the glory of God. Her light was like a most precious stone, like a jasper stone, clear as crystal.*
>
> *Revelation 21:10-11 (NKJV)*

Then I, John, saw the holy city, New Jerusalem, coming down out of heaven from God, prepared as a bride adorned for her husband. And I heard a loud voice from heaven saying 'Behold, the tabernacle of God is with men, and He will dwell with them, and they shall be His people. God Himself will be with them and be their God.'

Revelation 21:2-3 (NKJV)

John calls the New Jerusalem a mountain, and since a mountain is similarly shaped like a pyramid, it stands to reason this is the likely shape of God's city. A geometric pyramidal form that is 1380 miles high with a square base of 1380 miles per side has 876,024,000 cubic miles of total volumetric area.

If the city of New Jerusalem is similarly shaped and is this size, the volume of space apportioned per *Saint** within the city would equal 129 billion cubic feet. (The equivalent of 16,000 domed football stadiums—quite a 'mansion,' wouldn't you agree?)

*Based upon an estimated number of righteous people of all mankind since Adam, as suggested in Willmington's Guide to the Bible, this number exceeds 1 billion people (saints).

And behold, the word of the Lord came to him, saying, 'This one shall not be your heir, but one who will come from your own body shall be your heir.'

Then He brought Abraham outside and said,

"Look now toward heaven and count the stars if you are able to number them.' And He said to him, 'So

> *shall your descendants be.' And he believed in the Lord, and He accounted it to him for righteousness."*
>
> *Genesis 15:4-5 (NKJV)*

The occupation of the land is still an important part of God's plan for mankind. Abraham and his descendants were promised land, but Israel only enjoyed a partial blessing of the land even though God has always wanted to extend these blessings to include all lands.

In the city of New Jerusalem, there is neither marrying nor giving in marriage for those who live and dwell in the city are the righteous saints of God, the glorified 'sons of God' who have all received their inheritance from God as His heirs and joint-heirs with Jesus, and who also rule and reign over mankind.

But on the new earth, and eventually, throughout the universe, mankind will continue to marry, and procreation of humankind will continue on for the Aeon's of the Aeons' as the peopling of the universe(s) fulfill God's long-range plan.

There is, however, one vast difference with mankind during this perfect age, Man is sinless and, having been made perfect, is now an 'immortal being' who will live for all eternity in the fullness of God's abundant blessings.

> *"I will make a man more precious than fine gold; even a man than the golden wedge of Ophir"*
>
> *Isaiah 13:12, (KJV)*

Genesis 15:5 is the key to God's diary, in which, His long-range plan is identified. God took Abraham outside and said, "Look up at the heavens and count the stars…so shall your offspring be." God promised Abraham that He would make Abraham's descendants "as numerous as the dust of the earth; as numerous as the sands of the sea and the stars in the sky," and then added a phrase, "which cannot be counted."

Thus, I believe this scripture is informing us of God's desire for His creation to have the actual and spiritual children of Abraham to populate the earth and expand out into the billions and billions of galaxies, and into other habitable land's (Earths') throughout the universe, as the peopling of the universe progresses into a continuous eternal expansion without end.

With mankind expanding out into the whole universe, we, the inhabitants of the New Jerusalem, will also have our rule and reign with Jesus expanded forever and ever as His government and peace continue to increase without end. Thus, the descendants of Abraham populate the universe, and the "righteous saints of God," His children, and we, his kings, lords, and priests, reign over all of God's creation with our Lord Jesus Christ as it continues expanding forever.

Just as the 1000-year (Millennial) Reign of Christ provides natural mortal mankind an opportunity to grow and prosper in blessings from meaningful work, so will the perfect age increase mankind's abilities and greatly multiply their potential growth for unparalleled abundance, advancement, and honor. Perfected mankind will have no restraining hindrance over their creative ability to bring unprecedented glory to God.

Mankind will exercise 100% of their intellects as compared to Man today, who only uses an estimated one tenth of 1% of the brain's potential ability. Although Adam and Eve never experienced immortality but remained mortal and eventually died, they could talk to all of God's creatures and very probably to all of nature as well.

Remember, Adam named all the creatures created by God, and their total numbers amounted to somewhere around 17,000 different species. Adam could probably also personally communicate with each one of them while he was still in the garden.

We have previously mentioned that mankind today is probably 95% blind to the total color scheme that exists in God's creation and 98% deaf to the many sounds that exist in the creation. But this all changes on the new earth when mankind is made perfect, and God reveals to each person their own special assignment(s), and empowers them with His perfect ability to accomplish all that they can be, to bring Glory and Honor to the Father.

Humanity was originally created to become a powerful race of beings, not the weaklings they have become through sin. They were created to have and to use God's power of authority, spiritually, mentally, physically, and emotionally. The church, through Christ, has and is walking in this authority today, but only in a very limited way and without the total fullness God has always intended.

God still intends today for mankind as a race to have His complete power of authority over all of creation. He has assured Abraham's descendants' that this will become fully realized at mankind's' physical regeneration from mortality in the Millennial Kingdom to the state of immortality as humanity enters the perfect age and inhabits the new earth. (Habitations throughout the universe)

When Adam sinned, not only did he lose, but all of mankind lost the perfect state of authority that God placed in Adam. Humankind was intended to have dominion over all of God's creation and be in responsible charge of the entire earth and all of nature. But mankind's divine image and likeness were lost upon Adam's sin, and the human race became devil-centered instead of God-centered as Adam and Eve were lied, too, and tricked by Satan into handing the power and authority given by God over to the devil.

Jesus came and restored mankind back to a righteous relationship with God, and He also gave immortal humanity back His Godliness (holiness) and His authority (dominion). Jesus redeemed the earth and the human race itself from the cause of sin and the domination of Satan, and upon entering the new earth, God will return the absolute fullness of His divine nature to His 'elect,' His sinless, holy race of people—immortal mankind.

Neither Adam nor mankind have ever fully entered the fullness of the relationship that God has planned for Himself. Adam's earthly body was not a glorified body (John 7:39), but he had a perfect human body because there was no curse on the earth yet. Adam's body was neither mortal (from the seed of man) nor immortal, but his offspring were the first natural mortal humans to begin the population of the earth.

If Adam had instead chosen the Tree of Life, then he would have been sealed in a perfect relationship with God forever. But he chose the wrong tree, which brought sin and death to the human race. What do you think would have happened if Adam had eaten from the Tree of Life? He would have lived forever! Don't ever be angry with Adam, he sinned, but the "Devil made him do it!" We have all sinned! Most likely more than once.

That perfect relationship with God has been delayed over the past 6,000 years, and it will continue to be delayed for a little while longer to allow the 1000 year Millennial Reign of Christ to come into fruition, but then at its conclusion when the 7,000 years are passed, God will usher in the perfect age at the beginning of the 8th thousand years since Adam. It is interesting to note that the number 8 means 'a new beginning' (new birth), and the name 'Octavo' means eighth.

It is likewise interesting to know that 'octillion' is a word derived from 'Octavo,' and the actual quantified number scientists have concluded represents the "dust of the earth, is '20 octillions'—the number '20' meaning 'redemption.' And in Hebrew society, any forfeited land could be redeemed by the nearest of kin. Glory to God! It seems that the descendants of Abraham do just this with the land forfeited by their fathers.

What does this mean to you, dear reader? As kings, lords, and priests—joint-heirs with Christ who rule and reign with Christ forever? Well, just visualize the implication this number of Abraham's descendants will have on the government of the Kingdom of Heaven and the saints who are assigned to the vast populations of these nations of God's people.

As kings, lords, priests, and joint-heirs with Jesus, if each of 'us,' the saints, were apportioned an equal number of these, God's elect people, to shepherd and mentor under our reign with Christ, we would each receive responsibility for '20 quintillion' people (20 x 10^{18}) a number 500 million times greater than all humanity since Adam, and over 3 billion times more than all mankind alive on planet earth today.

Just imagine the government Jesus will have in place to maintain the smooth operation and performance of all the functions related to the universes' people, organizational systems, and public affairs. Knowing our Lord and King, it is certain to be just as harmonious and efficient as His organization during the feeding of the 5,000. It will, however, consist of a much greater total number of people as shown by the following illustration like the one shown to you earlier:

20,000,000,000,000,000,000,000,000,000 (20 octillion)
- 20,000,000,000,000,000,000 (20 quintillion)
apportioned to you)
19,999,999,980,000,000,000,000,000,000
- 20,000,000,000,000,000,000 (20 quintillion)
apportioned to me)
19,999,999,960,000,000,000,000,000,000* (apportioned to
all the other saints)

The above number is 19 octillions, 999 septillions, 999 sextillions, 960 quintillion more people than ever existed on the earth since Adam and Eve. Impossible, you say, not for *Our God* who created the Universe of Universe's where all immortal humankind shall continue to dwell forever.

Now, we know that God is not going to apportion out responsibility for His elect in this manner. Besides, this would not be in keeping with the way He has measured our blessings in the past. However, it is reasonable to conclude that He might assign and organize His elect, 'the descendants of Abraham,' in much the same way the talents were assigned to the faithful servants.

As you can now begin to comprehend the awesome magnitude of God's plan for peopling the universe, you can begin to see why the Scriptures infer something much grander in scale and glory than most people can imagine. The eternal world of God's realm is far more magnificent than the eternal world mankind has visualized in their mortal mind. It is obviously a world that only our God can 'see' not imagine, and *He* has plans to "see" this accomplished.

But glory to God, we the saints get to jointly participate with Christ in the development and manifestation of His long-range plan. We are gloriously blessed to be assigned the responsibility of guiding and mentoring natural immortal mankind on the path of continuing eternal accomplishment in fulfilling all that God has planned for His elect throughout the 'aeon's of the aeon's.'

As you were growing up, how many times do you remember hearing something negative about your peer group, those with whom you associated due to your status, age, or likeness? Look at those who have associated with their peers as the 'Generation X and Y groups, and Gen "Z," which identifies today's Generation—a peer group with some commonality of interests and beliefs, made up of a large number of Christian believers mentioned a few chapters ago.

Hanging this tag on all young people who belong to this peer group is an injustice, but it does present an interesting challenge to the 'saved' youth within the group. In these 'last days,' I believe this unique peer group has an unparalleled opportunity to become the Generation that will help spread the Gospel to *all* the Nations. I believe they have caught the vision of God's long-range plan and will be proclaiming the coming of "the Kingdom of Heaven."

This action would single them out as God's high-performance generation and would catapult this group into America's spotlight as a peer group with a commonality of purpose. A purpose of which no jaded and condemning society could sway them away from the truth. A purpose for which to live and die for—proclaiming the soon return of our Lord, Jesus Christ. Why? Because the finish line for this race of life is just ahead! Are you ready?

When we join all the other righteous saints in Heaven and receive our crowns and rewards, we will be joining with the largest peer group ever assembled, "The Sons of God." Have you ever before considered yourself to be a peer of Matthew, Mark, Luke, and John? What about Melchizedek, Methuselah, Abraham, Moses, David, and Solomon? Rehab, Mary (the Mother of Jesus), Sarah, or Elizabeth?

Your peer group will include all the billion or so righteous from Adam, you will know them, and they will know you. You will be known in Heaven just as all others will know you.

> *For now, we see through a glass, darkly; but then face to face: now I know in part; but then shall I know even as also I am known.*
>
> *1 Corinthians 13:12 (KJV)*

In addition to all these saints of old, you will be known and will know all your family from generation to generation throughout history. Then every day throughout eternity, you will be in the glorious presence of God, as will those around you, family and friends alike, who will all be manifesting the actual realized radiant reflection of His glory.

You and every Saint in your entire peer group will shine with the actual real quintessence* of His glory. (*The highest essence of God's nature and magnificence in its purest, holiest, and most concentrated representation.) Aside from the glorious existence of the supernatural saints, the nature of natural immortal mankind's life and the magnificent world within which they will live for all eternity is incredibly glorious beyond human imagination and is truly 'heaven on earth.'

In Revelation 21:1, we are told the first heaven and first earth were 'passed' away, not destroyed to annihilation, but changed from one condition of physical existence to another, a 'regeneration' or 'restoration.' The word "paliggenesia" in Greek is the same word Jesus used when He promised His disciples a 'regeneration' in the earth. Paliggenesia is also the same word Paul used in his letter to Titus (3:5) when he referred to the 'regeneration' of humanity.

The 'seventh day' of Genesis was connected to the 'old creation,' which was imperfect and pointed to the Millennium, but the 'eighth day' (new beginning) as mentioned a few pages back, has to do with God's perfect creation. The new heavens and the new earth are the symbols of what is called the 'perfect age.' They point to the new beginning and the start of eternity into the Aeons of the Aeons', i.e.: (the Ages of the Ages').

Since all the spirits of evil and mankind's sinful nature have been removed from the heavens and the earth forever, all those things that caused germs, sickness, death, and disobedience have been literally annihilated from the sphere of Man's existence and from the whole of creation.

There will never again be anything destructive in creation, no storms, earthquakes, floods, fires, plagues, famine, and no pests, etc., etc.—not even a fly or mosquito to pester or annoy mankind. The age-old characteristic word that best describes this perfect age is 'utopia,' a perfect, pure, and holy utopian society of Godly natural immortal human beings. The perfect age gives birth to a society established under God's ideal conditions of eternal life and advances His sinless, holy human race to exceedingly great heights of realized perfection and societal accomplishments. And throughout eternity, the billions and billions of nations within all His creation will bring God continually expanding and unprecedented honor and glory.

God's new habitation for mankind will be unparalleled in splendor and accomplishment. No doubt a fine mist will water the whole of the new earth as it did in the Garden of Eden, with plant and animal life in full, unparalleled Edenic beauty and glory. The whole 'habitation' will forever blossom with total complete health and vigor, with glorious green vegetation and beautiful flowers of colors we've never seen, covering the landscape of all earthly paradises throughout the new heavens.

There will be 'no more sea,' oceans will have even disappeared from Man's vocabulary, but there will no doubt still be an abundance of large bodies of water, rivers and streams, pools, ponds and lakes for their beauty, enjoyment, and for the fish and other aquatic creatures.

All the various multitude of creatures that will inhabit earth will be loving, domesticated, and beautiful, surpassing even all the beauty of the present earth's grand species. The whole earth will be like a marvelous animal sanctuary for mankind's pleasure, enjoyment, and love.

What a magnificent, breath-taking experience it will be as mankind is surrounded by such unparalleled beauty and glory. What a delight it will be to see children running and playing with all of God's creatures, without a care in the world for fear of anything or anyone—anywhere! For Man and all of nature will co-exist; in total complete harmony and grace.

As we previously discussed, there is to be an abundance of meaningful productive 'work' for natural mankind during the 1000-year Millennium that will bring great joy and satisfaction.

The work activities of mankind during the Millennium, after the initial cleanup, will also be an example of the glorious future they will enjoy in the perfect age with God. The very existence of righteous mankind during the Millennium will be a type and shadow of the complete fullness of purpose and ultimate magnificence that natural immortal mankind will enjoy throughout eternity on the new Earth.

The work of advancing mankind's achievements throughout the entire universe for the honor and glory of God and the continuous advancement of His long-range plan for peopling the universe is a highly esteemed objective for all of mankind. The fullness of joy and peace that will come with the satisfaction of accomplishing 'the work' assigned to mankind will be rewarded above and beyond any present earthly measure.

Mankind will immensely enjoy the work because of the wonderful satisfaction of knowing that God is so highly honored by their accomplishments. Besides, as they honor God, He honors them with His abundant blessings and showers them with His infinite love. With all immortal mankind's achievements throughout the new earth and the new heavens, the built environment of the eternal cities and the physical centers of activity throughout the habitations of the universe can't even begin to be imagined. Even with the aid of the world's most advanced computer graphics, it is impossible to visually portray the image and likeness of any part of this, the future glorious Kingdom of Heaven.

In my own mind's eye, I can picture a future city of enormous proportions due to the vast size of the city of New Jerusalem. Even though this is the eternal dwelling place of God and all the saints, its great magnitude suggests that cities of the future 'perfect age' will themselves be perfect in every detail. The absolute beauty of the natural landscape created by God is impossible for us to even imagine today.

With the actual physical extraordinary size of the New Jerusalem and the theorized ultimate size of the new earth that is regenerated from this present planet, the cities of the future will no doubt be multi-layered mega structures of perfect proportions and scale. Urban sprawl will be eliminated forever and replaced with beauty.

The building materials will be of an equally eternal quality themselves and very probably don't exist today. We know the city of New Jerusalem is transparent gold and precious stones, but the future cities of the nations will no doubt be of different materials but still of an eternal quality beyond human description today.

I firmly believe that the science fiction imaginations of the entertainment world have depicted many good examples of vastly enormous future cities that may be types and shadows of the probable ones that will come to fruition. These cities are themselves transparent with great cavernous volumes connected by moving walks and streets. They have been depicted with multitudes of flying and hovering vehicles of conveyance traversing the open cavernous spaces that even appear to ascend and descend into infinity.

One thing is certain, we can be assured that the Godly future cities will be absolutely nothing like our cities today. Our cities today are constructed of corruptible materials and house corruptible, sinful, mortal mankind, but there will be nothing corruptible in the future cities of the world. They will house the eternal activities of natural immortal mankind, and the presence of God's Glory will be everywhere and His Spirit dwelling in everyone.

The saints of God, His holy ambassadors to the people of the nations of the earth, will rule and reign over the nations with Christ and will freely go in and out of the New Jerusalem to abide with mankind. The reflection of God's Glory will radiate from the glorified bodies of the saints and the brightness of His glory will literally fill the space in which His Saint's occupy.

We, the 'saints' of God, His glorified children, 'the sons' of God', are wonderful reflections of His glory. Thus, within the sphere of our own glorified presence, the manifestation of God's Holy indwelling Presence is 'shone' through us, His children, who are the literal Holy reflection of His Brightness for all of eternity.

Wherever the saints of God are present, the reflection of God's Glory will literally shine like the stars in awesome splendor and heavenly glory and will be a witness forever of God's eternal love, honor, and presence.

The city of God itself, the New Jerusalem, will shine with the Glory of God Almighty and His saints with a brightness of His glory that will continuously illuminate the surrounding areas of the new earth and the nations closest to its walls.

Imagine the magnificently spectacular edifice such a city will present from great distances in every direction across the new earth and even into the new heavens. Its highly probable pyramidal top 'capstone' brilliantly illuminated by the Heavenly light of the Shekinah glory of God radiating like a guiding beacon throughout the cosmos.

A guiding light is leading the way to God's holy city, the holy place into which all the kings of the earth (the saints) are to bring the "glory and honor" of the nations. A beacon much like the star that pointed to Bethlehem and the glorious birth of our Lord and Savior, Jesus.

As Jesus' government continues to expand, colonies of God's holy race of people will also expand out into the galaxy and eventually throughout the universe. The 'saints' as Holy ambassadors of

God will be able to instantaneously, at the speed of thought, travel from the New Jerusalem to the many other habitable planets in far-off galaxies as their God-given assignments dictate.

In addition, with the expansion of God's 'sinless, holy race of people,' immortal Mankind will continue to populate the universe forever and ever. The 'saints' with their increased God-given knowledge and wisdom, will likewise continue to rule and reign over the ever-increasing multitudes of God's holy nations forever and ever. 'Immortal Mankind', will also have advanced superiority over the new heavens, and interstellar, intergalactic space travel will be developed that will allow humankind to quickly traverse the oceans of the cosmos as a Man today traverses the oceans between earth's continents. The actual speed of travel will be irrelevant in the future world of mankind, and the speed of light as a means of measurement will be as obsolete as the conveyance in which we today have imagined will be the physical mode of space travel.

With the glorified 'saints' heightened power and perfect love, along with the heightened abilities and capabilities of natural immortal mankind, the perfect unencumbered development of mankind within God's glorious creation comes into realization just as God planned from the foundation of the earth.

God's sinless, holy race of people will continue to bear wonderful fruit forever, as mankind will never be satisfied with his heart's desire to bring glory and honor to our Triune God. Likewise, God will never be satisfied with showering His blessings, upon blessings, upon unspeakable blessings to the billions and trillions and quadrillions of nations as their glory and honor are brought before God. Hallelujah, Amen.

Truly, Heaven will have come to 'all the earth'—all earthly habitations throughout the whole of God's glorious creation, forever expanding throughout eternity.

So, dear Saint, as you earnestly await His glorious appearing, continue in the things of God and diligently pursue the holy assignment, He has commissioned to you.

> *"And as you go, preach, saying, 'The Kingdom of Heaven is at hand.'*
>
> *Matthew 10:7, (NKJV)*

Although but a flicker today, you, dear Saint, surely are to become the glorious reflection…

OF HIS GLORY!

CHAPTER 20

Conclusion—We're big Winners!

Our present little earth and its 'solar system' is only in the very beginning phases of its development, just a baby, and the only one in the universe that, as yet, is known to be a habitable planet that will sustain human life. But our God does not plan things on a small scale. The whole of God's creation is to be regenerated to fulfill His plan and purpose for peopling all the new terrestrial habitations with a sinless, holy human race.

The suffering, death, and resurrection of Jesus were then accomplished for a much grander scheme than just the Redemption of a billion or so righteous saints, but also to redeem the whole cosmos and the entire human race that He made in His image and likeness from the awful curse of sin.

It is us, dear saint, the righteous sons of God who, in the end, will emerge victorious. Those of us whose hearts are turned to God and want above all else to be His children, will have a loving relationship with our Father, fellowship with Him, and obey His will.

Today, we must live in the world of the ungodly by faith in God the Father, Son, and Holy Spirit. By maintaining our complete steadfast trust in Him as Savior and Lord, we have become eternally related to Him and will receive the blessing of inheritance that only a Father can bestow upon His children. A blessing that is signed, sealed, and delivered to the righteous, we the saints await the Lord's coming appearance, at which time the full manifestation of our inheritance will be realized.

Unfortunately, the world is a stranger to us, and we are all like aliens awaiting the time in which we will go home. Because the people of the world have turned their back on their Maker and are busily engaged in doing the good things of temporal life, they have no time to honor or fellowship with God. They are too busy building a life for themselves through their vain pursuit of worldly careers and material possessions like homes, cars, boats, planes and things, things, things! So busy, in fact, that they are completely neglecting to secure a home in heaven for either themselves or their children.

> *"For where your treasure is, there your heart will be also. The lamp of the body is the eye. If therefore your eye is good, your whole body will be full of light. But if your eye is bad, your whole body will be full of darkness. If therefore the light that is in you is darkness, how great is that darkness!"*
>
> *Matthew 6:21-23 (NKJV)*

The people of the world are so concerned about the here and now that the hereafter, for many of them doesn't even come into mind. The mental block is so great they have become very foolish in rejecting the truth, mentally, physically, and spiritually concerning the things of God.

Then there are those who only partially retain a hold onto the things of God much the same as they might employ a 'hedge' against financial loss in the commodity market. But woe to these who are sitting on the proverbial fence, for Jesus has no use for the lukewarm in His kingdom.

> *"So then, because you are lukewarm, and neither cold nor hot I will vomit you out of My mouth. Because you say, 'I am rich, have become wealthy*

> *and have need of nothing'—and do not know that you are wretched, miserable, poor, blind and naked."*
>
> *Revelation 3:16-17 (NKJV)*

> *"I counsel you to buy from Me gold refined in the fire, that you may be rich; and white garments, that you may be clothed, that the shame of your nakedness may not be revealed; and anoint your eyes with eye salve, that you may see."*
>
> *Revelation 3:18 (NKJV)*

God couldn't be clearer in His instructions to mankind concerning His great desire to see all people of the world turn from Satan and the sinful nature that keeps them imprisoned.

But mankind, in their vision quest for the world's soulish pleasures and its temporal satisfaction, continues voluntarily and intentionally to commit spiritual suicide, with their only gain, in the end, being a most horrifying, intense, and eternal damnation as their reward.

> *"As many as I love, I rebuke and chasten. Therefore, be zealous and repent. Behold, I stand at the door and knock. If anyone hears My voice and opens the door, I will come into him and dine with him, and he with Me. To him who overcomes I will grant to sit with Me on My throne, as I also overcame and sat down with My Father on His throne."*
>
> *Revelation 3:19-21 (NKJV)*

God most definitely has a much grander plan for mankind than to allow the world to continue throughout all of eternity in its unfocused trivial pursuits. From Romans 14:17, we see that He expects

His redeemed to experience God's Kingdom in the 'here and now' and live a life of *"righteousness, peace, and joy in the Holy Spirit."*

He has also charged us all with an assignment to pass on to others that which we have had revealed to us through His Holy Spirit. As His followers, we are therefore admonished to do our part and proclaim the Gospel of Jesus Christ to all those yet unsaved prisoners of sin.

> *I charge you therefore before God and the Lord Jesus Christ, who will judge the living and the dead at His appearing and His kingdom: Preach the word! Be ready in season and out of season. Convince, rebuke, exhort, with all long-suffering and teaching.*
>
> *2 Timothy 4:1-2 (NKJV)*
>
> *"But you be watchful in all things, endure afflictions, do the work of an evangelist, fulfill your ministry" (2 Timothy 4:5, NKJV).*
>
> *Finally, there is laid up for me the crown of righteousness, which the Lord, the righteous Judge, will give to me on that Day, and not to me only but also to all who have loved His appearing.*
>
> *Timothy 4:8 (NKJV)*

God expects us to step out in faith with Him just as Abraham did after God told him to go. When he received God's instruction, he prepared his whole house, and in complete, total trust, he obeyed and left the city of 'Ur' without even knowing where he was going.

We do know, however, and since we have this knowledge, we should go forth as Abraham in faith and preach the good news to all the earth. All we must do is tell someone! In so doing, we will help bring all of God's people to the fullness of their inheritance, as a joint heir with Jesus, as kings, lords, and priests forever and ever.

Now, God doesn't expect you and me to single-handedly preach to *all* the earth (nations), but He does expect you and me to "preach, convince, rebuke and exhort" those who the Holy Spirit brings 'to us' as a specific part of our assignment.

As believers, we all have an assignment and a specific responsibility that God gives and entrusts to us. He even gives some believers more responsibility than others when He knows they can handle it, just as the example He gave us in the Parable of the Talents.

It is up to us to say, 'yes, Lord,' as we honor Him and step out in faith knowing it's not us alone that will be doing the Will of our Father, but 'Him in us,' who is working through us, as we diligently pursue the completion of our assignment.

As I mentioned in the beginning chapters of this book, mankind generally has no idea what their place is in God's Kingdom. Some Christians alike have not even begun to comprehend the fullness of eternal life God has prepared for us, His children.

Because mankind has a need to overcome the many deceptions perpetrated by so many anti-Christ groups, it is important to understand 'the plan,' God's long-range plan for His creation, His 'elite righteous saints' (the sons of God), and the human race in general.

By increasing mankind's knowledge of all those things 'to hope for,' they will have more strength and perseverance to overcome the temptations and romance of the new age of peace and humanism being promoted today. A movement being orchestrated by Satan himself in his last-ditch effort to prevent the people of the earth from hearing the 'Truth.'

Jesus Christ is the only way, the only truth, and only through Him can one attain true 'life.' God Himself became a flesh and blood man to lead mankind into the everlasting covenant that He promised to Abraham, Isaac, and Jacob. A covenant with a far greater promise than Abraham, the Hebrew Patriarchs, and all of mankind have ever imagined—a sinless, holy race of 'immortal sanctified children of God.'

This 'elect' holy race of God's people are the physical and spiritual descendants of Abraham, who enter into the perfect age in possession of God's very best—they possess the universe and all of God's creation and live eternally in complete, total harmony in God's will.

> *Your descendants shall be as countless as the dust of the earth, and you shall spread abroad to the west and the east and the north and the south; and all the families (nations) of the earth shall be blessed through you and your descendants.*
>
> *Genesis 28:14 (AMP)*

> *But you have said, 'I will surely do you good, and make your offspring as the sand of the sea, which cannot be numbered for multitude.*
>
> *Genesis 32:12 (ESV)*

The supreme test of Abraham's faith and obedience came after God's command that Abraham offers up his beloved son, Isaac, as a sacrifice to Him. Abraham, in complete obedience to God, was willing to give up his absolute greatest treasure on earth (Genesis 22:1-13), and by his own hand would have slain Isaac had the Lord not intervened at the very last moment.

Because of Abraham's great love of God and his total commitment to obedience, God's promise of descendants *"as numerous as the stars of the heavens"* was once again reaffirmed as God's promise to Abraham *(Genesis 22:16-18).*

> *And without faith it is impossible to please God, because anyone who comes to him must believe that He exists and that He rewards those who earnestly seek Him.*
>
> *Hebrews 11:6 (NIV)*

> *By faith Abraham, when called to go to a place he would later receive as his inheritance, obeyed and went, even though he did not know where he was going. By faith he made his home the promised land like a stranger in a foreign country; he lived in tents, as did Isaac and Jacob, who were heirs with him of the same promise. For he was looking forward to the city with foundations, whose architect and builder is God.*
>
> *Hebrews 11:8-10 (NIV)*

> *He remembers his covenant forever, the word he commanded, for a thousand generations, the covenant he made with Abraham, the oath he swore to Isaac. He confirmed it to Jacob as a decree, to Israel as an everlasting* covenant.*
>
> *1 Chronicles 16:15-17 (NIV*

> **Note: Everlasting—for all eternity, perpetual, without end.*

Our covenant, Father Abraham's great faith, and loving willingness to sacrifice his son, reminds us of our own Heavenly Father. God Himself, out of love for us, sacrificed His only begotten Son, so that we and all of mankind could return to a right-standing relationship with Him, and receive all that He has prepared for us from the foundation of the earth.

In addition, the sacrifice that was given for us brought total complete redemption to the whole of God's creation. It prepared the way for God's 'elect', His sinless holy race of people, planned from the beginning of time to populate the entire heavenly cosmos forever and forevermore, fulfilling God's covenant promise to His friend, Abraham.

> *But in keeping with His promise we are looking forward to a new heaven and a new earth, the home of righteousness.*
>
> *2 Peter 3:13 (NIV)*

Just as Jesus singled out the twelve and gave them the 'elite' status of disciples and then later sent them out as apostles; just as God will single out the 144,000 faithful Jews and send them out as evangelists during the Tribulation, just as God originally singled out Abraham and made him the father of the Jewish Nation whom God also singled out as His people, His 'elect' from all the nations of the world; He too has singled 'you' out, dear Saint. You are very special, and He has prepared wonderful blessings for you, befitting of your sovereign position in His heavenly Kingdom as a child of God and a reflection of His glory.

Only you, and you alone, can fill the position and fulfill the assignment He has selected just for you. He has chosen you as carefully as Jesus chose the twelve. He has ordained you to the highest calling in all His creation.

As a child of God, you dear saint, are His heir and a joint heir with His only begotten son Jesus, in the most 'elite' corps throughout

His whole Heavenly realm. You are the actualized personification of His glory, to be fully realized upon His glorious appearing.

> *For those God foreknew He also predestined to be conformed to the likeness of His Son, that He might be the firstborn among many brothers.*
>
> *And those He predestined, He also called; those He called, He also justified; those He justified, He also glorified.*
>
> *What, then, shall we say in response to this? If God is for us, who can be against us? He who did not spare His own Son, but gave Him up for us all—how will He not also, along with Him, graciously give us all things?*
>
> *Romans 8:29-32 (NIV)*
>
> *Dear friends, now we are children of God, and what we will be has not yet been made known. But we know that when He appears, we shall be like Him for we shall see Him as He is. Everyone who has this hope in Him purifies himself, just as He is pure.*
>
> *1 John 3:2-3 (NIV)*

Since man today only utilizes about one-tenth of one percent of his brain's total potential, this is one of the major causes of mankind being 95% blind to the total color scheme displayed in God's creation and 98% deaf to the world's sound patterns.

Knowing this tells us that today a very minimal amount of mankind's total created intellect is ever used. During the Millennial Reign of Christ, mankind's intellectual perfection will very probably begin to be expanded and developed into a far greater intellectual potential, just as God originally created in Adam.

As natural immortal mankind (God's 'elect,' physical and spiritual Israel), enter directly into the perfect age from the 1000 year Millennium (or shortly thereafter), all of mankind's five senses will no doubt be tuned to absolute perfection and will very probably utilize a full 100% of their total intellect, thereby maximizing their brains total abilities.

With the five senses tuned to absolute maximum perfection, 'mankind' will now perfectly understand both himself and his environment and will advance all of mankind's capabilities far beyond any previous level.

Along with humanities indwelling presence of God, the total elimination of the root cause of sin, and the divine guidance of God's Holy Spirit, human-race becomes a race of sinless, holy people that will become elevated to extraordinary heights of accomplishment and bring unprecedented honor and glory to God.

These future brilliant holy people of the new earth, being the physical and spiritual descendants of Abraham, will fulfill God's covenant promise as they continue to expand out into the cosmos, providing the literal peopling of all habitable lands within God's creation.

Abraham's descendants will therefore be continually evolving and expanding into incredible areas of achievement as God's holy nations of 'elect' people fulfill that which they have been assigned in God's magnificent long-range plan for all His creation.

This sinless ever-expanding holy race of people have the distinction of being the continuing and never-ending fulfillment of God's long-range plan for the literal 'Kingdom of Heaven'.

And the nations of those who are saved shall walk in its light, and the kings of the earth bring their glory and honor into it. And they shall bring the glory and the honor of the nations into it.

Revelation 21:24, 26 (NKJV)

The 'righteous saints,' God's glorified children, who dwell in the New Jerusalem with God, and who 'rule and reign' with Christ forever, are the 'kings, lords and priests' over the nations of all God's holy race of people. It is we, you and me, the 'sons of God' who are appointed by our Father God as 'kings, lords and priests' when the heavenly crowns and rewards are given out to the righteous at the judgment seat of Christ just before the marriage of the Lamb to His bride, the Church.

Therefore, we are the 'kings of the earth,' the ones blessed of the Lord who bring our own glory and honor to God as well as the glory and the honor of the nations' into the city of New Jerusalem and present *all* to God.

From these passages of Scripture we can see that within God's order of the literal 'Kingdom of Heaven,' there are many positions and places of service, a hierarchy of organization within His government that will carry over into each and every nation throughout His creation.

Of the increase of His government and peace there will be no end, upon the throne of David and over His kingdom, to order it and establish it with judgment and justice from that time forward, even forever. The zeal of the Lord of hosts will perform this.

Isaiah 9:7 (NKJV)

Even though there is a hierarchy in the order of His government, the rule and reign over all of God's people and God's creation is accomplished out of love, not an authoritarian rule.

Every saint's position and assignment, as well as every natural man or woman's position and assignment within the hierarchy of His government over the billions and billions of nations', is provided with the love of a servant's heart forever and ever.

> *"For who is greater, he who sits at the table, or he who serves? Is it not he who sits at the table? Yet I am among you as the One who serves. But you are those who have continued with Me in My trials. And I bestow upon you a kingdom, just as My Father bestowed one upon Me, that you may eat and drink at My table in My Kingdom and sit on thrones judging the twelve tribes of Israel."*
>
> Luke 22:27-30 (NKJV)

Most people believe in God, but the final deciding issue is their belief in Jesus Christ. Every false religious group or cult teaches erroneously about Christ, and most will certainly disagree that Jesus is God. The devil has tried time and again to delude the truth about Christ with false teachings, and his cults have professed the doctrinal belief that Jesus did not physically rise from the dead, that Jesus is not equal with God, and especially that Jesus is not God.

The delusions are often very subtle because even many of today's cults will agree that Jesus is the Son of God, and why shouldn't they, the devil's themselves, agree (Mark 3:11, 12). How He was conceived and why He really came to this earth is usually the area where the delusion is paramount. I have been told there are cults that profess that God came to earth, laid with Mary in physical union, and thus Jesus was conceived.

For any intelligent Christian to believe this sounds preposterous, but the devil is a thief and a liar and can take the facts and twist them just enough so that many people believe, and then propagate it among the nations. Preposterous? Yes! But very few people ever read the scriptures for themselves, never develop the ability to rightly divide the word of truth and rely on others for their understanding of religious doctrines.

> *"Jesus said, 'I am the way, the truth and the life: No man come unto the Father but by Me"*
>
> *John 14:6, (KJV).*

> *For by grace are you saved through faith; and that not of yourselves: it is the gift of God: Not of works, lest any man should boast.*
>
> *Ephesians 2:8, 9 (KJV)*

> *For the earnest expectation of the creature (creation) waits for the manifestation of the "sons of God." For the creation was made subject to vanity, not willingly, but by reason of Him who hath subjected the same in hope.*
>
> *Because the creation itself also shall be delivered from the bondage or corruption into the glorious liberty of "the children" of God.*
>
> *"For we know that the whole creation groaneth and travaileth in pain together until now"*
>
> *Romans 8:19-22, (KJV)*

Earthquakes, tornadoes, hurricanes, etc., are all manifestations of the earth's groaning to be redeemed, to be set free, and be changed.

If mankind paid a little more attention to the world and the frequency of the catastrophic world events, they too would hear all of creation groaning in pain, warning mankind of the impending tribulation.

God has told us throughout the Scriptures that there is coming a day when our bodies will be "raised back to life" again, and we will be Glorified. There is a double meaning here that I believe deludes mankind's understanding of exactly what this means.

If a natural mortal man has died a physical death, his body goes back to the dust of the earth from which it came. However, at the translation of the saints taken alive to meet the Lord in the air upon His return, mortal man's earthly body does not return to dust but is instantly 'changed' into a glorified heavenly body like Christ's and made incorruptible (unable to die).

The body of natural mortal mankind, which has returned to dust is likewise instantly 'changed' from the corruptible (dust) into a new heavenly body like Christ's and is likewise made incorruptible. Both groups of natural mortal mankind have therefore had their bodies 'raised back to life' and are like Christ's glorified heavenly body.

The word 'life' is the key to our understanding and likewise adds to our confusion. The Scriptures identify "Christ as the 'Light' of the world," and this word 'light' has a greater meaning called 'life.' Therefore, "Christ is really the 'Life' of the world." Being the 'life' of the world, when our bodies are 'raised back to life' again, whether we have died a physical death or not, means our natural mortal bodies are 'regenerated' to a different type of body, a heavenly body that is 'incorruptible'—No longer made of dust.

The Scriptures tell us this new body is like Christ's resurrection body. This body never dies unless it experiences the 'second death' at the Great White Throne Judgment, at which time the resurrection body will be taken away from the wicked by God. A horrible experience once the wicked have experienced the wonderful incorruptible body as they stand before the throne in judgment.

So, by being 'raised back to life,' natural mortal mankind experiences a regeneration from the corruptible to the incorruptible, from one state of life—'mortal earthly life' to a new state of life—'immortal heavenly life,' like Christ's.

But, in addition to receiving this 'new state of life,' when the saints are raised back to life, they also receive something special from God in addition to 'heavenly life.' Their new heavenly bodies are miraculously glorified, receiving the exaltation of, and the magnificent splendor of, God's very own radiance and celestial glory.

Imagine the awesomeness of so great a gift from our God, and just for you and for me, the sons of God, His glorious children, and heirs of the 'Kingdom of Heaven'—A supernatural immortal glorified heavenly body. Praise God in the Highest! Holy, Holy, Holy, Lord God Almighty, dear blessed Lord, and Father, we the saints are so blessed to soon become like Jesus—Glorified to be just like the Celestial magnificence and radiant reflection of His glory!

> *Now, therefore, you are no longer strangers and foreigners, but fellow citizens with the Saints and members of the household of God, having been built on the foundation of the apostles and prophets, Jesus Christ Himself being the chief corner stone, grown into a holy temple in the Lord, in whom you also are being built together for a dwelling place of God in the Spirit.*
>
> *Ephesians 2:19-22 (NKJV)*

Jesus is the Chief cornerstone, the crowning Capstone that all believers are joined under, and of which all believers are crowned together in victorious completion of purpose.

Natural 'mortal' mankind who goes into the promised new earth (land) and new heavens receives a new body like the body that Adam must have received from God. This new body is Perfect in every detail with respect to mankind's spirit, soul, and the immortal human body.

Mankind's new body is like Adam's with one major, significant difference—it is immortal and will live forever just as Adam's would have, had he eaten from the 'Tree of Life' instead of the 'Tree of Knowledge' of good and evil. So, this new race of people will populate the universe in fulfillment of God's promise to Abraham to truly enter 'The Promised Land'—heaven on earth, the literal magnificent and glorious Kingdom of Heaven that has no end.

Upon entering this 'Kingdom,' mankind as a race will have been absolutely purged of the sin nature inherited from Adam and will become God's sinless, holy race—God's elect people, physical and spiritual Israel. Therefore, natural righteous mankind who come out of the Millennial reign of Christ will likewise be translated into the Kingdom of Heaven with a new body.

Upon entering the perfect age, mankind's spirit and soul will eternally live in a sanctified, immortal human body, having the attribute of procreation and all human characteristics in perfect harmony with their spirit and soul forever bringing honor and glory and thanksgiving to Almighty God, whose Divine presence dwells with mankind forever throughout eternity.

In this age we currently live in, Satan uses the world's ideas, morality, philosophies, desires, governments, culture, education, science, art, medicine, music, economic systems, entertainment, mass media, sports, agriculture, and last, but by no means least, 'religion,' to oppose God, His people, His word, His righteous standards, and His long-range plan.

Satan makes an unceasing effort to destroy the life of God in the Christian, and he defies our direct fellowship with God through Jesus. He leads multitudes of people into spiritual destruction with some of the cleverest and most deceptive thoughts ever planted in the human mind.

However, the Bible supplies us with the answer. Jesus said it would not be *"He who will judge mankind on the last day, but His word."* In short, if we disobey His precept that we must be *born again*, there will be no need for Him to judge us. His word will do the judging, and the judgment will be automatic. We would be sending ourselves to hell (John 12:48). The only thing to be determined on this judgment day is 'the degree' of punishment each of the condemned will deserve and receive in hell.

So, let's not forget to remember the warning mankind received from Jesus:

> *"Enter by the narrow gate; for wide is the gate and broad is the way that leads to destruction, and there are many who go in by it. Because narrow is the gate and difficult is the way which leads to life, and there are few who find it. Beware of false prophets, who come to you in sheep's clothing, but inwardly they are ravenous wolves."*
>
> *Matthew 7:13-15 (NKJV)*

How do we obtain Eternal Life? By believing in Christ! (John 3:15, 16, 26) How do we receive Peace on the earth? Through Jesus Christ! (John 14:27, 16:33, Romans 8:8; Philippians 4:5-8).

We need to always remember the one vital all-important truth: Christianity is Christ! It is not a church, not a creed, not a religion, and certainly not beliefs contrary to God's word. The church is Christ, the living Christ that lives in 'born again' mankind. No additional human wisdom, technique, or theory is needed to complete the sufficiency of God's word that reveals mankind's perfect salvation in Christ. The words of Jesus, the New Testament apostolic faith, and God's grace were adequate in the early days of the church to meet the needs of the lost, and they are just as adequate today.

Absolutely nothing can even begin to offer more height, depth, strength, and help than what Jesus Himself proclaimed and provided and what the apostles testified to in Biblical revelation. Jesus Christ alone is *"the way and the truth and the life."* (John 14:6)

The *"mystery of Christ" is God's purpose to "bring all things in heaven and on earth together under one head, even Christ"* (Ephesians 1:10, 3:6) and to include people of all nations in the promise of life and salvation. If mankind walks in the light, they will have the assurance of eternal life. They will talk with God, and He will talk with them, for they will be the *'righteous of God in Christ Jesus,'* being made alive with Christ *"for He Himself is our peace"* (Ephesians 2:14). And *"He can never be replaced, or His Word nullified by any other revelation, testimony or prophecy"* (Acts 20:27-32; 1 Timothy 6:12-20).

To be effective in our families and in our communities, we need to have a common vision and common goals with other believers. We need to fully comprehend God's plan and purpose for our lives and *'catch the vision'* of what eternal life in the *'Kingdom of Heaven'* reveals in our spirit.

If mankind ignores His calling, the only alternative is to be *"destroyed with the brightness of His coming"* (2 Thessalonians 2:8).

I pray this encourages the spirits of all reader's, and especially those of you who have been tagged as any specific generational type. I pray that you *'catch the vision'* of this message, and as a child of God, you know your place in the *'Kingdom of Heaven'* as a righteous 'Saint' and a reflection "Of His Glory".

Let this supercharge your spirit, then put on the garment of praise and go forth in faith as the high-performance Godly Generation proclaiming—repent, for the Kingdom of Heaven is at hand! And just as Jesus has told us in Mark 1:15, *"The time is fulfilled, and The Kingdom of God is at hand. Repent and believe in the Gospel."*

We must all go forth now in faith and preach the Gospel to all who will hear. We must tell all people what the Spirit of God reveals to our spirit, for they too can receive the 'fullness of their inheritance' from God. They, too, can receive *'the spirit of adoption'* from Christ Jesus and be ordained as the 'sons of God.'

You too can become the *"righteousness of God in Christ Jesus"* and as an heir of God and joint-heir with Jesus, rule, and reign with Jesus as *'kings, lords, and priests,'* forever, to the eternal Honor and Glory of God.

You, too, can become the radiant magnificent reflection…

OF HIS GLORY!

BE HUMBLED BEFORE GOD

Revelation 7:9. Do you ever find yourself approaching God with a shopping list or your personal agenda? I pray this meditation from Revelation 7 will help you have an even greater longing to come near to your Creator. To submit yourself to the arms of God. To humble yourself in His presence. Kneeling as you look up into the loving eyes of God.

***COPY THE FOLLOWING ONTO YOUR BROWSER FOR ACCESS:**

https://encounteringpeace.libsyn.com/humbled-before-god

To receive a daily meditation from the scriptures.

http://encounteringpeace.com/

Note:

Encounter was launched with a mission to offer a safe space to encounter the transcendent God amid the noise of our daily routines. It is a podcast of sacred and mindful meditations to help you encounter the divine presence of God throughout your day.

In addition to the individual Meditations referenced within the book for your use related to specific topic's, the following application (APP) with access to all Encounter meditations quoted in my book "Of His Glory" has been authorized by the author and publisher of Encounter to bless your life and to share with all those our God leads you to pass this forward, too also bless others.

To obtain your own personal access to this new 'Encounter APP' of over 500 audio Meditations, please also consider subscribing to this new 2021 'APP' that will provide you with a wonderful library of over 500 Meditations that are available on demand. [7]

https://directory.libsyn.com/shows/view/id/encounterapp

*e-book readers may Ctrl + Click on the Links throughout this book to acquire additional information on the subjects presented.

*e-book is an electronic version of a printed book that can be read on a computer or handheld device designed specifically for this purpose.

SUMMATION

As previously quoted, Billy Sunday (cir. 1900) once said, *'If we could get a real appreciation of what Heaven is, we would all be so home-sick for Heaven the Devil wouldn't have a friend left on earth.'*

The heavens are part and parcel of God's creation, the universe, some of which is seen and some unseen. It will, however, become a most glorious visible paradise in the future age to come once all things are made new, and the universe is peopled with God's holy race of sinless mankind, as planned from the very foundation of the world. If only the people of earth could grasp the truth of this statement, they would be much more diligent in pursuing God's will in their own lives. They would be so much more devoted to teaching their children the importance of securing the significance of God's eternal rewards in the literal *"Kingdom of Heaven."*

Fully attaining the incredible magnificence of Eternal Life serving God's elect people. The doctrine of God's Glory encompasses the greatness, beauty, and perfection of all that He is. In everything that He is and in everything that He does, God is greater than human description. Every attribute and every action of God is stunningly beautiful in every possible way. Each characteristic of God and every accomplishment from His hand is totally perfect. This is what we mean when we talk about God's Glory.

The stunning reality of this universe is that there exists One who is the greatest, the most beautiful, and the most perfect in every way. God is gloriously great, gloriously beautiful, and gloriously perfect. There is none like him; He has no rivals, and no valid comparisons can be made to Him. He is the great Other, in a category of His own beyond our ability to estimate, understand or describe.

Every part of God is glorious in every way possible; there's nothing more to be said. And because God is glorious in every possible way, He alone stands in this vast universe as the only One who is worthy of the worship, surrender, and love of every human heart. We, the saints of God our Father, Jesus Christ our Lord, and the Holy Spirit, are ordained to bring unparalleled Glory to our Triune God as we are translated into the image of our God serving as kings and priests of our God throughout the Kingdom of Heaven for eternity.

DEFINITIONS OF GOD'S GLORY:

Bible verses about Glorification:

Beloved, we are God's children now, and what we will be has not yet appeared; but we know that when He appears, we shall be like Him!

with His Glory, "Amen and 2 Corinthians 3 "Blessed be His Glorious name forever; may the whole earth be filled Amen!

*Psalm 7.2:19 ESV**
:18 ESV

*"For all have sinned and fall short of the Glory of God" (Romans 3:23, ESV).**

Now the appearance of the Glory of the LORD was like a devouring fire on the top of the mountain in the sight of the people of Israel.

*Exodus 24:17 ESV**

That the God of our Lord Jesus Christ, the Father of Glory, may give you a spirit of wisdom and of revelation in the knowledge of Him, having the eyes of your hearts enlightened, that you may know what is the hope to which He has called you, what are the riches of His glorious inheritance in the saints, and what is the immeasurable greatness of His power toward us who believe, according to the working of His great might that He worked in Christ when He raised Him from the dead and seated Him at His right hand in the heavenly places, far above all rule and authority and power and domination, and above every name that is named, not only in this age but also in the one to come.

*Ephesians 1:17-21 ESV**

Then the cloud covered the tent of meeting, and the Glory of the LORD filled the tabernacle. And Moses was not able to enter the tent of meeting because the cloud settled on it, and the Glory of the LORD filled the tabernacle.

*Exodus 40:34–35 ESV**

Moses said, *"Please show me your Glory"*

*Exodus 3318, (ESV)**

"For the earth will be filled with the knowledge of the Glory of the LORD as the waters cover the sea" (Habakkuk 2:14, ESV).

"Then shall your light break forth like the dawn, and your healing shall spring up speedily; your righteousness shall go before you; the Glory of the LORD shall be your rear guard."

*Isaiah 58:8 ESV**

*"Having the Glory of God, its radiance like a most rare jewel, like a jasper, clear as crystal" (*Revelation 21:11, ESV)*"

"I Glorified You on earth, having accomplished the work that You gave Me to do. And now, Father, Glorify Me in Your own presence with the Glory that I had with You before the world existed"

*John 17:4-5 ESV**

And the Word became flesh and dwelt among us, and we have seen His Glory, Glory as of the only Son from the Father, full of grace and truth.

*John 1:14 (ESV)**

*"And every tongue confess that Jesus Christ is Lord, to the Glory of God the Father" (*Philippians 2:11, ESV)*

To them God chose to make known how great among the Gentiles are the riches of the Glory of this mystery, which is Christ in you, the hope of Glory.

*Colossians 1:27 (ESV)**

When the Bible speaks of God's glory, what is it talking about? The doctrine of God's glory encompasses the greatness, beauty, and perfection of all that He is.

In everything that He is and in everything that He does, God is greater than human description. Every attribute and action of God is stunningly beautiful in every way. Each characteristic of God and every accomplishment from His hand is totally perfect. This is what we mean when we talk about God's glory.

The stunning reality of this universe is that there exists One who is the greatest, the most beautiful, and the most perfect in every way. God is gloriously great, gloriously beautiful, and gloriously perfect. There is none like Him; He has no rivals, and no valid comparisons can be made to Him. He is the great Other, in a category of His own beyond our ability to estimate, understand or describe.

Every part of God is glorious in every way possible; there's nothing more to be said. And because God is glorious in every possible way, He alone stands in this vast universe as the only One who is worthy of the worship, surrender, and love of every human heart.

Note: The above (15) ESV Bible Verses are taken from the following link of 100 Bible Verses. Copy on your browser or/ click on the link if you are reading an e-book to check out all the other verses for your enlightenment.

https://www.openbible.info/topics/glory of god

*The English Standard Version (ESV), of the Bible is an English translation of the Bible published in 2001 by Crossway. It is a revision of the Revised Standard Version that employs an "essentially decorate" translation philosophy.

NOW ENVISION ETERNITY

Dina Janette was working as a street vendor to earn enough money to buy her own food to be able to eat each day. If she didn't make enough per day, she would not eat. No time for school or enough money to purchase the necessary supplies to go to school. In Peru, the government pays for the school sessions broken down into a morning session and an afternoon session. As our team exited our van on the third morning of our mission to minister to a large group of teen's I was led by the Spirit to a single cart with one lone person in the middle of a concrete plaza with only a small umbrella overhead for protection from the sun.

As my ministry partner, I, and our translator approached the cart, we recognized a lonely young girl at the cart. We spent close to thirty minutes visiting with and ministering to Dina Janette and personally witnessed the wonderful power of the Holy Spirit overcoming her with a glorious radiance, turning her dark black eyes into a radiant light the moment she accepted Jesus into her heart. At the exact time of her acceptance, our team was physically moved back at least three feet away from her cart as the Holy Spirit flowed into her heart. We continued to attend to her needs, gave her a small 'book of John' in Spanish, prayed with her for her physical and family needs knowing in our hearts the Lord had selected her as a disciple even before we arrived in Peru.

I received several letters from Dina through our translator for a few years but eventually lost contact with her. One of the letters I received from Dina about two years after our trip to Lima, she wrote that not only had God touched her life in glorious ways, she returned to school, her family was also likewise touched by the finger of God. The Holy Spirit continued ministering through Dina to her family, and they each opened their hearts to receive God's word and received their salvation. He knows where and to whom we are needed to minister His word. Thus, when we receive an anointing from the Lord and He equips us with the necessary knowledge and wisdom to do as He says, "Always believe it is the Lord God and pass it forward!"

With the Lord's imminent return, the primary vision we should all have for our ministry prior to the Millennial reign of Christ is a short-term vision. We all need to see our own ministry as an extension of Jesus' ministry. Whether here at home, church, or elsewhere in the nations, the vision for the children of God is the same. God expects us to support and propagate the ministry He has formed and knows that He has appointed you to be a friend and mentor to His children. Our continuing desire is to become an effectual minister of the gospel and persevere in winning the souls of boys and girls, men and women, to Christ. Preaching the literal "Kingdom of Heaven" is imminent.

I believe the training and expertise God has provided me through my professional career as well as the on-the-job training in the ministry, I have received His blessed preparation with a heart of compassion and love for God's people like Jesus' own heart. I am waiting on the Lord for the next step that He would have me take to increase my ministry to the next level He intends for me to go. My greatest desire is to do the Will of God, doing it with the power of the Holy Spirit and with love and a sound mind. I am never as alive in my spirit as I am when I am working in the ministry of which God has ordained for my life.

It is now the year 2021, and knowledge is now doubling at the rate of every thirteen months. I now know beyond any shadow of a doubt every person, man, woman, and child are all the children of God, and we as brothers and sisters are responsible for praying for them and all their family! God's salvation and healing power are always present and available to His children. He say's *"Ask, and you will receive!"* I have seen how marvelously true His Words are, and

I now believe you too will pass forward this truth, dear brother and sister in Christ.

> *Dear friends, we are God's children now, and what we will be has not yet been revealed. We know that when He appears, we will be like Him because we will see Him as He is.*
>
> *1 John 3:2 Christian Standard Bible (CSB)*

NOTE: Encounter was launched with a mission to offer a safe space to encounter the *transcendent God amid the noise of our daily routines. It is a podcast of over 500 sacred and mindful meditations to help you encounter the divine presence of God throughout your day. [8]

https://directory.libsyn.com/shows/view/id/encounterapp

What does it mean that God is transcendent? Copy the following *Got Questions link below onto your browser for a very concise definition.

* https://www.gotquestions.org/God-transcendent.html

> *And we all, with unveiled face, beholding the glory of the Lord, are being transformed into the same image from one degree of glory to another. For this comes from the Lord who is the Spirit.*
>
> *2 Corinthians 3:18 English Standard Version (ESV)*

> But we all, with open face beholding as in a glass the glory of the Lord, are changed into the same

image from glory to glory, even as by the Spirit of the Lord.

King James Bible (KJV)

And all of us, as with unveiled face, [because we] continued to behold [in the Word of God] as in a mirror the glory of the Lord, are constantly being transfigured into His very own image in ever increasing splendor and from one degree of glory to another; [for this comes] from the Lord [Who is] the Spirit.

Amplified Bible (AMP)

EPILOGUE

Signs God Cares for You (Psalm 8:3-4)

Have you ever felt completely alone and isolated against the pressures of the world? Have you perhaps felt life pushing you in a corner, with no place left to turn? Well, this meditation from Psalm 8 will help you remember that when the world pushes against you, God is the creator of that very same world.

I hope the following meditation will enable you to remember that nothing happens in all of creation without the knowledge and the will of the Creator of creation, the very One that made you and cares for you, our Triune God, the Father, His Son Jesus Christ and His Holy Spirit.

So, to begin, whether resting in the first rays of morning sun or the approaching shadows of evening, allow the next 15 minutes to be a retreat to contemplate seeing with new eyes, begin to rest in your restored life. As your eyes begin to close, center on this place of balance for a still moment, just let this be a time of yielding with a silent whispered prayer of reconciliation with the Holy Father, Holy Son, and Holy Spirit.

Resting now in this divine moment, listen and respond now to Romans 1, and as you are, read the following answer:

> Heavenly Father let me know of Your care for me. May the Lord bless the hearing and the reading of His word. For ever since the creation of the world, His invisible attributes, His eternal power, and divine nature have been clearly seen. So Heavenly Father, let me know of Your care for me. His power is understood through His work-

> manship, all His creation, the wonderful things that He has made. So Heavenly Father, in that, let me know of Your care for me.

His care is evident so that they who fail to believe and trust in Him are without excuse and without defense, so "Heavenly Father, let me know of Your care for me. For a moment longer, rest here in the divine presence, your body, and soul balanced and in harmony with God… Pause (30 sec)."

Take a moment to collect your thoughts. Do you feel backed into a corner? Do you feel isolated and uncared for? Well, no matter which, center your thoughts and feelings now in a moment of prayer. Just thankful for being in the presence of your creator God, guiding Spirit and transforming Son, still caring for you.

Take note of any thoughts, feelings, or deeds that are out of balance with God's plan, any thoughts of being uncared for. Don't be frightened by what comes to mind. Simply note your thoughts as the Holy Spirit brings them to mind. And for this next minute, continue in prayer, as you whisper, "Heavenly Father, let me know of Your care for me…"

Center now on the Holy Spirit transforming your mind and motivations to those of Christ. Center on being balanced and known and cared for. Your thoughts clash, or your mind becomes disturbed…not to worry, just pause, breathe, and center back on the centering presence of God. Take another moment in peace as you whisper your centering prayer, "Heavenly Father, let me know of Your care for me…"

Center too on your breathing, bring your attention to each breath, take several deep, slow breaths from your belly, just be aware of each of them. Be aware of the balance within your breathing. Breathe in, hold it, feel the tension, and now release it as you breathe out. Let even your breathing become your divine worship and a reminder of the care of God within you. As your thoughts drift and wobble, thank God for the reminder to see with new eyes. Take a minute now, and with each slow exhale, silently whisper your sacred prayer, "Heavenly Father, let me know of Your care for me…"

Continue as you center on God's message for you in this the first of three scripture readings from Psalm 8:3-4, and we will begin in the Amplified Bible.

> *When I see and consider Your heavens, the work of Your fingers, the moon and the stars, which You have established, what is man that You are mindful of him, and the son of earthborn man that You care for him?*

If any words resonate with you, well listen once more, carefully, and be mindful of how the Holy Spirit is guiding your thoughts.

> *When I see and consider Your heavens, the work of Your fingers, the moon and the stars, which You have established, what is man that You are mindful of him, and the son of earthborn man that You care for him?*

Did any ideas seem more fresh or novel or new from this second reading? Well, allow this next minute to be a time of surrendering your life to be in balance with the plans of God…

Listen once more now, but in an expanded version from the New King James:

> *When I consider Your Heavens, the work of Your fingers, the moon and the stars, which You have ordained. What is man that you are mindful of him, and the son of man that you visit him, You*

> *have made him a little lower than the angels. And You have crowned him with glory and honor.*

How can you apply this message to your life after listening again? And for this next minute, return to your breathing, as you center on being cared for, healed, and aligned with God…

In this third reading, let the scripture become a prayer as you listen from the New Living Translation.

> *When I look at the night sky and see the work of your fingers—the moon and the stars that you set in place—what are mere mortals that you should think about them, human beings that you should care for them? Yet you made them only a little lower than God and crowned them with glory and honor. You gave them charge of everything you made, putting all things under their authority—the flocks and the herds and all the wild animals, the birds in the sky, the fish in the sea, and everything that swims the ocean currents.*

This is the word of the Lord. Thanks be to God. What do you desire most from God currently? I want to give you this minute, for that to be your contemplation. And if your mind drifts, not to worry, just pause, breathe and return to the transforming work of God. The God that cares for you…

While resting now, in a moment of imaginative contemplation, I want you to find yourself in the story from the fourth chapter of the book of Mark. I want you to imagine yourself in a fishing boat, with Jesus and His disciples as evening comes. Jesus tells you to take the boat and steer it to the other side of the lake. But soon, a fierce storm comes up. High waves begin to break into the boat and fill it with water.

But you turn around, and you see Jesus sleeping at the back of the boat, with His head on a cushion. The disciples wake Him up, shouting, *"Teacher, don't you care that we're going to drown?"* When Jesus wakes up, He rebukes the wind and says to the waves, *"Silence, be still."* Suddenly, the wind stops, and there's a great calm, but then He turns and asks you, *"Why are you afraid? Do you still have no faith?"* Jesus falls back to sleep, and you can hear the disciples asking, *"Who is this man, even the wind and waves obey Him?"*

For this next minute, feel yourself abiding in the strong presence of your creator and remaining in His protective arms. Yes, you can feel the pushing of the waves, but feel too the security of His presence. He knows each wave; He created the oceans. So just remain there, cared for, and safe behind the pulsing forces of the world…

Now return and center once more on your breathing. And when you feel ready, not a moment before, slowly open your eyes to see the world anew. I pray your life feels a bit more balanced and cared for than when we began. And as you walk with new purpose, be aware of others you pass on your path, who may feel uncared for, ignored. Who do you know in your life that longs for the caring arms of God? Let me pray this closing benediction for you to remember that when you see and consider the heavens, they are the work of God's fingers. He established the moon and the stars, and just as those, He is mindful and cares for you as well.

Now may you know the compassion of Christ, feel the embrace of the Holy Spirit and encounter the care of the Holy Father now and always, and Lord God, hear our prayer, Amen.

The Encounter link's below will provide access to two audio meditations to bless you upon a new 'Journey.' Enter each Link in your Web browser or w/ e-Book click on the Links.

https://encounteringpeace.libsyn.com/signs-god-cares-for-you

https://encounteringpeace.libsyn.com/new-creation

*See 'page 16' in the front matter for additional information.

A Journey to our Galaxy's center:

A comparison of the Milky way Galaxy viewed edge-on from the inside. Structural details of the Milky Way Galaxy are depicted in this illustration. Out in the Cygnus-Orion arm of the milky way Galaxy, where the sun resides, there is one star for every 400 Cubic Light-years. The next spiral arm inward, 6000 light years from us, is the Sagittarius Arm, the Galactic landscape would appear noticeably brighter than the sky in our region of the Galaxy.

The Centaurus Arm is next, about 8000 light-years farther in toward the Galaxy's Nucleus. Centaurus Arm, a Galactic traveler would see a wall of stars ahead—emerging from the Centaurus Arm, a galactic central bulge. From this distance (less than 10,000 light years), the core region has a rich golden glow, the combined light of billions of stars far more closely packed than anywhere in the spiral arms.

A few Blue Giants are seen. Instead, the brightest stars are red giants like Betelgeuse and Antares. The vast majority are of stars that are yellow or orange. Unlike the most luminous parts of the spiral arm, the nucleus does not derive its brilliance from the short-lived Blue Giants but, rather, by brute force from thongs of lesser suns, whose combined light creates a dazzling scene, like hundreds of bursting skyrockets superimposed and frozen in time.

Revelation 21: THE PASSION TRANSLATION

A New Heaven, a New Earth, the New Jerusalem

21 Then *in a vision* John saw a new heaven and a new earth. The first heaven and earth had passed away, and the sea no longer existed. [2] I saw the Holy City, the New Jerusalem, descending out of the heavenly realm from the presence of God like a pleasing bride that had been prepared for her husband, *adorned for her wedding.* [3] And I heard a thunderous voice from the throne, saying:

"Look! God's tabernacle is with human beings.

God is the 'epitome' of organization, He always plans ahead and is not wasteful, of any of His creation, Galaxies collide and the material from two or more Galaxies merge together and make a new but larger Galaxy increasing the size of the universe preparing for the expansion of His elect people, Jews' and Gentiles', for evermore.

God commanded Abraham to leave his birthplace and go…to the land that I will show you. This bond between the People of Israel and their land was reaffirmed to succeeding generations through his son **Isaac** and his grandson **Jacob**: The land that I assigned to Abraham and **Isaac** I assign to you and to your offspring to come.

"A NEW BEGINNING"!

I suspect that God has planned for the new Heavens and Earth to begin from the physical matter of our Milky Way Galaxy providing for the new beginning of the Aeon's of Aeons' for Eternity. Imagine the probability of our Milky Way Galaxy and Andromeda merging.

ANATOMY OF OUR ANATOMY OF OUR GALAXY
<u>Home</u>; The Beginning Journey's, Galaxy

ENDNOTES

1 https://www.spacetelescope.org/news/heic1406/

2 https://encounteringpeace.libsyn.com/knowledge-of-gods-glory

3 www.encounteringpeace.org or/ http://encounteringpeace.com/

4 https://www.amazon.com/Astronomy-2019-Terence-Dickinson/dp/0228100372
https://www.thriftbooks.com/a/terence-dickinson/211961/
https://books.google.com/books/about/Exploring_the_Night_Sky.html?id=SegOAQAAMAAJ

5 https://svs.gsfc.nasa.gov/13510
https://www.cnbc.com/2020/01/10/17-year-old-discovers-planet-on-third-day-of-internship-with-nasa.html
https://www.nasa.gov/feature/goddard/2020/nasa-s-tess-mission-uncovers-its-1st-world-with-two-stars

6 https://encounteringpeace.libsyn.com/blessing-of-gods-grace

7 https://directory.libsyn.com/shows/view/id/encounterapp

8 https://directory.libsyn.com/shows/view/id/encounterapp

Rev. Jon C. Crowdus
Jon Crowdus Ministries
joncrowdus@gmail.com

I pray that you will be blessed by this work and will "pass it forward" to bless all those who will run with His vision.

Trust God to show you the way!

Back Cover

The "Back Cover" of this book is a photo from Shutterstock of a sunset settling over a horizon with hands opened, and palms turned up as one receives God's blessing of an encounter with God's Holy Spirit providing His "Revelation Knowledge" and His "Wisdom" to fully understand the reality of Eternal Life upon receiving your overwhelming TRANSFORMATION… "Of His Glory"!

CPSIA information can be obtained
at www.ICGtesting.com
Printed in the USA
LVHW052107211021
701096LV00006B/21

9 781637 691441